The United States and the Americas

Lester D. Langley, General Editor

*This series is dedicated to a broader
understanding of the political, economic, and
especially cultural forces and issues that have
shaped the western hemispheric experience—
its governments and its peoples. Individual
volumes assess relations between the United
States and its neighbors to the south and north:
Mexico, Central America, Cuba, the
Dominican Republic, Haiti, Panama,
Colombia, Venezuela, Peru, Ecuador, Bolivia,
Brazil, Paraguay, Argentina, Chile, and Canada.*

# Ecuador and the United States

Ronn Pineo

# Ecuador and the United States: Useful Strangers

The University of Georgia Press
Athens and London

Set in 10/14 Palatino by Newgen.
Printed and bound by Integrated Book Technology
The paper in this book meets the guidelines for
permanence and durability of the Committee on
Production Guidelines for Book Longevity of the
Council on Library Resources.

Printed in the United States of America

11   10   09   08   07   C   5   4   3   2   1
11   10   09   08   07   P   5   4   3   2   1

Library of Congress Cataloging-in-Publication Data

Pineo, Ronn F., 1954–
    Ecuador and the United States : useful strangers / Ronn Pineo.
      p. cm.
    Includes bibliographical references and index.
    ISBN-13: 978-0-8203-2970-3 (hardcover : alk. paper)
    ISBN-10: 0-8203-2970-3 (hardcover : alk. paper)
    ISBN-13: 978-0-8203-2971-0 (softcover : alk. paper)
    ISBN-10: 0-8203-2971-1 (softcover : alk. paper)
    1. United States—Foreign relations—Ecuador. 2. Ecuador—Foreign
relations—United States. 3. Balance of power—History. 4. United States—
Relations—Ecuador. 5. Ecuador—Relations—United States. 6. National
characteristics, American. 7. National characteristics, Ecua-dorian. 8. Ecuador—Civilization. 9. Ecuador—History. 10. Ecuador—Politics and government. I. Title.
    E183.8.E2P56 2007
    327.730866--dc22

                                                          2007010389

British Library Cataloging-in-Publication Data available

To Ardis and Tomm

# Contents

# Maps

# Acknowledgments

Work on this project was supported by a Towson University Summer Stipend Grant, a Fulbright Lecturing and Research Award, and a grant of sabbatical leave by Towson University. I am most grateful for this generous support.

For their help, wise counsel, and most of all for their friendship, I would like to thank Pablo Núñez Endara, María Elena Porras, and Rocio Rueda Novoa at the Archive of the Ministry of Foreign Relations in Quito. Larry Clayton and Lester Langley, general editor of this series, gave close attention to the manuscript, and it improved as a result of their efforts. Polly Kummel, an exceptionally talented and most insightful editor, helped me so much. And I would like to thank my brother, Smith Pineo, for his help with this project. One could not ask for a better friend.

**Ecuador and the United States**

# Introduction

To some, the story of Ecuadorian-U.S. relations might appear to be a tale that does not need to be told. The United States has long regarded Ecuador as one of the least important Latin American nations, although Ecuador is larger than many people may suppose. While it is geographically small (about 100,000 square miles, or about the size of the state of Oregon), Ecuador has a surprisingly large population; at nearly thirteen million, Ecuador today has a population larger than each of the nations of Central America and the Caribbean, and Ecuador is nearly as populous as Chile.

Nonetheless, it has been the Caribbean states, so near the United States, that have been defined traditionally as falling within the U.S. sphere of influence. Mexico, neighbor and leading trade partner, has been of utmost importance to the United States. Big nations like Brazil and Argentina loomed large. Those countries that served as cold war staging zones—El Salvador, Nicaragua, Guatemala—sometimes found themselves at the center of events. And the present-day war on illegal drugs has made Peru, Bolivia, and especially Colombia key U.S. concerns. But Ecuador has historically met none of these conditions. From the U.S. perspective Ecuador has been a distant, small nation, one never really at the center of foreign policy concerns. Moreover, given the great disparities in the size and power of the two nations, it might seem safe to assume that in all exchanges the United States must always have had its way, that studying the relationship between Ecuador and the United States could be of little benefit. The goal of this book is to show the mistake of such thinking.

If it is true enough that the United States has rarely focused its attention on Ecuador, from the Ecuadorian perspective the United States has nearly always mattered, and mattered a great deal. Moreover, it would be unwise to assume that, in relations between the two nations, the United States always has bested Ecuador. Ironically, because the United

States was generally preoccupied with affairs elsewhere, and because it was ignorant about Ecuador, when the United States inevitably did have reason to deal with Ecuador, it could sometimes significantly outmaneuver its big neighbor to the north. In the various contests of wills Ecuador often got what it wanted. This book is about the dynamics of power in the relations between a very large if distracted nation when dealing with a very small but determined nation, an investigation that reveals a great deal about both.

Beginning especially in the late nineteenth century, when the United States came to be more consistently involved in and concerned with Latin America, U.S. policy goals for Ecuador were generally the same as those for the region as a whole, from the age of economic imperialism, the Good Neighbor policy, the cold war, and the war on illegal drugs to the process of democratization and adoption of neoliberal economic policies. Within this context the United States sought to influence political, economic, and cultural developments in Ecuador.

Yet despite the great power advantage of the United States, Ecuador was never merely a passive recipient of U.S. policy or actions; Ecuadorians always sought to modify U.S. plans. Ecuadorians played this game with great skill and sometimes manipulated U.S. officials so masterfully that they never realized what had happened. This study seeks to examine the influence that ran mostly north to south and will assess Ecuador's successes in containing, controlling, bending, distorting, or even thwarting U.S. influence. Certainly U.S. power influenced Ecuador but often only in ways that Ecuadorians themselves wanted. Factions within Ecuador, especially regional ones, saw the United States as an outside force that could be used as a potential ally in Ecuadorian domestic political disputes. To Ecuador the United States could be a powerful and useful stranger.

The United States too found benefit in dealing with Ecuador. Ecuador historically has served the United States as a supplier of raw materials, as a site for important military bases, and as a voting supporter for U.S. positions in world and regional organizations. For the United States, Ecuador too could be a useful stranger.

## Themes

Ecuador provides an excellent context in which to explore several critical issues in Latin American–U.S. relations, issues that would not receive adequate coverage if we were to consider only the largest Latin American states. One feature that makes the Ecuadorian case especially intriguing is that in general the United States historically played a rather different role in the Ecuadorian economy than it did in the economies of many other nations of Latin America. From the early twentieth century forward Ecuador came to depend on U.S. imports, and the United States also became the leading purchaser of the various Ecuadorian exports— cacao until the 1920s, bananas in the 1950s, and oil since the 1970s. But the United States made less direct investment in Ecuador than it did in most other Latin American nations.

The producers of cacao and bananas were Ecuadorian, not foreign nationals operating on Ecuadorian soil. Even with oil, where the United States exerted significant economic influence, the Ecuadorian government maintained ultimate ownership. Ecuador never became a mere outpost for U.S. companies. So while the United States carried on a lively economic exchange with Ecuador, the few U.S. investors in Ecuador could not drive the needs and concerns of U.S. policy.

This book offers a survey of the history of Ecuadorian-U.S. relations, focusing on the critical political and economic relations, both official government policies as well as unofficial economic or nongovernment exchanges and influences. I also address certain aspects of cultural exchange, especially where Ecuador offers something beyond the all-too-familiar story of the domination of U.S. consumer culture: rock music, Coca-Cola, and McDonald's. Because Ecuador is a small nation, one less studied and less well understood, I provide in each chapter background information about the nation's changing economic, political, and social context.

For this study I work from the best available empirical evidence to build interpretive arguments in an effort to offer an explanation of Ecuador's unique relationship with the United States that fleshes out some of the pathways of resistance available to smaller states when dealing with much larger ones. From this analysis I seek to offer a larger comparative contribution to our understanding of interstate relations, that is, a contribution to theory construction. One of my main goals is to illustrate some of the ways in which the less powerful are not powerless.

In exploring the larger contours of Ecuadorian-U.S. relations, I give special emphasis to several episodes. Chapter 1 looks at the ways the United States provided encouragement and assistance to Latin America in its struggle for independence, and how Ecuador fit into the larger process. Ecuadorian-U.S. relations developed slowly in the early nineteenth century, a time of political chaos in Ecuador. This situation was greatly exacerbated by Gen. Juan José Flores's repeated efforts to return from exile and fight his way back into power. The United States offered the Ecuador government some support, at least at points, in responding to the Flores challenge. Yet by the mid-nineteenth century Ecuadorian-U.S. relations had become increasingly strained. Chapter 2 looks at this period, one of rising concerns about U.S. imperialism in Mexico, Central America, and the Caribbean, focusing on Ecuadorians' growing fears that the United States had designs on the Galápagos Islands.

The early twentieth century, covered in chapter 3, brought new areas of tension between the two nations. Even when the United States was attempting to help Ecuador, misunderstandings and considerable bitterness could sometimes result. This was certainly the case when the Rockefeller Foundation took the lead in ridding the port city of Guayaquil of yellow fever in 1918–19. Great controversy and considerable disappointment also attended the U.S. role in the building of the Quito-to-Guayaquil railroad.

Complications surrounded other developments in Ecuadorian-U.S. relations. In the late 1920s the Princeton economist Edwin Kemmerer sought to help Ecuador reform its finances and banking practices, but Ecuador's motives in inviting Kemmerer were less than pure, and its embrace of Kemmerer's recommendations was at best half-hearted. Chapter 4 looks at developments before the mid-twentieth century, a time of war for Ecuador and the world. When Peru invaded Ecuador in 1941 and seized valuable territory, the United States helped arrange the

Peruvian withdrawal. Yet Ecuador was never satisfied with the treaty it signed and came to blame the United States for the role it played in getting Ecuador to agree to the accord. During World War II Ecuador cooperated with the Allied war effort, providing two important air bases for the forward defense of the Panama Canal. After the war, however, many difficulties emerged in the process of handing the bases over to Ecuador.

Chapter 5 examines the cold war years, a time when the U.S. anti-Communist crusade brought increased U.S. interest in Ecuador's internal politics. This chapter explores several U.S. foreign policy initiatives for Ecuador and Latin America, especially the Alliance for Progress, following the story from the initial high hopes for the program through its subsequent failure. I also assess the implications of U.S. anti-Communist policy, in particular the actions of the Central Intelligence Agency in Ecuador. Chapter 6 explores relations from the mid-1960s to the 1980s, looking especially at the battles between the United States and Ecuador about fishing rights in the Pacific, known as the "tuna wars," before turning to the controversies surrounding the role of U.S. companies in the development of Ecuadorian oil exports.

Chapter 7 takes up the years from the 1980s to the present, a time when Ecuador and most of Latin America were swept along in a global stampede toward free-market economic policies—neoliberalism—and democratic political forms, both ardently championed by the United States. Washington's motive was ideological, the abiding belief that free trade, free societies, and an open political process are positive goods and that the United States ought to seek to advance these goals everywhere.

Yet as is ever the case in Ecuador, all grand notions imported from without have to undergo some modification and refitting to match the distinctive shape of Ecuadorian reality. Ecuador has stubbornly remained Ecuador, always only partially budged by the great winds of world change. Ideological proscriptions must be translated into "Ecuadorian," refracted through the prism of Ecuadorian culture. Ecuadorian acceptance of neoliberalism and democratization has been highly selective, a process shaped by the pull of competing political interests that liked bits of ideas here and there in these policies. Ecuador has demonstrated only a shallow and highly provisional commitment to democracy and an indifferent dedication to free-market policies.

In recent years Ecuador and most Latin American nations have struggled to cope with the burden of massive foreign debt. In order to gain access to new loans to pay the interest due on their older debts, these nations have had to win the approval of the International Monetary Fund and follow its mandates for fiscal austerity. The epilogue closes by offering an assessment of this situation and some critical reflections on its implications for the construction of democracy in Ecuador.

## Geography and Culture: The Ecuadorian Setting

To understand the history of a nation's foreign relations, one first needs to understand something about its national context, its land and people. Nowhere is this more true than in Ecuador, a special place of spectacular beauty and unique culture. Ecuador is a nation divided by deeply held sentiments of regional difference, feelings that originate in its extraordinary geography. It would be impossible to exaggerate the centrality of geography in shaping Ecuadorian economic, political, and social reality.

The towering Andes mountain range runs through Ecuador from north to south, splitting the nation into sections (see map 1). The Andean highlands—the sierra—occupy a quarter of the nation; to the west along the Pacific Ocean tropical lowlands—*la costa*—make up another quarter of Ecuador's national territory; and stretching to the east the sparsely populated Amazon tropical rainforest—known as the Oriente—covers the other half of Ecuador.

In the Ecuadorian sierra the Andes form into two distinct rows punctuated by thirty volcanoes. The highest peak is Mount Chimborazo, at 20,577 feet, near the central highland city of Riobamba. Between the two chains of the Andes lie eleven fertile intermontaine basins, each averaging about fifty miles in width east to west, nestled at elevations ranging from seven thousand to ten thousand feet above sea level. At this altitude the climate of the tropical equator turns temperate—for every

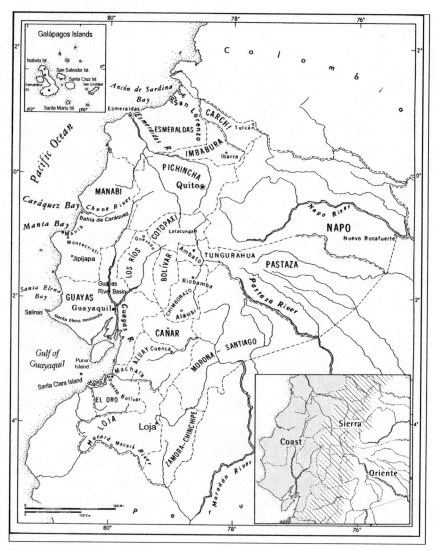

Map 1. Ecuador

three-hundred-foot increase in elevation the temperature drops one degree Fahrenheit—and each step up or down in elevation provides a different ecozone for specialized agricultural production.[1]

The temperate mountain basins are the heart of the sierra, offering arguably the most agreeable climate found anywhere on Earth. Every day the temperature warms up to about 78 degrees, and every night it cools to the 50s. Seasonal variation is nil; it is always springtime. It is also excellent country for agriculture: since ancient times the valleys of the sierra have been crowded with people and farms. Late afternoon rainfall is a near daily occurrence, and the rich volcanic soil yields bountiful harvests of a host of grains, fruits, and vegetables. The major cities of the Ecuadorian sierra are located right in or adjacent to these valleys, from the capital, Quito (at 9,300 feet), in the north; to Cuenca (8,500 feet), the third-largest city in the country, in the south; to Ambato (8,400 feet) and Riobamba (9,000 feet) in the central highlands. Streaming down from the sierra, stretching toward the Amazon or the coast, hang many lush, warm valleys. These produce vegetables, cotton, sugar, oranges, pineapples, and other tropical fruit.

The coast is a different world. For the most part *la costa* is flat, low, hot, and very humid, with vast reaches covered with tropical forests. The sole exception to this is the arid Santa Elena Peninsula, which juts out to the west from the port city of Guayaquil. The region around and upriver from Guayaquil has long been the most productive and populated zone of the coast. This area, the Guayas River basin, covers twenty-five thousand square miles and is blessed with nearly ideal conditions for tropical export agriculture. The river complex—the Guayas, Vinces, Daule, and Babahoyo, among countless other wide streams—provides a natural transportation system: the Guayas River basin is the largest navigable fluvial system on the Pacific side of Latin America. Moreover, the soil of the basin is among the best in the world. Accordingly, export crops, especially cacao—chocolate beans—and bananas, along with sugar, tobacco, coffee, and tagua—vegetable ivory once used to make buttons—have flourished in this region.[2]

The remaining areas on the edges of Ecuador hold less than 4 percent of the population and have been important mostly for their symbolic meaning. To the west, more than five hundred miles offshore, lie the Galápagos Islands. Largely devoid of freshwater and thinly populated even today, these remote, arid islands have nevertheless figured prominently in U.S.-Ecuadorian relations. At the other extreme is the vast Amazon tropical rainforest. Until recently the few Indians who made this area their home were not integrated in any significant way into national life; even today some people living there are outsiders within their own country. Still, the Amazon has large symbolic significance to Ecuadorians—here is a land with boundless potential that one day, perhaps, could make Ecuador great. The Amazon, this symbol of hope, was not something Ecuador could give up easily, and whenever Peru tried to take away any of this territory claimed by Ecuador—a frequent occurrence—Ecuador would go to war. In 1967 Ecuador found oil in the Amazon, near the border with Colombia. A petroleum boom began, a development that had far-reaching implications.

Grounded in this geographic reality, the two most populated regions of Ecuador, the sierra and the coast, developed different demographic circumstances and social arrangements. The population of the sierra has historically been a good deal larger than that of the coast. In the period before the Spanish conquest, the sierra's fertile, temperate valleys supported a thick population of native Americans. During the colonial period indigenous people continued to make up the bulk of the population in the rural zones, while the cities of the highlands came to be home to the white population and an ever-growing number of mestizos. These racial patterns within the sierra persist even today, although overall the region now holds a slightly smaller population than does the coast.

The coast, hot, wet, and tropical, lacked zones ideal for temperate agriculture and food production and as a result probably did not support a large native population before the Spanish conquest. During the colonial and early national periods the coast continued to be thinly populated, especially in comparison with the sierra. Only in the late nineteenth century did the coastal population begin to grow rapidly as cacao production and export soared, inducing streams of Indian migrants to travel down from the sierra. Coastal Ecuadorians are a miscegenated people, with *montuvios*—a mixture of Indian, white, and black—predominating.

The coast also has a small population of African Ecuadorians (they comprise 5 to 10 percent of the total population of Ecuador today) located chiefly in and around the northern coastal city of Esmeraldas. The historical origins of this African Ecuadorian population in Esmeraldas remain something of a mystery, for the region supported no plantations or other economic enterprises using African slaves during the colonial period. Many scholars guess that the roots of Esmeraldas's African population may lie in a foundered slave ship, driven off course by a storm or, perhaps, commandeered.

While each zone has a distinct racial composition, Ecuador's sense of regionalism has also been rooted in the different relations of production that developed. In the sierra, especially the central and northern regions, labor was nearly always in great oversupply, and the indigenous people suffered under generally coerced labor arrangements until well into the twentieth century. On the coast, however, labor was relatively scarce, at least until the late nineteenth century, and was generally not coerced. Likewise, the two zones showed different market orientations: in the sierra, chiefly for local consumption; on the coast, principally for the international market. To the extent that the sierra exported its agricultural or textile production, it delivered goods from the northern and central sierra to Colombia, whereas goods from the southern sierra went to Peru. Products from the sierra almost never made it down to Guayaquil or the coastal region of Ecuador. Likewise, the coast's trade was chiefly with Peru or, in the case of cacao, Europe, but not up to Quito or the Ecuadorian sierra.

Historically, transportation between the two regions has been difficult and at times really just not possible. Until the late nineteenth century Ecuador had only a primitive footpath linking Quito and Guayaquil. Even after a road was completed in the 1870s, it was so badly maintained that travel between Quito and Guayaquil still took two to three weeks. The rainy season, every February to May, left the dirt road from the coast into the Andes absolutely impassable. Ecuador completed a railway to the sierra in 1908, but mud slides, washouts, and endless delays plagued the line. The two principal regions of Ecuador would continue to grow apart, not together.

Ecuador's geographic reality found further expression in the nation's customs, for each region holds a unique set of social values. The white elite of the sierra shows a marked tendency to be more conservative, traditional, devoutly religious, and socially reserved. The elite of the coast is less uniformly white than the elite of the sierra, showing more representation from Ecuadorians of racially mixed backgrounds. The *costeño* (coastal) elite tends to be more cosmopolitan, liberal, business oriented, and much less inclined to go to church on Sunday. Even today there remains considerable intolerance between the people of all social classes from the two regions; in the past it was even worse. Too many people of the sierra, especially the white elite, continue to refer to the coastal *montuvios* as a racially inferior breed, as *monos*, monkeys. In response, many people of the coast see *serranos* (people from the sierra) as arrogant, aloof, supercilious, and racist. Moreover, people from the coast have historically resented that Quito, the capital, has usually gotten to decide how to spend the nation's tax revenue, money generated mostly by the busy commerce of the coast.

This complex regionalism has often placed Ecuador on a separate historical path from other Latin American nations. However, the U.S. officials who had dealings with Ecuador were usually blithely unaware of all this. The Americans who came to Ecuador seemed to think that what they did not understand about Ecuadorian history and culture would not hurt them. But it did.

# 1     From Colonies to Young Republics: Independence to the 1850s

Relations between Latin America and the United States developed slowly and sporadically from the days of independence to the mid-nineteenth century. As a young nation the United States focused its interest chiefly on those Latin American lands adjacent to its borders, and by the mid-nineteenth century a good deal of that territory would come to reside within U.S. borders. South America tended to matter a good deal less to the United States, and Ecuador, small and remote, figured perhaps least of all in U.S. thinking.

The logistics of travel did little to encourage the development of ties between the United States and Ecuador. The problem was not just the vast distance between the two nations, although this was certainly part of it. The British Pacific Steam Navigation Company dominated ocean transportation to Ecuador, and the British set routes to suit their convenience. They began to provide regular service to Guayaquil only at mid-century, and even then they sent only one ship per month. Mail from Ecuador to the United States had to travel first to Liverpool. Mail from the United States to Ecuador went by way of Valparaíso, Chile. It took a month to send a communication from one nation to the other—and another to get a reply.

Travel within Ecuador was even more difficult. As the nineteenth-century adventurer and travel writer William Eleroy Curtis noted: "The road to Quito [from Guayaquil] is a mountain-path . . . traversed only on foot or mule-back, and then only during six months of the year; for in the rainy season it is impassable, except to experienced mountaineers."[1] Even during the dry season the trip usually took eight or nine days, with no lodging to be found along the way. As a weary and discouraged

Curtis discovered when he arrived in Quito, it too had no hotels. "[Evidently] few people ever go . . . here," he rightly concluded.[2]

Ecuador and the United States established limited diplomatic contact during the nineteenth century. For the first part of the century Ecuador did not have any diplomatic representation in the United States, leaving all Ecuadorian matters to be handled by the Chilean minister to the United States. Ecuador finally opened a legation in Washington, D.C., in 1853, but it closed soon thereafter and did not reopen until 1870. The post frequently fell vacant. From 1890 to 1895 Mexico represented Ecuador's interests in the United States.

In the early years of nationhood only a handful of states sent diplomatic representatives to Quito: Colombia, Peru, France, and the Holy See but not the United States.[3] As U.S. Secretary of State John C. Calhoun explained in 1845, "The state of our relations and the commerce between the two countries, do not, it is considered, warrant either the establishment, on our part, of a formal mission at Quito or the employment there of a formal diplomatic agent of any grade."[4] The United States finally opened a legation in Quito three years later, sending Vanburgh Livingston of New York as chargé d'affaires.[5] But U.S. representation was inconsistent, and years could pass with no one in the job. When in 1870 the State Department again placed a representative there—this time after a three-year lapse—the official sent, Rumsey Wing, could not even speak Spanish. After that, the United States had no foreign minister in Ecuador from 1876 to 1892, maintaining only a lower level consular office.

The lack of U.S. diplomatic representation in Ecuador was largely a matter of money—the potential benefit did not justify the cost—and reflected just how little Ecuador mattered to the United States. In truth, most Americans had never even heard of Ecuador. Similarly, most nineteenth-century Ecuadorians gave little thought to the United States or the wider world. In the uncharitable words of Curtis, Ecuador was "a hermit nation" preoccupied with internal issues and only rarely peering outward.[6] Curtis added, "There is not a newspaper printed outside the city of Guayaquil, and the only information the people have of what is going on in the world is gained from the strangers who now and then visit the country."[7] Yet despite these many obstacles, the political, commercial, and cultural interchange between the two nations slowly took more precise form and character. This chapter examines the implications of the limited but formative links between Ecuador and the United States as relations developed between these two useful strangers.

## From Colonialism to the Age of Independence

Through the colonial era Ecuador stood very much on the economic periphery of the Spanish empire. While the vast silver deposits of Peru and Mexico generated fantastic riches, Ecuador could offer little more than good farmland and available workers. In time a trade in textiles developed, with many small factories (*obrajes*) in Quito and its surrounding hinterland producing coarse cloth and woolen ponchos to be sold to clothe mine workers in Peru and Bolivia. However, a series of devastating epidemics led to the collapse of the *obraje* complex during the 1690s. Any hope for the industry's revival was crushed by the subsequent commercial reforms enacted by Spain's Bourbon kings in the eighteenth century, especially the free trade laws of 1788, which served to greatly increase competition from European cloth producers.

Colonial Guayaquil developed as a shipbuilding center, but this industry declined after the 1720s when bigger vessels from Europe began to clear Drake's Passage and arrive in the Pacific. Guayaquil also exported modest, if ever-rising, quantities of cacao to Mexico, where it was consumed as a luxury item, brewed into a rich, bitter beverage. However, Guayaquil's cacao trade usually had to be conducted clandestinely; under Spanish law most intercolonial trade was illegal for much of the colonial period.

Colonial Spanish political authority in Ecuador centered in Quito, the seat of an *audiencia,* a high court and governing political body. When the Audiencia of Quito was established in 1563, it was placed within the Viceroyalty of Peru and therefore technically came under the authority of Lima, although as a practical matter the viceroy was too far away to exercise real control. Distance created autonomy, and so while Quito could usually ignore the viceroy in Lima, this also meant that Guayaquil and other Ecuadorian towns could generally ignore Quito. During the eighteenth century Spain repeatedly modified Ecuador's political disposition, creating the new Viceroyalty of New Granada, first temporarily in 1717 and then permanently in 1739, including what is today Colombia, Panama, Venezuela, and Ecuador, with the capital in Bogotá. Guayaquil's place in all this was never settled. In 1803 Spain toyed with the idea of having Guayaquil partially attached to both the Viceroyalty of New Granada and the Viceroyalty of Peru but in 1810 removed the city from New Granada and reattached it to Peru. This lasted until 1819, when Guayaquil was given to New Granada. The situation grew even more unclear during the struggles for independence.

Quito and Guayaquil followed distinct pathways to independence, which both reflected and reinforced the deep sense of regional difference in Ecuador.[8] Ecuadorian independence originated as a response by *criollos* (whites born in the Americas) to the imposition of tighter royal control and heavier taxes in the late eighteenth century. Ecuador's *grito*, or first cry of independence, is generally dated at August 10, 1809, although the wealthy *quiteños* (people from Quito) who launched the revolt against the royal *audiencia* claimed only that they should have the right to govern in the name of King Ferdinand VII (1808, 1814–23), who was in French captivity. Quito stood alone in insurrection; the other cities of Ecuador did not join the movement. Even in Quito few people took part in the revolt. Royal troops swiftly moved on Quito, coming up from Lima and down from Bogotá, smashing the small uprising. The two subsequent Quito revolts against local royal authorities, one that began on August 2, 1810, and another on February 15, 1812, also proved short lived, with Guayaquil and other cities again declining to join the Quito rebels.

Ecuador's achievement of independence came less because of developments within Ecuador itself than spillover from events in Chile and Venezuela. After Chile fell to José de San Martín's invading forces from Argentina in 1817, Spain increasingly lost control of the waters of the Pacific Coast of South America. Guayaquil merchants recognized that their cacao sales—on the rise in the last half of the eighteenth century—now were in peril. The prosperity of the city depended on cacao: shipments made up at least two-thirds of all Guayaquil exports from the 1770s through the 1830s. Unless Guayaquil joined the cause of independence, the city would be vulnerable to rebel blockades or attacks that would shut down the cacao trade. The cacao merchants and great landowners of the coast decided to throw in with the rebels, and Guayaquil declared itself an independent city on October 9, 1820.

José Joaquín de Olmedo, a local lawyer, reform advocate, and rather accomplished poet, emerged as leader of the free city-state. However, the liberator Simón Bolívar had already decided that Guayaquil was going to be part of his new nation, Gran Colombia, while to the south San Martín thought that Guayaquil would be part of Peru. By late 1820 local opinion in Guayaquil was divided among four options, in descending order of preference: continuing as a free city, joining Peru, remaining royal, or becoming part of Gran Colombia.

In 1821, with most of the Ecuadorian sierra still under royal control, Bolívar named Antonio José de Sucre to lead the campaign for liberation. The decisive battle came on May 24, 1822, when Sucre defeated Spanish forces at the Battle of Pichincha, on the edge of Quito. But as the historian Roger Davis has noted, "Ironically, the liberation of Quito signaled the demise of Guayaquil's autonomy."[9] As Bolívar wrote to the Guayaquil junta in 1822: "You surely know that Guayaquil is a complement of the territory of Colombia; that a province does not have the right to separate from an association to which it belongs."[10] To Olmedo, Bolívar added privately, "You know my friend that a city on a river cannot form a nation."[11]

Bolívar vowed that he would never allow the "political absurdity" of Guayaquil as an independent city-state.[12] When he arrived in Guayaquil on July 11, 1822, he placed the city under the "protection" of his three thousand Colombian troops. Guayaquil could do little to oppose Bolívar; Olmedo's troops were too greatly outnumbered. Still, the pro-Peru faction in the city hoped things would be different when San Martín arrived.

San Martín landed in Guayaquil two weeks later, on July 25, 1822, and met with Bolívar on July 26 and 27. But San Martín would not help

Guayaquil. He was much more concerned with securing support for the liberation of Peru and would accept whatever conditions Bolívar demanded. And so, as some angry locals wrote on walls across the city, Bolívar's victory marked "the last day of despotism and the first day of the same."[13]

## The United States and the Independence of Latin America and Ecuador

Many leading Ecuadorians, including Olmedo, praised the United States for its support in Latin America's struggle to secure its independence. The United States was the first nation to establish formal diplomatic relations with the newly formed Latin American states, the first to send diplomatic representatives, and the first to sign trade treaties. Many in the United States approved of Latin American independence, seeing in its fight for liberty an obvious parallel to America's own earlier struggle against the British. Many Americans thought that the Latin Americans also had the right to a future free from the interference of the decadent old monarchies of Europe. A growing sense of a shared American fate began to emerge, an America of sister republics.

Perhaps even more important, leading business interests in the United States believed that they had spotted some trade opportunities in Latin America, provided, that is, that the region could first be freed from Spanish colonial control. The European wars of the early nineteenth century had already disrupted established trade and supply routes to Latin America, and as a consequence some commercial opportunities—some legal, some not—had opened up for U.S. merchants. U.S. trade with Latin America was picking up; by 1821 about 13 percent of U.S. exports went to Latin America. However, most of that trade went to Cuba and hardly any to Ecuador.[14]

American traders, especially those sailing out of Boston, helped to encourage the spirit of independence in Latin America. As some leading Latin Americans got to know the Bostonians, the Latin Americans came to see a connection between U.S. independence and its growing prosperity. As the events of independence started to unfold in Latin America and Spain, the United States began to establish official representation in several Spanish American cities. In 1810 the United States sent diplomatic agents to cities in Cuba, Mexico, Venezuela, Argentina, Chile, and Peru, instructing them to show goodwill to the Latin American people as they contemplated separation from Spain. The United States wanted to start out on friendly terms with the young republics of Latin America, should they be created, lest U.S. traders lose out to the British, who might move in and snap up all the good business opportunities.

Still, Americans were conflicted about how far they wanted to go in assisting Latin American independence. In 1815 the U.S. government issued a statement of neutrality, but not all agreed with this stance. In 1816 Speaker of the House Henry Clay (1811–14, 1815–20, 1823–25) advocated assisting the rebels directly, by all means short of war. President James Monroe (1817–25) chose to maintain U.S. neutrality, although this meant he would permit rebel vessels equal access to U.S. ports. Rebel insurgents purchased arms from private U.S. merchants and even from the U.S. government, with some war materiel advanced on credit.

The official U.S. position was that the Latin American wars of independence were civil wars, therefore requiring that the United States take a stance of neutrality. While Washington was deeply sympathetic to the insurgent cause and willing to try to aid the rebels if it could do so and maintain neutrality, the United States did not want to go to war to help Latin America win its independence. As Richard Rush, the interim secretary of state, wrote in 1817: "As inhabitants of the same hemisphere, it was natural that we should feel a solicitude for the welfare of the colonists. It was nevertheless our duty to maintain the neutral character with impartiality and allow no privileges of any kind to one party, which were not extended to the other."[15]

By 1817 Monroe had begun to consider recognizing the independence of the newly forming Latin American states. The U.S. Congress held its first debate on the topic in 1818. Speaker Clay led those favoring recognition, but the measure failed, 115–45. The United States instead dispatched three commissioners to report on whether Latin America was ready for recognition, but they issued conflicting reports. Some criticized the rebel governments, holding that they did not really control the territory they claimed, that they had not yet really defeated the Spanish. It seemed best to advance cautiously. Many Americans worried that recognition of Latin American independence would bring immediate war with Spain and perhaps other European states as well.

But whereas in 1820 only Argentina, Chile, and parts of Venezuela and Colombia were free of Spanish authority, two years later all of Colombia and all of Venezuela, Ecuador, and Mexico had achieved their independence. Monroe now realized that if the United States did not extend recognition to the new Latin American states, they might begin to establish stronger trade ties with Great Britain. In 1822 the United States recognized Gran Colombia (the republic that included Venezuela, Colombia, Panama, and Ecuador), then Mexico, as well as Argentina and Chile in 1823, Central America and Brazil in 1824, and Peru in 1826. And although promoting republican forms of government was an important U.S. goal, Washington nevertheless recognized Mexico and Brazil, both of which were monarchies. Monroe's secretary of state, John Quincy Adams (1817–25), concluded that the successful U.S. War for Independence had supplied the inspiration for the Latin American independence movements. Writing in 1823, he said: "The sentiments of the Government of the United States have been in perfect harmony with those of . . . [the people of Latin America], and while forbearing, as their duties of neutrality prescribed, from every measure which could justly be construed as hostile to Spain, they have exercised all the moral influence which they possessed to countenance and promote the cause of independence."[16]

The United States took a special interest in the young nations, at least in the first part of the nineteenth century. Of the ten diplomatic legations that United States established by 1824, five were in Latin American cities: Santiago, Buenos Aires, Mexico City, Bogotá, and Lima. The United States set up a permanent Pacific naval force operating out of ports in Peru and Chile, one of the four it established around the globe during the nineteenth century. A deeper measure of the special interest of the

United States was the unilateral foreign policy statement it issued regarding Latin America, a pronouncement that would come to be known
as the Monroe Doctrine.[17]

In his speech to Congress in December 1823 Monroe asserted twin
doctrines: U.S. opposition to the recolonization Latin America, and the
concept of two spheres, the Old World and the New World, with the
latter regarded as a special American zone that Europe would have to
refrain from entering. Monroe believed that any transfer of the Latin
American states to the hands of the European powers could threaten
U.S. security by making the New World part of the great powers' chess-
board. Accordingly, he declared that henceforth if any European state
attacked Latin America, or tried to claim or reclaim colonial holdings
there, the United States would oppose such actions in any way it chose,
including force of arms, if this served Washington's interests. In short,
the United States would view as an unfriendly act any European effort
to control the new Latin American states. Monroe did not want places
near the present or future boundaries of the United States to ever be
subjected to transfer to European powers. The Monroe Doctrine was a
U.S. assertion of its right of self-defense.

Monroe's message was also intended to shore up U.S. friendship in
Latin America, to encourage republican forms of government, and to
stimulate profitable trade relations. His declaration was not, however, an
inviolable pledge to fight for any Latin American nation attacked from
outside the hemisphere. Monroe's words did not commit the United
States to be the protector of Latin America's independence. He also did
not ask the Latin American nations to join with the United States to defend themselves against any European efforts to reconquer them.

Nonetheless, the Latin American states did not understand Monroe's
message in this way. In 1824 the Colombian government proposed a
military alliance with the United States. Washington rejected the idea.
Brazil also suggested an alliance, and the United States again refused.
No matter what some Latin American leaders thought Monroe had said
or meant to say, the United States had no desire to enter into mutual defense pacts with Latin American nations. In 1826 the Guayaquil newspaper *El patriota de Guayaquil* openly questioned whether the United

States would really come to the aid of small nations, noting that it had not helped Italy or Greece when they were attacked by larger European states.[18]

In actuality, three days after Monroe sent his message to Congress, the "Greek Question"—whether to aid the Greeks who had been trying to throw off Turkish rule for two years—prompted an outcry from members of Congress who believed that the United States had as much in common with Greece as with any of the Andean republics. The debate ended with no congressional endorsement of Monroe's "doctrine."

Monroe himself did not make any effort to realize the goals of his message, and during the nineteenth century several occasions seemed ripe for implementation of the Monroe Doctrine, but each passed without U.S. action. Indeed, Monroe's declaration was not considered a "doctrine" at all; by the 1840s his pronouncement had been all but forgotten. Europe intervened in Latin America sixteen times in the nineteenth century, with the British acquiring territory along the Gulf coast of Central America and taking over the Malvinas/Falkland Islands in 1833; repeated French and British interventions in Argentina, between 1838 and 1850; French attacks on Veracruz in 1838; Spain's reacquisition of the Dominican Republic (1861–63); British, French, and Spanish intervention in Mexico in 1861; French intervention in Mexico in 1862; placement of the European monarch Maximilian on the throne of Mexico (1864–67); and repeated European actions to collect debts in Venezuela, Colombia, and Haiti in the second half of the nineteenth century. Clearly, Latin America would have to arrange for its own security.

## Bolívar's Panama Conference

In a December 1824 letter to other Latin American chiefs of state, Simon Bolívar proposed a pan-American conference to discuss the formation of a confederation of American states, an effort to Latin Americanize the Monroe Doctrine and to plan for the liberation of Cuba and Puerto Rico from Spanish authority. As José R. Revenga, Gran Colombia's secretary for foreign affairs, reported, Bolívar was determined to "remov[e] . . .

the enemy [Spain] from all this hemisphere."[19] Bolívar did not want the United States at the meetings, but the other attendees asked that it be included. But the liberation of Cuba and Puerto Rico was a topic that the United States wanted nothing to do with. Washington preferred that Cuba remain a colony of Spain, believing that a weak but independent Cuba could be easy prey for a European aggressor. U.S. officials worried too that the pan-American meeting was going to take up anti-slavery measures, something that would be especially troubling to the U.S. South.

Despite its misgivings, the U.S. Congress approved funding to send two delegates to the convention. As it turned out, the U.S. mission never arrived at the conference in Panama. One U.S. representative, Richard C. Anderson, died on the way to Panama from Bogotá, and the other, John Sergeant, learned that the meetings had concluded even before he left the United States. Attendance at the conference, held in June and July 1826, was pretty thin anyway, with just Peru, the Republic of Central America, Mexico, and Bolívar's Gran Colombia represented. Great Britain sent a nonvoting observer. Chile and Argentina had trouble arranging travel and did not send anyone. Brazil declined. Conference planners somehow forgot to invite Paraguay. In the end the meetings led to nothing substantive, although some say the conference promoted a worthy, if ephemeral, spirit of inter-American cooperation. However, such rosy claims seem more like retroactive wishful thinking, given that the nineteenth century was a time of incessant warfare among the Latin American states, the recurrent bloodshed vividly demonstrating the absence of any meaningful sentiment of inter-American cooperation.

## From Gran Colombia into Ecuador

At times even intranational cooperation was hard to find. Bolívar's creation, the republic of Gran Colombia, lasted but eight years, 1822 to 1830, enduring only as long as Bolívar was alive. Its three southern departments, Guayaquil, Quito, and Cuenca, had trouble with the Gran Colombian state right from the start. Military rule remained in place even after the Spanish forces were defeated, with Ecuador's governors and intendants all appointed by the executive in Bogotá. Ecuadorians saw the soldiers, nearly all Venezuelans and Colombians, as an army of occupation. Worse, when the troops went too long without pay, they began to prey upon the locals. Authorities in Bogotá ignored all complaints.

The problems were plain to see. "The present system of government," wrote Beaufort T. Watts, U.S. chargé d'affaires in Bogota in 1827, "has proved inadequate to the general welfare of the country." Given the "unsettled state of the country," Watts added, "a seperation [sic] of the three great Provinces, Quito, . . . [Bogota] and Venezuela, into independent States is the most probable event."[20] Editorial opinion in *El patriota de Guayaquil* concurred, holding that Gran Colombia would be better off adopting the federal political structure of the United States.[21] Objections in Ecuador to government from Bogotá, especially the imposition of forced loans, became more vigorous when Guayaquil's cacao exports stalled in the late 1820s. In the Ecuadorian coastal zone landless *montuvios* revolted. Soon cities across Ecuador were issuing *pronunciamentos* (revolutionary declarations) decrying the illegitimacy of the Bogotá government. When Venezuela pulled out of Gran Colombia in November 24, 1829, Ecuador saw its chance and left too, on May 13, 1830. Ecuador was at last free to try to chart its own course, but this did not mean it found a better direction.

## Young Ecuador

U.S. merchants had long expected a surge in trade with Latin America once it became independent, and many in Ecuador believed the same thing. By 1832 Aaron H. Palmer was already advertising in the Guayaquil newspaper *El colombiano*, offering his services in arranging commerce between New York and Guayaquil.[22] But the commercial bonanza that Latin Americans and Ecuadorians hoped would develop with the United States did not. No sooner had Latin Americans secured their independence than U.S. interest in the region began to fade. Ironically, for Guayaquil and the central coastal zone of Ecuador, the years following independence actually brought a blossoming of the cacao economy. Cacao export sales doubled from 1830 to 1857, with chocolate beans' making up half of all Ecuadorian exports in that period.[23] But the ships loaded with cacao sailed for Spain, Chile, and Peru, not the United States.

Few U.S. vessels came to Ecuador. From time to time a U.S. whaling ship might stop at the northern port of Esmeraldas, and sometimes U.S. traders bound for Asia took on supplies in the Galápagos Islands. But otherwise only the occasional stray U.S. ship would find its way to far-off Ecuador; of the 109 vessels that called at Guayaquil in 1856, only seven sailed from the United States.

Only the most intrepid U.S. entrepreneurs set up shop in Ecuador. In 1824 three opened Ecuador's first sawmill. At mid-century the nation's only foundry was run by an American. In 1859 the Baltimore and Guayaquil Light Company began to provide gaslights for the city of Guayaquil. In the same year several Americans took the lead in setting up the Empresa Vapores del Guayas (the Guayas Steamship Company), providing steam-powered vessel transport in the Guayas River basin.

But overall there was not much trade between the nations. In the early years of the nineteenth century, Ecuadorians sent to the United States small quantities of cacao, some straw hats, and pitch for patching ships and in return received a few pieces of farm equipment, some seed, flour, liquor, paper, drugs, furniture, and soap. Guayaquil residents (the only Ecuadorians in a geographic position to import much of anything) preferred goods imported from Europe. At mid-century most of Ecuador's imports came from Great Britain and most of its exports still went to Spain.

Given the weakness of trade ties, Ecuador and the United States established fairly limited consular representation. At first Ecuador set up consulates in several U.S. cities, including Baltimore in 1839; Washington, D.C., Philadelphia, and New York in 1842; Boston and Norfolk, Virginia, in 1846; San Francisco in 1852; and New Orleans in 1853. But there was just not enough trade to justify maintaining these posts, and in the 1870s and 1880s Ecuador cut back its consulates to New York, Philadelphia, Chicago, and Washington, D.C. The first U.S. consul in

Guayaquil, William Wheelwright of Massachusetts, came to Ecuador in 1824 (when the nation was still a part of Gran Colombia). However, the United States did not open additional consular offices in Ecuador until the 1880s.

Early diplomatic exchanges between Ecuador and the United States were likewise limited. The nations entered into the Treaty of Peace, Friendship, Navigation and Commerce in 1839 (formalized 1842), but this document was not much more than a call for normal business exchanges to proceed smoothly. During the nineteenth century the United States signed a dozen more treaties with Ecuador, covering naturalization, extradition, postal conventions, and similar matters. The attention of the United States was elsewhere. Ecuador, for its part, was looking inward, absorbed by its own problems.

## Ecuador's Political Dilemmas

When delegates met in Riobamba from August 11 to September 5, 1830, to draft Ecuador's first constitution, they decided to call their new nation Ecuador. The old title, the Kingdom of Quito, would never work: Cuenca and Guayaquil could not accept the nation's being named after Quito. Yet this gesture did little to reduce Ecuador's regional animosity, and the many problems that would beset the young nation stemmed principally from the continuing regional rivalry. In fact, the coming of independence had served to exacerbate contentious sentiments, exciting each region's desire for greater autonomy. If Latin America could be free of Spain, and Ecuador could be free of Gran Colombia, why couldn't Cuenca be free of Quito, or Guayaquil be free of both?

The unevenness of economic advance in Ecuador further increased regional tensions. In the first half of the nineteenth century the economy of the sierra stagnated and in some districts actually retreated. The key problem continued to be transportation. As U.S. Consul Alexander McLean noted, even as late as the 1880s the vegetables consumed on the coast came from farms in Peru or Chile, "while abundance rots in the interior because there are no roads . . . to [coastal] market[s]."[24] The coast grew economically and the sierra did not, and an ever-growing stream of migrants departed the impoverished highlands for the more prosperous coast. Whereas in the 1780s about 92 percent of Ecuador's population lived in the sierra, by the 1880s only 70 percent did.[25]

Political disputes in Ecuador pitted the sturdy old sierra landholding class against the entrepreneurial business and landholding elite on the coast. This was a long-standing dispute. As the U.S. diplomatic representative Delazon Smith noted in 1845, "A settled spirit of animosity and rivalship . . . has always existed between the Citizens of Guayaquil and those of Quito."[26] On one side, the sierra elite fought to hang on to its coerced labor force and to continue tariff protection for what was left of its textile industry and its internal markets for grain and other farm products. Meanwhile the coastal elite wanted access to sierra labor, for workers were scarcer on the coast. The coastal elite favored free trade and opposed the sierra's insistence on protective tariffs that benefited only the sierra haciendas and remaining textile industries. But most of all, *guayaquileños* bitterly resented Quito's seizing of nearly all the import and export taxes collected at the Guayaquil customhouse—the key source of government revenue. Quito took the money and spent it on itself. The *serrano* elite was not inclined to compromise, a habit hardened over countless generations. The sierra *hacendados* were a force unto themselves, with total legal, social, political, and economic power in their fiefdoms. *Hacendados* completely controlled the lives of their peons: they could beat them; they could lock them away in their private hacienda jails. As a result members of the *serrano* elite were quite used to having their own way.

In this regional rivalry the sierra had a much larger population and the heavy weight of tradition on its side, but the coast, growing and prosperous, was not without resources. So this was the problem: neither region was strong enough to just smash the other and impose its will, and so the two fought ceaselessly. In 1870 Rumsey Wing, the U.S. minister to Ecuador, offered a different take on the endemic political violence he found: the factionalism and fighting that Ecuador had been subjected to since its inception was chiefly the result of "the fact that many of the principal citizens have had literally nothing else to do."[27]

There was no real chance that these regional disputes could be amicably worked through using the political institutions of the young republic. Formal politics was deeply corrupt. Petty acts of extortion or unrestrained theft of the national treasury seemed to occupy most of the energy of too many public officials. While elections were frequent, they were hardly ever honest. Almost no one was allowed to vote anyway, least of all illiterates, the landless, peons, slaves, women, the poor—the great mass of ordinary Ecuadorian people. Less than 1 percent of the population enjoyed suffrage rights. Only the prosperous, mainly the leading landowners, were permitted to hold office. Most presidents were selected by special constitutional assemblies anyway, not general elections: between 1830 and 1859 six of the nine presidents were picked by such special assemblies of notables, and for the whole of the nineteenth century ten of the eighteen presidents had the assemblies to thank for their office.

Government in this era had a very limited reach. It usually fell to the church, not the state, to provide public education, orphanages, and medical care. The state handed over a good deal of its political authority to decentralized independent juntas (special commissions) to handle public works projects. The juntas had their own special tax resources, their own budgets, and no duty to report to anyone—ever. Likewise, it fell to each city to organize, carry out, and pay for road construction in its district; in the sierra, cities and towns usually relied on the ancient, pre-Inca, *minga* road gang system. Much of Ecuador during the nineteenth century was so atomized that it lacked even a national currency or anything that might have functioned as one. Foreign currency, especially from Colombia, Spain, Venezuela, Peru, and Chile, was more widely used for interregional trade.

Ecuador's governments were constantly on the verge of bankruptcy. The many civil wars were bad for business, tearing up infrastructure, conscripting the workforce, and, worst of all, leading to the blockade of the port. Moreover, all this fighting produced a steady drain on meager government financial resources: by one illegal means or another, the government was cheated out of at least half its anticipated tax revenue. In the days of the young republic nearly all revenue went to pay the military and the government bureaucracy. In some years, for example, from 1830 to 1860, nearly all government revenue went only to military spending. Yet these sums never seemed to buy much, the money allocated seldom finding its way down the chain of command. Forced recruits made up the rank and file, and if they did not receive their pay (a frequent occurrence), they used their arms to informally collect from handy innocents whatever they felt might be due them. Armies lived off the land; all nearby farms suffered their predations. Too often officials relied on forced loans to fund the government. All governments operated in the red. As the U.S. diplomatic representative Delazon Smith put it in 1845, Ecuadorians were "a people almost constantly harassed by civil discord and violent revolutions."[28] He was right. Young Ecuador was a nation in name only, with feeble national governments and bitterly opposed, yet fairly evenly matched, regional interests locked in a deadly embrace.

Ecuador's internal weakness led to its defeat in several wars during the nineteenth century, losing in the process about half the territory it claimed when it came to nationhood in 1830. With their government perpetually in a state of chaos, Ecuadorians could not spare much attention for events and places beyond their own shrinking borders. To the extent that leading Ecuadorians thought at all about the United States, it would be to seek its assistance against foreign invasion and encroachment by its neighbors.

## The Age of Caudillos

Accordingly, the early years of the republic proved to be a time of endless struggles between regionally based, opportunistic, and highly charismatic caudillos (warlords). Although the disputes generally pitted regional interests against one another, at times the conflicts were driven by the personal ambitions of battling caudillos. One such was Gen. Juan José Flores. From Ecuador's inception and for the next thirty years, Flores would be the central figure in the nation's history.[29]

Flores, a Venezuelan, came to Ecuador in 1826 to serve as Bolívar's governor for the southern departments of Gran Colombia. When war broke out in 1828–29 between Gran Colombia and Peru, Flores won wide acclaim for defeating the invading Peruvians. Even more important for the advancement of his career was Flores's marriage to Mercedes Jijón y Vivanco, the daughter of notables, a liaison that won the young commander a place within aloof Quito society. Flores governed as military authority until 1830, but with the breakup of Gran Colombia he became Ecuador's first president. He was only thirty years old and did not make a good impression on everyone. Thomas P. Moore, the U.S. minister to Gran Colombia, reported to the State Department in 1830, "[Flores] is extremely ambitious and very vain."[30]

The central issue facing Ecuador was the same one facing all newly created nations: the construction of viable national political institutions. But in Ecuador the depth and bitterness of regional differences made this a particularly difficult challenge. The early years of the nation sometimes saw a new uprising every week. If President Flores left to deal with rebellions on the coast, revolts immediately sprang up in the sierra. Ecuador frequently had two national governments, each proclaiming loudly, and all too convincingly, the rank illegitimacy of the other. The fighting never stopped, and the endless disputes threatened to rip the country apart.

One of the most serious revolts, the Revolution of los Chiguaguas, was launched in Guayaquil in October 1833 by Flores's lifelong nemesis, Vincente Rocafuerte y Bejarano, the leading representative of coastal landholding interests. The fighting ended in 1834 when Flores and Rocafuerte came to an agreement: henceforth they would take turns in the presidency under the Convenio de Paz (Compact of Peace), which provided for the Quito-based and Guayaquil-based elites to alternate in power.

Vicente Rocafuerte got his turn in the presidency from 1835 to 1839. A great admirer of the U.S. Constitution, Rocafuerte thought that the United States offered the world's best example of democracy—he just believed that Ecuador was unsuited for it. He began his tenure in office with the writing of a new constitution for Ecuador, the nation's second. This would establish a pattern for Ecuador: incoming leaders prefer to start off fresh, with their own constitution. There have been many constitutions in Ecuadorian history.

A key foreign policy issue facing Rocafuerte was the diplomatic challenge raised by the creation of the Peru-Bolivia Confederation (1836–39), under the leadership of Mariscal Andrés Santa Cruz. Chile saw the union of its neighbors as a great threat, and war resulted, a conflict that threatened to draw in other Latin American states, including Ecuador. Rocafuerte sought to maintain Ecuador's neutrality, offering to mediate the dispute. However, his efforts were greatly complicated by the maneuverings of ex-president Flores.

Exiled Peruvian president Agustín Gamarra, who opposed Santa Cruz, sought Ecuadorian assistance. Gamarra approached Flores with an offer that played directly to the general's oversized ego: Flores would command a combined force of Chileans, Ecuadorians, and exiled Peruvians, the army to be paid for and supplied by Chile. But Chilean strongman Diego Portales had never agreed to this. He sent word to Flores: Chile would not pay for Ecuadorian forces and, moreover, no foreigner could command Chilean troops. When Rocafuerte learned what Flores was up to, the president was furious. To Rocafuerte it was Flores's vanity that had led him to consider taking Ecuador into a war against Santa Cruz and the Peru-Bolivia Confederation. Rocafuerte knew that his nation was not ready for war because of its internal strife. When Santa Cruz's forces began to lose in January 1839 and Bolivia withdrew from the confederation, Santa Cruz abandoned the project and left for exile in Ecuador. Peru protested and for a time contemplated going to war, but Ecuador refused to hand over Santa Cruz.

As called for in the Convenio de Paz, Flores followed Rocafuerte in office, serving as president from 1839 to 1843. At the end of his term, however, Flores moved to fix his own reelection, a clear violation of the Constitution, and, more seriously, a double-cross of Rocafuerte. Rocafuerte tried to lecture Flores on his civic duty, using the example of U.S. President George Washington, who, Rocafuerte pointed out, had stepped down after a second term. Unmoved, Flores continued his drive for a third term anyway, and in the inevitable warfare that ensued, Flores drove Rocafuerte into exile. Coastal and Cuenca elites regarded the Constitution that followed as an another unfair power grab by Quito, opening a period of intensified regional conflict. When Flores sought to impose new taxes on the populace, a broad-based and violent social revolt erupted as well.

In the midst of all this, U.S. Special Agent Delazon Smith arrived from Ohio to negotiate U.S. debt claims against the Ecuadorian government.[31] The case, as summed up by the historian George Lauderbaugh, involved U.S. merchant "ships that had been confiscated during the wars [of independence] by Gran Colombia and placed in service against the Spanish Navy."[32] The U.S.-based insurance companies had paid the claims of the owners of the *Ranger, Morris,* and *Josephine,* but, as Lauderbaugh notes, "had not been able to collect from Ecuador although Venezuela and New Granada had paid their share of the claims."[33]

Named to his post on December 28, 1844, Smith took eighty days to travel from Norfolk, Virginia, to Lima, "by far the most speedy passage on record," he boasted.[34] He then left Peru for Ecuador, traveling overland from Paita to Quito and avoiding the port of Guayaquil because "the yellow fever was raging most fearfully [there]."[35] Working his way up along the length of highland Ecuador, Smith got a good look at the nation in the middle of another civil war. He had enormous difficulty deciding which of the warring factions represented the legitimate government. At length, Smith decided that it was probably not the best time to push for collection of the debt and decided to just go home. This was surely preferable, he felt, to "remaining here for an indefinite number of months in waiting upon an ignorant, a selfish, a pennyless [*sic*], and a rebellious people for the formation of a Government which I can properly address. . . . At present there is neither legitimate Government or money adequate for the days wants in the Republic of Ecuador."[36] Smith departed, continuing to avoid Guayaquil by taking the arduous land journey up through Colombia and out.

The civil war that Delazon Smith witnessed was a successful effort to root Flores out of office. "When in Lima," Smith noted, "I saw and conferred with Mr. Rocafuerte, formerly President of the Republic of

Ecuador, I found that he was deeply and warmly engaged in the then existing revolution. He bitterly denounced Gen. Flores, the late President, as a foreigner, a usurper, a tyrant, a mulatto, a thief & &."[37]

On March 6, 1845, three wealthy Ecuadorian businessmen, José Joaquín Olmedo, Vicente Ramón Roca, and Diego Noboa, launched the Marcista (March) movement against Flores. They took some inspiration from the United States: in making their case for rebellion, they quoted directly from the U.S. Declaration of Independence. Flores recently had suffered battlefield reverses, and the payment of twenty thousand pesos induced the general to accept exile. After two brief civilian governments, Roca (1845–49) and Noboa (1849–50), a renewed scramble for power ensued. By 1851 Gen. José María Urvina Viteri had gained power. Either directly as president (1852–56) or as the power behind the presidency of Gen. Francisco Robles (1856–60), Urvina would dominate Ecuadorian politics until 1860. Yet this did not end the challenges, both internal and external, to Ecuador's political peace.

## The Flores Threat

When Flores left in 1845, he went with the promise that he would be paid 20,000 pesos in cash every year. Flores did receive the first installment, but after that he got nothing. He began to plot a comeback. His political goal, it seems, was not so much a dictatorship of his own but the imposition of a foreign monarchy for Ecuador. The indefatigable Flores and his supporters put together nineteen invasion plans in a two-year period, 1846–48. Although all his invasion attempts ended in failure, his efforts nevertheless proved extraordinarily disruptive and costly for Ecuador. In large part because of Flores's actions, most Ecuadorian national governments would find themselves totally overwhelmed by the first task of any government: staying in power.

Flores's monarchical schemes typically involved putting a Spanish prince on the throne of some recombined trans-Andean superstate. In 1846 the ordinarily frugal Spanish monarch, Queen Christina, advanced Flores $2 million in the belief that he was going secure thrones for her three children, placing them in Colombia, Peru, and Ecuador. Flores assembled an army of about six thousand men. In response, Ecuador's political leaders undertook a desperate quest for assistance from any external power that might come to their aid against Flores.

Peru took the Flores threat seriously too, and in November 1846 President Ramón Castilla issued an invitation for a pan-American conference in Lima. Castilla wanted to arrange for a united defense against Flores, although he also sought to use the meetings to discuss the implications of the British and French military intervention in Buenos Aires and the U.S. attacks on Mexico (1846–48). Castilla invited Argentina, Bolivia, Brazil, Central America, Chile, Colombia, Venezuela, Ecuador, and the United States to the meetings. While Ecuador, Bolivia, Chile, and Colombia accepted immediately, U.S. President James Polk (1845–49) saw no real threat from Flores, did not care to be lectured about the Mexican War, and decided not to send an official delegate. Instead, the U.S. chargé to Peru, John Randolph Clay, sat in informally on the discussions. By 1847 Peru, Ecuador, and Chile had agreed to cooperate in a collective defense against Flores's planned invasion, the forces for which were being outfitted and assembled in Spain. But Flores needed more money before he could make his move. He traveled to the United States in an unsuccessful bid to meet with Polk and acquire more money and war materiel for his invasion effort. When Flores's efforts to secure ships in London were uncovered by an Ecuadorian agent, the British authorities seized the vessels. This halted Flores's plans to invade South America, if only temporarily.

During the peak of the crisis Ecuador formally requested that U.S. warships be brought to the defense of Guayaquil. Whether the United States would have complied with this request is not clear. In an 1847 internal memo Secretary of State James Buchanan (1845–49) wrote:

> We . . . received information that the projected expedition of General Flores against Ecuador had exploded. May this ever be [the] fate of all such attempts to interfere with the sovereignty and independence of the American Republics! . . . Our warmest sympathies were enlisted on the side of Ecuador. . . . This will ever be the case when any attempt shall be made by the Powers of Europe to interfere with the independence of any of the

nations of this continent. . . . It did not, however, become necessary for this Government to adopt any measures in consequences of the movements of General Flores, because we never apprehended serious danger from his expedition.[38]

Buchanan told Vanburgh Livingston, U.S. chargé d'affaires in Quito, to inform the Ecuadorian minister of foreign affairs "that the intervention or dictation, direct or indirect of European governments in the affairs of the Independent States of the American Hemisphere, will never be viewed with indifference by the government of the Untied States. On the contrary, all the moral means, at least, within their power, shall upon every occasion be employed to discourage and arrest such interference."[39]

Ecuadorian Foreign Minister Manuel Gómez de la Torre was quite pleased with this statement and expressed Ecuador's "sincere and just gratitude."[40] In his presidential address in 1848 President Ramón Roca echoed this sentiment, expressing his thanks to the United States. Still, it is worth pointing out that the United States had not actually done anything. In fact, even its words of support did not come without some contradiction. In 1850 the U.S. chargé d'affaires in Quito, John Trumbull Van Alen, wrote Washington that Flores had actually been very popular as a leader and had been unjustly ousted by a small clique of opportunists. Flores's return would be a good thing for Ecuador, Van Alen thought.[41] Two years later Courtland Cushing, the new chargé d'affaires in Ecuador, wrote Washington to contradict Van Alen. Cushing said that Flores was, as a matter of fact, enormously unpopular in Ecuador and that his return would be a disaster.[42]

At the time Flores was already preparing his next attack on Ecuador. Cushing told the Ecuadorian foreign minister: "The United States cannot view with indifference such an attempt to interfere with the independence and sovereignty of this Republic."[43] Cushing received a letter from John Randolph Clay, U.S. chargé d'affaires in Lima, detailing Flores's plans to launch an invasion of Ecuador from there. Cushing immediately shared the information with the Ecuadorian Ministry of Foreign Affairs, demonstrating that at least some U.S. officials were committed to helping Ecuador against Flores.[44]

In the spring of 1852 Flores anchored three warships near Puna Island, at the mouth of the Guayas River. Guayaquil stood but forty miles away. From this position Flores tried to turn back all the ships headed for Guayaquil, and commerce in the port city halted. When a privately owned U.S. ship, the *Silas Marine,* slipped past Flores's ships and headed for Guayaquil, Flores fired five shots, missing each time.[45] Yet U.S. officials near the scene remained divided about what to do. Cushing wanted the United States to assist in the defense of Guayaquil. The USS *Portsmouth,* a sloop of war, lay at anchor in Guayaquil, and the USS *Raritan* stood nearby at Paita, Peru. Cushing urged his counterpart in Peru, John Clay, to join him in requesting that the *Raritan* be sent to Guayaquil, but Clay refused.[46]

By mid-1852 the Ecuadorian government had four vessels, perhaps five, that could be made serviceable for war and began planning to sail down the river and attack Flores.[47] Meanwhile a ship carrying about forty U.S. adventurers arrived to join Flores's forces. Ecuadorian Foreign Minister José Villamil wrote Cushing to protest.[48] Fortunately for Ecuador, Flores's invasion was beginning to fall apart. Many of Flores's soldiers had already been killed or captured in skirmishes south of Guayaquil, and most of the other men had deserted. Then one of Flores's ships blew up while lying at anchor, killing fifteen to twenty of the U.S. filibusterers. Flores, sensing that it was now or never, moved his ships in late June 1852 to within six miles of Guayaquil. Cushing wrote Capt. Thomas A. Dornin of the *Portsmouth,* urging him to stay in Guayaquil and attack Flores. The *Portsmouth* was scheduled to leave Guayaquil for Panama, but when Dornin saw Flores coming up the Guayas toward Guayaquil, he brought the *Portsmouth* around and returned to port. Flores sat near Guayaquil cogitating for a couple of days and then turned around and went back to Puna Island.[49] At last, on July 4, 1852, Flores attacked Guayaquil. Cannon shot from his vessels killed three civilians in the port city. Reported Cushing, "Two 18 pound balls passed through several rooms of my house one of them after killing my nearest neighbor Mr. Reina on his balcony, passed through my bedroom and parlor and lodged in an adjoi[ni]ng room."[50] For a time the USS *Portsmouth* and some French vessels sat in front of the Guayaquil shore battery, blocking its line of fire. Whether this action was intentional or accidental will probably never be resolved, but more important was that most Ecuadorians believed it was intentional. Still, it is hard to see what motive the United States would have had to frustrate Ecuadorian efforts at self-defense. In any event, at length the port's defense cannons were able to get some shots off and succeeded in driving Flores away.

The United States could have played a more active military role in the defense of Guayaquil, which was under attack by invaders who were supported by foreigners. Perhaps the United States declined to act because Flores had support from France and Spain. If the United States had intervened, it could have been drawn into combat with the French and the Spanish. Nevertheless, Cushing simply could not fathom why the United States had not cooperated more in defeating Flores. Others shared this view. Ecuadorian President José María Urvina wrote in 1853: "The conduct observed by the naval forces of the United States with respect to the piratical forces of Flores has been truly unfortunate for the interests of both Americas!"[51]

In late 1852 Ecuadorian authorities wrote to the United States to complain that Flores was putting together yet another invasion attempt—and this time he was plotting and gathering supplies in California.[52] U.S. Secretary of State William L. Marcy (1853–57) offered only a perfunctory reply, saying that Washington was looking into the matter and would be sure to take care of it.[53] In 1854 Philo White, the U.S. minister to Ecuador, told Marcos Espinel, Ecuador's minister of foreign affairs, that U.S. naval authorities in California believed that no expedition of adventurers was headed for Ecuador at the time. He had heard that some group was heading for *Mexico*, but those efforts had already been thwarted. Cdre. B. Dulaney, in command of U.S. vessels stationed in Callao, wrote from the USS *St. Lawrence*, his flag ship, on June 1, 1854, to say that he had no knowledge of any filibuster attempt against Ecuador. Dulaney pledged to send an armed vessel to Guayaquil to protect U.S. citizens and property if Flores did attack.[54] U.S. intelligence was accurate: Flores was not coming back.

Still, Ecuador's outlook toward the United States had begun to shift. Ecuadorian authorities were not pleased with the limited U.S. reaction to the Flores threats. They wanted U.S. warships to help or, at the very least, stay out of the way. Soon Ecuador would have further grievances against the United States.

## Conclusions

Both trade and diplomatic relations with the United States were slow to develop in Ecuador's early years. The country was too chaotic, too inward looking, to have much to do with the rest of the world, including the distant and as yet not particularly important United States. Ecuador did not even send a diplomatic representative to Washington, and it was not until the mid-nineteenth century that the United States sporadically began to place diplomatic officials in Quito.

Yet the United States and Ecuador formed some nascent contacts in the first half of the nineteenth century. From this Ecuador developed some good feelings toward the United States, at least at first. Ecuadorians certainly welcomed U.S. support during Ecuador's Wars of Independence, and many Ecuadorians were deeply grateful when the United States offered strong words of friendship, solidarity, and support in response to the initial Flores threat. But by the mid-nineteenth century Ecuadorian attitudes toward the United States had begun to change. In the wake of the Mexican War, fears of further U.S. imperialism were emerging. After Flores's attack on Guayaquil, Ecuadorians widely believed that the United States had directly hindered their efforts to defend the port, which generated considerable resentment and concern. But what would do the most to strain relations between Ecuador and the United States was the growing perception in the second half of the nineteenth century that the United States had plans to seize the Galápagos Islands.

## 2 Establishing an Unsettling Relationship: The 1850s to the 1890s

During the first half of the nineteenth century Ecuador had maintained a generally positive outlook regarding the United States. Even the U.S. invasion of Mexico (1846–48) did not evoke negative comment from Ecuador, at least initially. Context was everything, and the Mexican War came just as Ecuador was facing Flores's first invasion attempt. The United States had promised military support, Ecuadorian leaders believed, and although U.S. officials had not actually said this, the belief that they had led Ecuador to overlook U.S. actions in Mexico.

But elsewhere in Latin America, U.S. imperialism was already evoking concern. Some Caribbean and Spanish newspapers suggested that Latin America ought to unite under Spain's leadership to protect itself against the United States.[1] For Ecuador this was a nonstarter because Spain had supported Flores.[2] Seeking to address the threat of U.S. imperialist aggression, in 1856 Chile called for a meeting of the Latin American states, at what it dubbed the Inter-American Continental Congress. The Latin American nations were troubled not only by the U.S. annexation of half of Mexico but also by the repeated filibustering expeditions into Central America led by William Walker, the Tennessee adventurer who also had tried to invade Baja California in 1853–54. The Santiago conference, attended by Ecuador, Peru, and Chile, led to a continental treaty for mutual defense. Although the document was never formally ratified, the meetings signaled that Ecuador's thinking about the United States had changed, not least because many leading Ecuadorians now feared that the United States was interested in acquiring the Galápagos Islands.

Yet at the same time the second half of the nineteenth century brought closer ties between the United States and Ecuador. Nascent trade links developed, with more Ecuadorian agricultural exports shipped to the United States and more U.S. goods arriving at the docks in Guayaquil. Some U.S. companies came to Ecuador, especially to help in the construction of public works. Both nations opened more consular offices and placed their diplomatic relations on a firmer and more regularized basis. But although Ecuador and the United States were building a relationship, it proved to be one that was rather more vexing than both would have preferred.

## A Shift in Attitude

The troubles regarding the Galápagos Islands began in 1853 after the new Ecuadorian minister to the United States, Gen. José Villamil, informed the Franklin Pierce administration (1853–57) that the islands held thick deposits of guano and that Ecuador was interested in cooperating with the United States in undertaking the exploitation of this valuable resource. The offer looked very attractive to the United States, especially given the rising price of Peruvian guano, an essential fertilizer for cotton production in the slave South. Courtland Cushing, U.S. chargé d'affaires in Ecuador, aroused further interest, advising that "I have seen private letters recently, stating that guano has been discovered on one of the [Galápagos] islands. . . . The Government of Ecuador is too helpless to take care of the Gallapagos [sic] Islands, and . . . might be disposed to cede them to the United States upon reasonable terms."[3] Secretary of State William L. Marcy was intrigued, suggesting in August 1854 that "perhaps the Ecuadorian Government would prefer to grant, for a fair consideration, to the United States, the right to exclusive possession of its islands, for a long term of years, or in perpetuity with an unrestricted right to take away the guano found thereon."[4]

That year Pierce empowered Philo White, who had replaced Cushing as chargé d'affaires, to negotiate a convention with Ecuador that would grant the United States sole rights to mine guano in the Galápagos. Villamil hired a U.S. steamship captain, Julius de Brissot, to take him and the U.S. consul in Guayaquil to the Galápagos to determine just how vast the guano deposits might be. After this fact-finding mission Brissot traveled to New Orleans, where he announced that Ecuador's guano beds were in fact much larger than those in Peru. But Brissot's claims were simply false. White informed Marcy in September 1854 of "the unwelcome fact, that, after a thorough exploration, *no* guano can be discovered on the Galápagos Islands."[5] There had never been any guano on the islands, nor was there any guano anywhere in Ecuador.[6]

Nevertheless, as news of the proposed transfer of the Galápagos Islands began to leak out, the Ecuadorian public responded with outrage. Ecuadorians certainly blamed their leaders, but more important was that the story lent credibility to Ecuadorians' fears that their powerful neighbor to the north was turning its imperialist gaze toward them. If the United States might take the Galápagos Islands, what would stop it from acquiring even more of Ecuador? After the Galápagos episode many Ecuadorians began to rethink their views of the U.S.-Mexican War. Viewed in this new light, the United States now seemed a most warlike and expansionist nation, one that had proved itself fully capable of attacking its Latin American neighbors and taking their land. Ecuadorians could only hope that U.S. territorial ambitions would remain close to its own borders. As the historian Joedd Price has correctly summed up: "Only *after* the Galápagos scare were Ecuadoreans critical of past United States territorial expansion into Mexico in 1846–1848. Also after 1854, they were quite concerned with and opposed to any Yankee intervention in Central America, Panama, Santo Domingo, and Cuba."[7]

### Ecuador's Nadir

On the heels of this new realization about the United States came deeper troubles for Ecuador, both foreign and domestic. In 1854 President José María Urvina Viteri offered the British territorial concessions in Esmeraldas and the Oriente (the Amazon territory) in exchange for reduction of the debt that Ecuador owed Great Britain—the Espinel-Mocatta accord. The trouble with Urvina's land-for-debt swap proposal was that much of the territory in question was in dispute—it probably really belonged to Peru.

The debt to the British had long historical roots. During the wars of independence Gran Colombia had borrowed about $30 million from the British, and when Ecuador gained its independence from Gran Colombia, it inherited 21.5 percent of that debt. Ecuadorians believed that this share of the burden was far too large and that the British had grossly overcharged for war materiel, dishonestly inflating the amount owed. Nevertheless, when Ecuador opted out of Gran Colombia, it had formally accepted its part of the debt obligation, even though no one from Ecuador had been on hand in Bogotá in October 1830 when shares of the debt had been apportioned. At the time the Flores government had no choice, because it was completely preoccupied with putting down an internal revolt. Following Flores's lead, in 1837 Vincente Rocafuerte had officially reaffirmed Ecuador's responsibility for its part of the debt.

When Peruvian President Ramón Castilla learned that a deal between the British and the Ecuadorians was in the offing and that it involved Peruvian land, he ordered an immediate blockade of Guayaquil. Then, in 1858–59, he launched a strike deep into Ecuador, occupying the port city. Given the preexisting weakness of government of Ecuador, Peru's invasion was more than the nation could bear, and Ecuador fell apart, disintegrating into multisided civil war. Ecuador now faced the ugliest possibility for any nation: partition. In 1859 five leaders vied for control of Ecuador: Gen. Francisco Robles; Gabriel García Moreno, who controlled the northern and central sierra; Jerónimo Carrión, in the southern sierra region near Cuenca; Guillermo Franco, who held most of the coastal region; and Manuel Carrión Pinzano, who held the extreme south around Loja and Túmbez, sierra and coast. This was not the proudest hour for Ecuadorian nationalism: Loja and Cuenca each declared independence, Guayaquil petitioned to join Peru, while in Quito García Moreno proposed that Ecuador become a French protectorate. García Moreno would later also consider joining Ecuador to Colombia.

Colombia had previously agreed to a mutual defense pact with Ecuador, promising to provide military assistance in the event of outside attack (spelled out in treaties signed in 1832, 1836, and 1856). But Colombia now refused to come to Ecuador's aid, claiming rather disingenuously that the war was a purely internal matter. Instead, Colombia's president, Tomás Cipriano Mosquera, joined with Castilla of Peru in 1859 and began to work out the details for partitioning Ecuador, splitting the territory between them. In the end they decided not go forward with this scheme, held in check by the fear that their actions might provoke Bolivia and Chile into war against both.

In the midst of this chaos the Ecuadorian faction led by García Moreno invited former president Flores back to command its army. This proved the turning point in the civil war as Flores valiantly led the Quito forces to victory. Surprisingly, Flores proved loyal to García Moreno, no doubt figuring that he would follow him in office, although Flores died before this could happen. In the end Castilla of Peru agreed to a negotiated settlement with García Moreno: in exchange for Ecuador's promise not to turn over the disputed Amazonian territory to the British, the Peruvian navy left Guayaquil in 1860. Of course, as soon as Peru withdrew its forces, Ecuador repudiated the deal, establishing a pattern closely followed in subsequent Ecuadorian diplomacy.

## The French Protectorate Proposal

During the darkest hours of the civil war, García Moreno wrote several letters to France, dated December 7, 14, and 21, 1859. Sent through the French chargé d'affaires, Émile Trinité, the letters from García Moreno proposed making Ecuador a French protectorate. García Moreno saw this as a way to save his nation from partition by Colombia and Peru, although his concerns about the United States were also a motivation. García Moreno believed that if the United States got the Galápagos Islands, the Americans soon would return for the rest of Ecuador—and Ecuador's neighbors as well. García Moreno thought that the United States might soon begin to apply its Monroe Doctrine unilaterally, imposing its political hegemony southward on the people of Latin America, pressing its dominant Protestant religions upon those of the Catholic faith.

What García Moreno had in mind was an Ecuadorian arrangement with the French that would be similar to Canada's relationship with Great Britain. But Ecuador's protector would have to be France. Becoming a Spanish protectorate was not a viable option, García Moreno explained, because Ecuadorians held too much lingering resentment against their old colonial master. The British would not do, either, García Moreno said, for they were of a different race, religion, culture, and language. The United States was not even in the running.

France took García Moreno's protectorate proposal seriously and by June 1861 was seeking more information from the Ecuadorian government. The French showed a special interest in learning what natural resources might be available for exploitation. French authorities also wanted to know how the Ecuadorian people would feel about the presence of foreign troops in their territory. García Moreno assured the French representative, E. Farbé (Émile Trinité had gotten the fever and died in Guayaquil), that the Ecuadorian people would cheer the French, welcoming them as their protectors.

García Moreno was wrong, of course, and when his secret letters to the French somehow came to be published widely in Lima and Panama newspapers, a popular uproar commenced at once. As the Ecuadorian people rallied angrily against the proposal, García Moreno had no choice but to back down. The matter also reached the attention of the United States, where policy makers regarded García Moreno's offer as a violation of the Monroe Doctrine. García Moreno publicly renounced the notion of a French protectorate on December 24, 1861, finding it wiser to continue to explore the idea in secret. As research by George Lauderbaugh has uncovered, "On 15 March 1862, [French Emperor] Napoleon III met with Ecuador's minister resident, Antonio Flores [Jijón, the son of Juan José Flores], who offered him the Galápagos Islands and portions of lands on the Amazon River in exchange for French protection against Peru."[8] García Moreno also directed Flores Jijón to float the idea of making the French protectorate a multistate Andean monarchy, the king to be picked by Napoleon III. But by 1861 French thinking had turned away from Ecuador and toward Mexico. France had more people and commercial interests in Mexico than in Ecuador and in the end went in that direction.

Still, it seems quite likely that Ecuador would have become a French protectorate if not for the pessimistic attitude taken by the French officials charged with making recommendations to their king. French authorities noted that while they would like to help the South American republics become more "civilized," they thought it would be too difficult to bring Ecuador up to this level. France would have to station too many troops there, and the whole thing would cost too much money. It was not worth it, the advisers told the king—Ecuador lacked any readily exploitable natural resource. So in the end Napoleon III rejected all of García Moreno's overtures, also turning down a more limited proposal for trading the Galápagos Islands for French help with military training and supplies. In the aftermath of this episode, García Moreno came to be widely reviled across Latin America. When he publicly backed Napoleon III's efforts to place the Archduke Maximilian on the throne of Mexico, Latin American leaders despised García Moreno even more.

## Continued Troubles

One might think that the national disgrace of near partition would have put the Ecuadorian elite on notice about the cost of their endless internecine fighting. Yet their ceaseless wrangling continued; the threats to Ecuador's survival were by no means over. In view of Ecuador's weakness and vulnerability, García Moreno tried a new initiative, this time involving Colombia, whose president, Tomás Mosquera, had been eager to work with Castilla of Peru to carve up Ecuador three years earlier. García Moreno wrote Mosquera on April 10, 1862, to explore the possibility of reconstituting Gran Colombia, reasoning that this would protect Ecuador from Peru. And it might have, but it would not protect Ecuador from Colombian soldiers, who in mid-1862 suddenly invaded Ecuador's northern sierra.

The trouble had started with a civil war in Colombia that pitted General Mosquera against forces led by Gen. Julio Arboleda. On June 19, 1862, Arboleda had passed into Tulcán in northern Ecuador in an effort to catch Mosquera and his fleeing troops. García Moreno had led the Ecuadorian forces north from Quito to Tulcán, where he was rapidly defeated, captured, and held prisoner. García Moreno gained his release only after the U.S. minister intervened. In exchange for his freedom García Moreno signed a peace treaty recognizing Arboleda as the leader of Colombia. Moreover, as Lauderbaugh has discovered, "in addition to this public treaty, García Moreno agreed secretly to provide Arboleda with arms and $20,000 in cash."[9] As soon as García Moreno arrived safely home in Quito, he forgot all about these promises and instead raised an army of 7,500 men and invaded Colombia. At the battle of Cuaspud on November 26, 1863, Ecuador's army suffered a complete rout, with 1,500 killed and wounded, 2,000 taken prisoner, and all its artillery seized.

With foreign protection no longer an option, García Moreno decided that the only remaining solution to Ecuador's perpetual political chaos and vulnerability to outside attack was the construction of a powerful, sierra-based dictatorship—one with him in charge. The distinct possibility of a new alliance between Peru and Colombia in 1863 renewed the threat of partition and finally forced most of the various regional elites in Ecuador to reluctantly back García Moreno. If elite coastal interests were especially unhappy with this arrangement, they at least saw in García Moreno someone who might provide a measure of stability for the nation. García Moreno would serve as president from 1861 until 1865 and again from 1869 until 1875; between his terms García Moreno tried to control two weak presidents, Jerónimo Carrión (1865–67) and Javier Espinosa (1867–69). Yet even the imposition of a strong García Moreno dictatorship would not bring an end to the severe challenges that Ecuador would have to face.

## Spain, Ecuador, and the United States

The 1860s brought foreign threats to several nations of Latin America. Deeply troubling was the presence of French troops in Mexico in 1862. Another Latin American concern was the Spanish reacquisition of the Dominican Republic, in 1861–63, an action that seemed to signal a broader Spanish desire to retake more of its former colonies. Then, in April 1864, Spain seized the guano-rich Chincha Islands of Peru.

In response to these developments Peru called for the fourth (and the last, as it turned out) Bolivarian conference (so called in recognition of Bolívar's pan-American dream). This was a meeting for Latin America only; the United States was not invited. The continent was under attack by a European power, and the Latin American nations were arranging for their mutual defense; they were not looking to the United States to invoke the Monroe Doctrine. Represented at the meetings in Lima in November 1864 were Argentina, Bolivia, Chile, Colombia, Venezuela, and Peru. Ecuador's attendance was problematical. García Moreno had declared Ecuador's neutrality in the Spanish-Peruvian conflict, offering to serve as mediator. Peru responded angrily, asserting that Ecuador had an obligation to stand in solidarity with the other Latin American republics. Peru withdrew its diplomatic representative from Quito in July 1864 and informed Ecuadorian officials that they would not be welcome at the conference in Lima. Other nations joined in the complaint against Ecuador, holding that Ecuador would have to affirm the cause of Latin American unity before it could be admitted to the conference. By allowing Spanish warships to obtain provisions in Ecuadorian ports, they argued, Ecuador had violated its alliance with the other Latin American republics, as agreed to at the congresses of 1848 and 1856. Other Latin American nations also maintained a good deal of lingering resentment because of García Moreno's scheme to try to make Ecuador a French protectorate. At length, however, convention delegates relented, conceding that no Latin American nation should have to agree to preconditions or offer explanations just to attend a conference. They grudgingly admitted the Ecuadorian delegation. Once at the meetings, Ecuador was persuaded to drop its position of neutrality and joined in condemning the Spanish occupation of the Chincha Islands. By early 1866 Peru, Chile, Bolivia, and Ecuador had entered into a mutual defense convention, the Quadruple Alliance. Ecuador declared war on Spain on February 27, 1866.

In late March 1866 a squadron of nine Spanish men-of-war cruised into the Pacific, headed for the port of Valparaíso, and let go a withering bombardment, reducing much of the Chilean city to smoking rubble. Sailing up the coast a month later, they moved on to shell the Peruvian port of Callao on May 2, 1866.[10] For Ecuador it was at about this time that two unrelated issues somehow came to be linked. One was Spain's attacks on Chile and Peru; the other was Ecuador's failure to keep up its debt payments to the United States. Under a convention signed with the United States on November 25, 1862, Ecuador had finally agreed to make good on various old claims. A commission with both U.S. and Ecuadorian members stipulated that Ecuador owed the United States $94,800 and that a payment of one-ninth of the sum ($10,533) would fall due on February 17, 1866. When the time came to pay, however, Ecuador could not come up with the money. Manuel Bustamente, the Ecuadorian minister of foreign affairs, wrote U.S. Secretary of State William H. Seward (1861–69) on April 25, pointing out that the Ecuadorian Treasury Department had instructed the governor of Guayas to turn over customs receipts and salt tax revenues, just as soon as they might become available.[11]

This is where the matter stood until the war with Spain broke out. After the attacks on Valparaíso and Callao in early 1866, residents of Guayaquil figured they would be next. When the Spanish squadron set sail from Peru, Guayaquil panicked. Shopkeepers boarded up store windows, rich merchants fled, taking as much merchandise as they could to store on their upriver estates. Writing on May 13, the U.S. representative in Guayaquil, L. V. Prevost, told the secretary of state:

> Two months ago I had requested the commander of the United States naval forces on the station to order one of the vessels under his command to this place to protect American property and interests. Again, on the 1st instant, learning that he was at Callao, I addressed him another communication, urging upon him the necessity of detaching one of his vessels with orders for this place. Up to this date no vessel has reached this port; and in case of a bombardment or other trouble, the Americans here, notwithstanding the large squadron on the station, will be without protection.[12]

García Moreno arranged for the rapid delivery of Chilean arms and munitions for the defense of Guayaquil, while soldiers under the command of General Ignacio de Veintemilla readied the city for Spanish attack. Veintemilla mined the waters of the approaches to Guayaquil and scuttled ships to block entrance to the port. Nearly all commerce halted; the human suffering began.

But on June 5 Seward told Prevost, acting secretary of the U.S. legation: "Information here leads me to believe that the Spanish fleet are not meditating an attack on Guayaquil."[13] He was right. After the bombardment of Callao the Spanish squadron, in need of supplies, left for the Philippines. The Spanish never attacked Guayaquil.

What happened next might best be termed accidental gunboat diplomacy. Prevost wrote from Guayaquil on July 5:

> During the period that the Spanish squadron was expected here I had requested the commander-in-chief of our naval forces on the station, in view of the circumstances, to send one of the vessels under his command to this port. The United States steamer Mohongo arrived here about the 1st of June. . . . It was at that time that I had made a peremptory demand on the government for the immediate payment of the amount due under the convention of 1862. The public prints, in noticing this, said also that the President of the United States had asked the Senate for more energetic measures to collect the amount due by Ecuador. The newspapers of this city also said that there was no doubt that the presence of a man-of-war in this port at the present time was sent for [the] purpose of forcing the government of Ecuador to pay the amount past due. . . . There is no doubt . . . that the presence of a man-of-war here always has, and may have had epecialy [sic] at that time, its moral effect.[14]

By August 1866 Ecuador had made its first payment in full, plus interest, and early in 1867 made its second payment to the United States. In the end it remains uncertain why Ecuador suddenly paid up. It could well have been that the presence of the U.S. ship convinced Ecuador's leaders to find the money. Of course, another possibility is that Ecuador paid in an effort to court U.S. help in the event of war with Spain. Still another possibility is that it was just a coincidence that Ecuador paid at this time, just as it really was a coincidence that the U.S. warship came into port just as Prevost was renewing the demand that Ecuador pay the money due the United States. Later, as events quieted down, Ecuador's debt repayment policy returned to normal: it stopped paying. The foreign debt would remain in default from 1868 until 1890 and would continue to be a key source of unease.

## More Troubles

There were other points of friction between the United States and Ecuador. Of special U.S. concern was García Moreno's rather extreme religious views. A fiercely devout Catholic, García Moreno entered Ecuador into an agreement with the Holy See in 1862 that Ecuador formally accepted as law in 1866. The accord established Catholicism as the formal state religion of Ecuador, banned the practice of all other faiths, empowered the Catholic Church to set school curricula, and gave the church a free hand to censor all reading material. To be a citizen of Ecuador one had to be a Catholic. It became all but impossible for Protestants to get married in their faith in Ecuador. When these government policies created an atmosphere of extreme anti-Protestantism, leading to acts of desecration of the few Protestant cemeteries in Ecuador, Washington lodged official protests.

Another problem area in U.S.-Ecuadorian relations developed around the case of the river steamer *Washington,* a vessel registered in Ecuador but with some minority owners who were U.S. citizens resident in Ecuador. In June 1865 former presidents José María Urvina and Francisco Robles sought to overthrow the García Moreno dictatorship, seizing the *Washington* in the process. But when García Moreno put down the rebellion, he decided to keep the vessel rather than return it to its owners. García Moreno's view was that the ship's owners had given the *Washington* to the rebels in support of their actions and it was therefore booty. García Moreno made some repairs to the vessel and began to sail it around. The original owners wanted it back.

The Ecuadorian high court, handpicked by the dictator, agreed with García Moreno's position. Judge Pedro José de Acteta found that the captain of the vessel, Francis Game (son of the owner of the Guayas Steam Navigation Company), had freely given the *Washington* to be used by revolutionary forces. As the court reconstructed events, the rebels were supposed to have paid Game $10,000 for this act of trea-son. Because the *Washington* had enjoyed neutrality rights of passage on the Guayas River system, Game had maneuvered the vessel right next to the unsuspecting crew of an Ecuadorian war steamer, the *Guayas*. The revolutionaries, commanded by Urvina and Robles, boarded the *Guayas* and killed the captain. Later García Moreno sailed out to meet the *Washington* in the Gulf of Guayaquil and defeated the revolutionar-ies in a sea battle, seizing the *Washington* and other vessels. The judge concluded that "the revolutionists could never have taken possession of the steamer *Washington* if it had not been for the connivance and co-operation of the captain."[15]

Frederick Hassaurek of the U.S. legation in Guayaquil was furious about Ecuador's handling of the case, arguing that a fair disposition of the matter was not possible—such could "hardly be expected in a coun-try without an independent judiciary," he said in disgust.[16] To Hassau-rek, the court's ruling in favor of García Moreno was in "utter disregard of all principles of good faith, reason, and justice."[17] But U.S. Secretary of State Seward was unmoved and reminded Hassaurek that the *Wash-ington's* U.S. connections were, after all, only minority owners living in Ecuador. Seward sided with García Moreno, finding that Ecuador did indeed have the right to seize the ship. Seward suggested that the own-ers seek a small financial settlement from the Ecuadorian government. While the case was still in litigation, the *Washington* caught fire and sank, a total loss. This, and Seward's attitude, effectively ended the matter. The United States would not intervene in Ecuador to protect U.S. eco-nomic interests if the holdings involved were too small to bother with.

Ecuador had its own diplomatic concerns with the United States, bringing to Washington's attention a matter involving claims of U.S. citizenship. Some people living in Ecuador asserted that they were, in fact, U.S. citizens and should therefore be excused from the military draft and from all Ecuadorian taxes. To deal with this situation the two nations reached a naturalization agreement on November 6, 1873, that stipulated that all naturalized U.S. citizens would lose their U.S. citizen-ship rights if they returned to their native land, stayed for two years, and showed no intention of returning to live in the United States. Unfortunately, most disputes between the two nations would not be resolved so easily.

## The End of the García Moreno Years and After

As with most dictatorships, that of García Moreno became increasingly unpopular with the passage of time. He certainly was hated by the Indian underclass of the sierra, especially for laws that had made it more difficult to leave for the coast, and the higher taxes and forced labor demands fed numerous protests, notably in 1871 and 1872. Ecuador's indigenous people launched seven major uprisings during García Moreno's time in power (1860–75). Characteristically, U.S. diplomats showed little sympathy for the Indians' plight. Wrote Rumsey Wing, the U.S. minister to Ecuador, in 1871: "These usually humble, passive Indians equaled, if they did not surpass, their red friends of North America in the devilish ingenuity of their barbarity. . . . They were not lacking in any element of aboriginal cruelty."[18]

Several revolts against García Moreno also occurred along the coast; the most significant was led by Eloy Alfaro Delgado in 1864 in Manabí, on the central coast. Although many in the Guayaquil elite were comfortable enough with García Moreno, a group of radical liberals came to violently oppose him. Ironically, by fostering economic progress García Moreno had helped create new social forces, groups that now demanded greater political clout. These new middle-ranking groups would not support his dictatorship. In the end García Moreno was pulling the nation in two directions at once, condemning and embracing modernization: favoring reforms while supporting a church that opposed them, pushing for higher literacy and then throttling the press. The end came in 1875 when García Moreno had himself reelected. An assassin, Capt. Faustino Lemus Rayo, caught García Moreno on the steps of the presidential palace and hacked him to death with a machete on August 6, 1875.

The bitter interregional combat resumed. The considerably less assertive Antonio Borrero y Cortázar from Cuenca followed García Moreno in office. Borrero lasted but eight months before a new civil war in Ecuador broke out, pitting the landowning sierra elite and the church against coastal merchants and cacao estate owners. Gen. Ignacio de Veintemilla, the *jefe militar* (military chief) of Guayaquil who had readied the city for Spanish attack back in 1866, led the coastal forces to victory. Underscoring the shift in power, Veintemilla formally assumed office in Guayaquil, not Quito. Long excluded coastal liberals were ebullient, believing this would be their chance to push through their agenda. The liberal leader Pedro Carbo especially held out this hope and worked, at least initially, with the caudillo Veintemilla (1876–83). But to the dismay of Carbo and others, Veintemilla was more violent opportunist and libertine than he was liberal reformer. According to Borrero, Veintemilla "lived his nights playing and drinking, and his days sleeping." [19] It was this unprincipled dictator who had the task of dealing with Ecuador's next series of foreign policy crises.

## Ecuador and the War of the Pacific

When the War of the Pacific, pitting Chile against Peru and Bolivia, broke out in 1879, both sides sought to enlist Ecuador's support. Chile made the most determined effort at wooing Ecuador, sending a representative to Quito in 1879 to make the pitch. Chile suggested that Ecuador might want to use the war as an occasion to secure a more favorable boundary with Peru. Chile asked Ecuador to commit two thousand to three thousand troops and send them to attack the three northern provinces of Peru, Jaén, Túmbes, and Maines. It was a tempting offer. President Veintemilla well understood that Chile had a special relationship with Ecuador: Chile had supported Ecuador's positions at the 1864 Lima conference and had supplied war materiel to Guayaquil when it was under threat of Spanish attack. In the end, however, Veintemilla had his doubts about whether Chile could win this war, and he worried too that his grip on power in Ecuador was too weak to risk sending several thousand men to make war on Peru. Veintemilla pledged his solidarity to Chile, but Ecuador would remain neutral in the conflict. Ecuador tried to mediate the dispute, but Chile refused Veintemilla's offer.

Veintemilla's dictatorship coincided with economic good times for Ecuador, with cacao prices rising and strong performances registered by other coastal export products, such as tagua, coffee, and rubber. If nothing else, Veintemilla knew how to spend money to have fun, and he came to be loved by those who took part in his grand fiestas and lavish public ceremonies. He may not have been honest, but he could be munificent with the money he stole, allowing his cronies to help themselves generously from the public till, while public works built in the García Moreno years deteriorated. Fed-up, disillusioned liberals backed a rebellion (1882–83) launched from Esmeraldas and led by Eloy Alfaro Delgada and Pedro Carbo. Veintemilla fled to Guayaquil where he robbed a bank to help cover his military expenses. He was defeated nonetheless and went into exile.

Historians have labeled the subsequent period, 1884–95, Ecuador's "progressive age." The label is not especially apt (and certainly does not resemble the period in U.S. history of the same name). Still, these years did bring a few important changes. Previously, from 1830 to 1884, Ecuador had experienced seven revolutions, twelve constitutions, and fifteen presidents. The progress in the "progressive period" was chiefly that all three subsequent presidents came to office through elections, not by war. Two actually completed their terms: José María Plácido Caamaño, 1884–88, and Antonio Flores Jijón, 1888–92. The Luis Cordero government that followed (1892–95) brought a return to form, falling to a corruption scandal in 1895. But as cacao exports, especially to France and Spain, continued their steady upward climb and provided larger sums of tax revenue, the national government began to command sufficient financial resources to do something beyond paying the military and trying to cling to power. Money can help purchase political stability; Ecuador's increased trade revenues were beginning to make this possible.

## Ecuador-U.S. Trade in the Second Half of the Nineteenth Century

The second half of the nineteenth century brought increased commercial competition between the British and the United States in parts of

Latin America, although this contestation was not much about Ecuador, a land that still held little attraction for either. There was hope in 1871, however, that Ecuador had found the product that would generate significant trade with the United States: cundurango, a plant native to the southern highlands of Ecuador. Country doctors firmly believed that cundurango could cure cancer. When one U.S. physician, D. V. Bliss, heard about cundurango, he tried it and quickly became convinced of its curative properties. Bliss was not without influence; he served as the private doctor to Ecuador's minister to the United States and to Hannah Stryker, the mother of Schuyler Colfax, the U.S. vice president. Bliss treated Stryker, a cancer patient, with cundurango and soon announced that she had been cured. The good news of her recovery touched off something of a sensation, and in 1871 requests poured in to the Ecuadorian legation in Quito for Ecuador to export more of the miracle drug. Things started to go badly, however, when Dr. Thomas Antisell and the medical society of the District of Columbia concluded that cundurango did not work. Bliss was kicked out of the medical society, and others—including the U.S. House of Representatives—soon joined in denouncing both him and cundurango. Stryker succumbed to her illness in 1872, and cundurango sales dried up.

Yet despite the cundurango boomlet, or perhaps because of it, trade between the United States and Ecuador remained limited, the products and commercial exchanges still relatively minor. The United States was the sole supplier of lard to Ecuador and sold some canned goods in Guayaquil, although as Alexander McLean, the U.S. consul there, noted in 1880, contents often arrived so badly rotted no one would eat them.[20] Also imported were Remington rifles, a popular choice for the recurrent civil wars. In the late nineteenth century the breweries in Quito imported hops from the United States, arranging to have them hauled all the way up to Quito on the backs of porters. Chairs made in the United States were imported too, disassembled in Guayaquil, and carried up in pieces and reassembled in Quito. The presses and type used by Quito's sole newspaper were also purchased in the United States. Otherwise, not much came from the United States. Guayaquil newspapers in the 1880s and 1890s offered few advertisements for U.S. imports, aside from a few for cure-alls, other assorted pills, and policies from the New York Life Insurance Company.[21]

There was not much to ship, but even so transport between the United States and Ecuador went badly. In 1879 three vessels sailed from the United States for Ecuador, but one burned and sank on the way. As William Curtis wrote of Ecuador in the late nineteenth century, "Nearly all the merchants . . . [are] foreigners, most English and German, with one or two from the United States."[22] The British continued to control shipping. In 1878, for example, all one hundred of the steam-powered ocean craft that called at Guayaquil had embarked from Great Britain.[23] Their monopoly made the British something less than fully attentive to customer needs, and Ecuadorians voiced many complaints about service. The British still charged more for the journey from Ecuador to the United States than for the more distant voyage to Great Britain. Cargo had to pass through Panama, and if it missed its connection, something that happened often, thieves would loot aggressively, leaving the remains to decompose in the tropical sun. By the late 1880s some vessels from San Francisco were heading for Guayaquil with cargoes of lard, flour, and kerosine, a journey that still took at least forty days at sea.

Nor did Ecuador generally attract much investment from U.S. businesses, although toward the end of the century some arrived, especially in connection with public works projects. García Moreno brought in more than forty U.S. citizens to provide technical assistance on a wide array of undertakings. One such was the proposed railway linking the sierra to the coast, a project begun in 1873 under the direction of U.S. construction engineers. U.S. engineers also carried out the survey for another planned line linking Quito to the Bay of Caráquez on the central coast, although the railway was never built. Other U.S. engineers worked on a road from Quito down to Esmeraldas and also on the main Quito highway through the heart of the sierra and toward the coast. In Guayaquil the Baltimore Gas and Light Company started streetlight construction in 1870, importing all the equipment from the United States. In the 1870s Guayaquil built a new customhouse, using wood and iron imported from Seattle and San Francisco. In this decade Ecuador also imported U.S. steam engines, railway equipment, saw mill equipment, and by the 1880s streetcars and ice plant equipment, all for use in Guayaquil. Workers completed a telegraph line linking the capital and Guayaquil in 1884, and by 1885 messages could arrive via undersea cable all the way from the United States. In 1886 Guayaquil opened its first brewery, the Guayaquil Lager Beer Brewery Association, built entirely with machinery imported from the United States. In 1887 a U.S. firm got the contract to expand Guayaquil's potable water supply. And by 1887 a U.S.-owned enterprise, the West Coast Telephone Company, boasted two hundred paying customers in Guayaquil.[24]

Now both Ecuador and the United States set up more official trade offices. In the 1880s the United States opened consulates in Chone, Bahía de Caráquez, Manta, Esmeraldas, and Quito. In the 1890s Ecuador expanded its consulates to include representation in Cincinnati, New Orleans, and Los Angeles. Yet despite this activity, at the end of the nineteenth century U.S. investments in Ecuador totaled but a third of those in neighboring Colombia. Even grander U.S. efforts to stimulate increased trade links, such as the Inter-American Congress of 1889–90, would also not have much impact.

## Blaine's Inter-American Conference

U.S. Secretary of State James G. Blaine (1881, 1889–92) regarded Latin America a great potential market and place for investment of excess U.S. capital, and he therefore actively championed the creation of a Latin American customs union. To achieve this Blaine called for a pan-American conference in 1881, but his plans fell through. When he became secretary of state for a second time in 1889, he was at last able to arrange for the inter-American meeting he so ardently sought. The conference took place in Washington, D.C., bringing together representatives from most of the nations of the Americas. Once they were assembled, however, Blaine found scant Latin American interest in lowering Latin American tariffs for U.S. goods, especially because the United States already allowed most Latin American tropical imports to enter duty free. The conference's results were feeble: a recommendation to adopt the decimal system and so forth. None of the attendees ever ratified the international arbitration agreement that came out of the conference. Little of value for Ecuador derived from the meetings. Reports sent by the Ecuadorian representative, ex-president José María Plácido Caamaño, were devoid of substantive content, instead overflowing with his obvious delight at attending opulent banquets, riding in trains, and relaxing in posh hotels.[25] To be sure, the meetings did at least bring the first call for creation of an inter-American free trade zone, an idea that continues to hold enormous appeal in some quarters. The conference also led to the formation of the Commerce Office of the American Republics (the forerunner of the Pan-American Union), which published tariff, regulation, and trade information. Yet these were modest accomplishments, and as the nineteenth century drew to a close, the United States still had only weak ties with most of Latin America, and especially Ecuador.

## Mutual Misunderstandings

Few people traveled between the United States and Ecuador during the nineteenth century. At mid-century the U.S. diplomatic representative, Delazon Smith, noted that he could find but five people in Quito who spoke English.[26] Efforts to bring more Americans to Ecuador came to nothing. In keeping with a proposal by President Abraham Lincoln (1861–65) to relocate former slaves to Latin America, an Ecuadorian private citizen, Benigno Malo, wrote the U.S. government with an offer to sell fifty thousand acres on the left bank of the Suya River near the Gulf of Guayaquil for that purpose. The U.S. government was not impressed with Malo's idea, and Seward wrote to Hassaurek on November 6, 1862, stating that any such a proposal would have to come from the Ecuadorian government itself. The Ecuadorian government also did not like the proposal. García Moreno, an avowed racist, had no interest in bringing blacks to Ecuador, telling U.S. Minister Hassaurek that "there were too many of them in Guayaquil already."[27]

Not many Americans, black or white, came to Ecuador. About twenty Benedictine nuns from New York and New Jersey relocated to Manabí in the late 1880s. They had come to serve as teachers, but the low pay and poor working conditions quickly left them disillusioned. They departed Ecuador after a couple of difficult years. In all of Guayaquil in 1883, then a city of about thirty-six thousand people, there were only twenty-eight U.S. citizens; in Ecuador as a whole there were perhaps one hundred U.S. citizens. Four years later Guayaquil could count only seventeen U.S. citizens.

Americans who visited Ecuador in the nineteenth century usually came away with inaccurate and uncharitable impressions. Delazon Smith, the special agent sent to Ecuador from Washington, reported at mid-century that "in travelling nearly five hundred miles on the territory of this republic, I witnessed little else than ignorance, indolence, wretchedness, dishonesty, and misery, on the part of the great mass of the people, and selfishness, low-cunning, sordid [sic] ambition, avarice, and blood-thirsty revenge on that of those who either lead or force the unconscious, unthinking multitude. The country too, is nearly as miserable as those who inhabit it. Nineteen-twentieths of the surface of the earth is insusseptible [sic] of cultivation, and forty nine-fiftieths of its inhabitants cannot read." [28] Ecuador was, Smith believed, a nation sorely vexed by "an ignorant, illiberal, indolent and licentious priesthood." [29]

People who could not travel to Ecuador had few sources of information about the place. Those who thought they knew anything about Ecuador might well have acquired such knowledge as they had by viewing the paintings made of the region by Frederic Edwin Church (1826–1900), probably the most accomplished of the Hudson River School of artists. Church, arguably the best-known artist in the United States in the mid- to late nineteenth century, traveled twice to South America, in 1853 and 1857, painting fantastic landscapes of the Andes. Inspired by the example of Alexander Von Humboldt, Church followed the German explorer's route, traveling the length of Ecuador. Exhibits of Church's Andean paintings drew great crowds in New York, where people lined up for blocks to view his work.

Literate Americans might learn about Ecuador by reading travel accounts, including especially those of William Eleroy Curtis. Curtis traveled across Latin America, visiting nearly every nation of Central and South America, and in the late nineteenth century he came to be widely regarded as one of the foremost authorities on Latin America, publishing more on the area than any other U.S. author of his day. Unfortunately, Curtis's widely read tracts were founts of significant misinformation, smeared throughout with ugly prejudice. Of Ecuador he said: "The priests control the Government in all its branches, dictate its laws and govern their enforcement, and rule the country as absolutely as if the Pope were its king." [30] There was more: "There is an unaccountable prejudice against water. I do not believe a Quito woman ever washes her face." [31] Men fared no better in Curtis's judgment: "He will stab you or rob you as soon as your back is turned." [32] Of Guayaquil: "The streets are dirty and have a repulsive smell, and the half-naked Indians which throng them are continually scratching their bodies for fleas and their heads for lice." [33] Guayaquil, he went on, "is the only place in Ecuador in which modern civilization exists; the rest of the country is a century behind the times." [34] As for Ecuador as a whole: "[It was] the most backward, ignorant, and impoverished [country] in all America." [35]

Of course, even literate Ecuadorians could be just as ignorant about the United States. Those few rich Ecuadorians who went abroad typically stopped in the United States only briefly, usually on their way to Paris. Yet given the difficulty of transport within Ecuador, even the well-off Ecuadorians seldom traveled. Quito stood in isolation from the rest of the world. For most of the century there was no regular newspaper in the capital; even by the 1880s the only paper in Quito was a three-times-a-week handbill that printed government notices. Guayaquil had newspapers but not many foreign ones. Peruvian papers were usually banned, and other foreign newspapers cost so much that few could afford them. Once in a great while a Guayaquil paper would reprint a story from a U.S. newspaper, but readers were not necessarily better informed for this, with stories claiming that bigamy was widely practiced in the United States and other similar salacious untruths.

The historian Joedd Price, in his careful study of cultural attitudes, notes that Ecuadorians tended to be sharply critical of the "Yankee, his love of money, his family life, and his Protestant religion." [36] Ecuadorians typically thought Americans to be crass and uncultured, quite in contrast to Ecuadorians, people who knew how to live, how to enjoy life. In explaining why Ecuador had so many constitutions and the United States but one, some Ecuadorians decided that the reason was that people in the United States were just lazy and uncreative. For the United States and Ecuador, even at the close of the nineteenth century, there continued to be a good deal of misunderstanding on both sides.

## Conclusions

Connections between the United States and Ecuador grew during the second half of the nineteenth century, although the political and economic links between the nations remained limited. For U.S. diplomats Ecuador was scarcely a coveted posting. Appointees understood that a job in Ecuador would not put them on the career fast track at the State Department, although many in the diplomatic corps avoided assignment in Ecuador out of even graver concerns. Diplomats and others harbored enormous fears about passing through, or—worse—being stationed in, the disease-infested port of Guayaquil. Such concerns were amply anchored in fact. There were many examples. U.S. Consul Louis Victor Prescot took ill and died of yellow fever in Guayaquil in May 1867. When the new U.S. minister to Ecuador, Thomas Biddle, met with Ecuadorian president Gabriel García Moreno in Guayaquil in April 1875, García Moreno spoke "of the pestilential climate of Guayaquil at this season, and advised our moving to Pasorja . . . six hours' sail from this city," Biddle said.[37] But Biddle had already stayed too long in Guayaquil; he died from what was probably yellow fever within a few weeks. He would not be the only U.S. diplomat to be lost in this way. Thomas Nast, the political cartoonist who became consul general in Guayaquil in May 1902, died there of yellow fever before the year was out. The wife of Consul General Frederick W. Goding died of yellow fever in Guayaquil in June 1918.

The U.S. representatives who at length began to arrive in Guayaquil and try, sometimes successfully, to make their way to Quito, made plain in the dispatches they sent home just how unimportant and frankly dull they found the place. Their letters usually had little to say about relations between the nations and instead were filled with racist slurs, snide asides, snobbish amusement at Ecuadorian customs, and the Americans' dismay with and anger at Ecuadorians' failure to conform to proper rules of social conduct as the writers had learned them in Kentucky or Minnesota.

Ecuador's foreign relations officers did not spend much time thinking about the United States; they were much more concerned about Peru and Colombia. What mattered most to Ecuador did not matter that much to the United States. The United States took no concrete action to stop or slow the renewed Flores invasion attempts or the Spanish attacks of the 1860s, despite Ecuador's pleas for help. Washington could have invoked the Monroe Doctrine in these cases, but it did not.

However, as the century drew to a close, a change in the relationship between the United States and Latin America began to emerge. As Peter Smith has noted, "Toward the end of the nineteenth century the United States shifted its strategy toward Latin America. . . . Washington turned principally from the acquisition of territory to the creation of a sphere of interest."[38] The United States focused on opening up the heretofore European lake of the Caribbean but would also come to play a larger role in South America as well. In 1895 the United States became involved in a Venezuela–British Guiana border dispute. When Great Britain accepted U.S. arbitration, it was evident that the United States would now assert its rising power in the western hemisphere.

At the very end of the nineteenth century Ecuador began to turn increasingly toward the United States. Cacao sales to the United States surpassed all previous levels. Imports from the United States rose steadily and would soon outdistance those from Britain. But most of all, the United States would come to be deeply enmeshed in the bewildering, frustrating, at once successful and profoundly disappointing, business of building Ecuador its first railroad.

# 3 The Railroad Age: The 1890s to the 1920s

Although Ecuador had developed only a limited relationship with the United States during the nineteenth century, this situation began to change at the turn of the century. Ecuador's cacao exports soared from 1895 to 1925 and ties to the United States grew stronger. By 1915 the United States had become the number one buyer of Ecuadorian exports, a position it retains today. Ecuador's import trade rose as well, and by the 1890s the United States was a leading source; by the end of World War I the United States was by far the most important supplier, a position it also retains today.

Beyond greater commerce with the United States, Ecuador looked increasingly to the United States for technical support, from advice on building highways and construction of new government office buildings to putting up electricity lines. Cultural exchanges increased too, most notably in the field of medicine. Most aspiring Ecuadorian physicians traveled to the United States to receive their professional training. But the foremost involvement of the United States in Ecuador in this period came in building a railway line, first as a partner in a private business arrangement and then, as things went seriously wrong, in nation-to-nation diplomacy. This story was heavily freighted with symbolic meaning: for Ecuador building the rail line represented nothing less than the nation's entry into the modern world. But the whole affair ended badly, an outcome that would complicate relations between the two nations for many years to come.

## The Economic and Social Context

The late nineteenth and early twentieth centuries brought a boom for Ecuadorian cacao exports. What triggered this welcome development was a change in how cacao was consumed. Formerly cacao had been used only to brew a bitter hot beverage, its flavor certainly an acquired taste. This, plus its high cost, made cacao a luxury that few cared to indulge. But in the 1860s global appetites for cacao increased dramatically when the Swiss hit on the idea of combining milk with chocolate. Now everyone, and especially Americans, wanted cacao. In the United States the number of chocolate factories increased from 949 in 1869 to 2,391 in 1914. Demand for chocolate soared, and the value of Ecuadorian cacao exports rose 700 percent from the 1870s to the 1920s. Overall, cacao made up three-fourths of all Ecuadorian exports in these years. Cacao estates in the Guayas River basin greatly expanded production. The export hub, Guayaquil, increased in population from 50,000 in 1895 to 120,000 by 1925.[1]

France, not the United States, was the largest purchaser of Ecuadorian cacao at the turn of the nineteenth century and in the first decade of the twentieth century. Spain, previously the leading buyer of Ecuadorian exports, retreated in importance, while Germany, Great Britain, and the United States became key purchasers. By 1900 the United States bought more Ecuadorian cacao than any other nation except France. When World War I disrupted trade with Europe, the United States took over as the leading buyer of Ecuador's cacao.

Imports kept pace with cacao exports but showed a somewhat different pattern. Until the 1880s only Great Britain ran commercial steamers into Guayaquil, and the British made effective use of their shipping advantage. Great Britain supplied from one-quarter to more than one-third of Ecuador's imports for most of this period. Over time, however, as U.S. imports became increasingly competitive, Great Britain's position eroded. Whereas in the 1880s the United States had provided only about half as many imports to Ecuador as did Great Britain, by the 1890s the two nations had pulled even, each providing about one-quarter to a third of Ecuador's imports. The products imported from the United States were chiefly food supplies—butter and flour from California, lard from the East—and inexpensive textiles. But ads in turn-of-the-century Guayaquil dailies also featured other U.S.-made products: Smith and Wesson revolvers, Gillette razors, Royal typewriters, Stetson hats, and other goods. These print ads, created for buyers in the United States, could really miss the mark when published in Ecuadorian newspapers. The pen-and-ink drawings of happy, satisfied, customers featured people whose physiognomy did not much resemble that of most Ecuadorians.[2] Sometimes even the ad text was in English: "Dr. Williams' Pink Pills for Pale People."[3]

U.S. culture was inexorably making its way into Ecuador, or at least to Guayaquil. The first movie theater in Ecuador, the Teatro Olmedo in Guayaquil, opened its doors in 1903, and feature films from the United States quickly became popular favorites. Advertisements in Guayaquil dailies in 1923 offered foxtrot lessons to be held at American Park; others encouraged young men to join the Boy Scouts.[4] But although this was a time of increasing U.S. influence in Ecuador, the growth was uneven. Major Ecuadorian papers still carried news about the United States only occasionally, with events from other Latin American nations and Europe getting more ink.[5]

World War I proved an important economic watershed for Latin America and Ecuador, disrupting normal patterns of international commerce and opening the way for U.S. domination of the import-export trade. Even after the war Ecuador and other Latin American nations did not resume their former trading partnerships with Europe. Henceforth Ecuador's export and import trade would focus on the United States, while France, Germany, and Great Britain were all reduced to minor roles. Whereas the United States had supplied but 27 percent of Ecuador's imports in 1911, by 1917 it supplied 59 percent, and whereas the United States had purchased 25 percent of Ecuador's exports in 1911, by 1917 it purchased 78 percent. The reign of the British Pacific Steam Navigation Company was also over. In its place New York's Ward Line Steamship Company came to enjoy a near monopoly of Guayaquil shipping.

The vibrant growth of the Guayas River basin's cacao industry, set against the continued economic somnolence of the sierra, triggered a demographic transformation in Ecuador, a mass migration to the coast. In 1887 Ecuador's coastal region held a population of about 240,000, or 18 percent of the nation's total of 1.3 million, but by 1926 the population of the coast had grown to more than 1.1 million, or 38 percent of Ecuador's population of 2.9 million. There was much to want to get away from in the sierra, especially the abusive labor conditions. When Indians journeyed into the nearest town to attend Sunday mass, they could be arrested, kept in jail overnight, and on Monday chained together at the waist and marched out to do road work.[6] The coast, in contrast, had much to offer. One advantage was higher wages. The historian A. Kim Clark found that in 1895 daily wages in the highlands averaged 2 to 5 centavos, while on the coast they reached 80 centavos or as much as 100 centavos (one sucre).[7] Workers streamed down from the sierra, arriving at the coast in search of greater economic opportunities and greater personal freedom. As the coast bloomed with cacao, people came from the sierra to share in the bounty of the harvest.

## Ecuadorian Patterns of Politics

The large economic and demographic changes in Ecuador in these years led to a reconfiguration of the social structure, resulting in new patterns of political contestation. The era of booming cacao exports brought a time of retreat for the sierra landowning elite and the emergence of an increasingly unified coastal agricultural and business elite. Owners of the great cacao estates and leading cacao exporters functioned as Ecuador's modernizing elite class fraction, seeking to lead the nation into the twentieth century. The sierra oligarchy still had a much larger population at its command and the weight of tradition on its side, but the emerging merchant and cacao-growing elite of the coast had more money—much more money. In Ecuador's endless regional rivalry the growing riches of the cacao age were now tipping the political balance toward the coast. The national government relied on taxes levied on coastal exports and imports: between 1895 and 1914 Guayaquil customhouse receipts, especially from taxes on imports, accounted for 70 percent to 80 percent of all national tax revenues.[8]

Because the sierra elite could not keep pace with coastal money making, some leading Ecuadorian political observers, especially those from Quito, believed that the coastal banking and cacao elite secretly ran the country, led by the plutocrat Francisco Urvina Jado, chief of the nation's largest bank, Banco Comercial y Agrícola (Commercial and Agricultural Bank). But what Ecuador's changed economic circumstance really meant was that the national government had to pay rather more attention to the coast, striking a greater balance between the two rival regions. Coastal-born Eloy Alfaro Delgado and Leonidas Plaza Gutiérrez would seize the presidency, but conservatives from the sierra still controlled the legislature, for the highlands' larger population meant that they could place more of their own in office. The sierra elite used its political strength, especially in the legislature, to block or slow down enactment of the coastal reform agenda.

Eloy Alfaro and Leonidas Plaza Gutiérrez, the most important liberal leaders, would take turns in the presidency, Alfaro (known to Ecuadorians as the *viejo luchador*—old campaigner—from 1895 to 1901 and 1906 to 1911, and Plaza from 1901 to 1905 and 1912 to 1916. Alfaro, a lifelong opponent of Ecuador's conservatives, took inspiration from U.S. federalism, a system of government that he recognized would give greater local autonomy to regional interests. Alfaro's first campaign came in 1864 when he was only twenty-two and led the revolt against García Moreno in Manabí on the central coast, and during Alfaro's long violent life he fought against García Moreno, Veintemilla, and many, many other presidents. In all he participated in eleven military struggles in Ecuador alone, for even during his years in exile Alfaro kept fighting, participating in civil wars in Central America and in Cuba.

The military campaigns that brought Alfaro to power relied on considerable support from the underclass, people who saw in Alfaro hope for reform and improvement in their lives. Some historians emphasize Alfaro's social commitment to the poor, but more see him as a crass opportunist. But whatever Alfaro might have intended to do, nearly all historians agree that he managed to accomplish little in the way of actual social reform.[9] Eloy Alfaro spoke of liberalism but in practice he could be a tyrant. Alfaro gangs attacked newspaper offices, and he exiled or jailed the editors.

One area in which Alfaro's effort was consistent was his crusade against the church. It would be fair to say that Alfaro hated the clergy and that the Catholic Church responded in kind, repeatedly bankrolling violent insurgencies against him. Furious, Alfaro kicked the foreign-born clergy out of Ecuador, correctly observing that they played a leading role in inciting the faithful to rise up against his authority. But it was not just Alfaro, for Ecuador's anti–Catholic Church measures continued when Plaza was in office. In 1902 Plaza pushed through a law that, for the first time, allowed non-Catholic burials and civil marriages in Ecuador. When Alfaro came back into office, he fanned the antichurch impulse and in 1908 seized church land, closed monasteries and convents, initiated the practice of secular registrations of births and deaths, and also removed the church from participation in public education.

Under Alfaro and Plaza, Ecuador for the first time granted entry to representatives of Protestant churches. From the United States arrived members of the Gospel Missionary Union of Kansas City, the Christian and Missionary Alliance of New York City, Methodists, Presbyterians, Seventh Day Adventists, and the Latter Day Saints. Reaction by some Ecuadorians was less than welcoming. The Cuenca newspaper, *El heraldo de la hostia divina*, wrote in 1898, "Protestantism is . . . a cadaver of outright putrefaction. . . . Their conquests . . . will involve only those venal souls, which are without character nor energy, and which have been long corroded by vices." [10] In 1899 E. B. Tarbox and W. G. Fritz of the Christian and Missionary Alliance of New York wrote to Archibald J. Sampson, the U.S. representative in Ecuador, complaining that "the priests [in Ecuador] were using the pulpit of the cathedral to excite the people to kill us." [11] The missionaries reported that one local priest had threatened that "if the Virgin Mary does not convert them [the Protestants] it is necessary that they be taken out of the city, and if not, they must be destroyed." [12] Moreover, Tarbox and Fritz said, a large crowd gathered at a missionary's home, yelling, "Kill the Protestant devils." [13] The mob threw stones through the windows before the police showed up and chased everyone off.

U.S. intervention brought this matter to the attention of the archbishop, but the troubles continued. In 1909 the Reverend Harry F. Compton, a missionary for the Methodist Episcopal Church in Quito, traveled with his family to the town of Malchingui, near Quito. According to a

State Department report, "about midnight 500 or more persons forced their way into the house, pounded upon their bedroom door, and threatened the family with violence if they did not depart immediately. . . . The Americans hastened to leave on their mules, stones and epithets being hurled at them as they fled." The report concluded: "It appears that the populace had been roused against 'the Protestant' Compton by a fanatical and threatening sermon of the village priest."[14] This would not be the last time that Ecuadorians would abuse missionaries from the United States.

In 1911 Alfaro completed his second term, with warfare again attending the transfer of power. When Emilio Estrada, chosen to replace Alfaro, died of a heart attack on December 21, 1911, Alfaro saw his chance to reclaim power. Plaza objected and in the ensuing combat defeated Alfaro. Alfaro and his fellow revolutionaries—Gen. Pedro Montero and Gen. Flavio Alfaro, Eloy Alfaro's nephew—were taken prisoner in January 1912 in Guayaquil. Immediately after Montero was tried and convicted, he was seized by a crowd and brutally murdered. Street violence erupted in Guayaquil and continued through the night of January 25, 1912. The U.S. legation on the scene showed little sympathy, writing that the "pandemonium let loose . . . only too clearly laid bare the brutal passions of a semi-civilized people."[15] Amid the chaos authorities spirited the Alfaros out of town, placing them under guard and on a train to Quito. A mob awaited them there. When the Alfaros arrived, the crowd pulled the former president and his nephew from the train and beat them mercilessly before murdering them. The crowd then fell upon the bodies and mutilated them, burned them, and dragged them through the streets of the capital on January 28.

The civil war slowly burned out and Plaza returned to office, serving on this second occasion from 1912 to 1916. Plaza proved less autocratic than Alfaro. He was probably more inclined to seek compromise between coastal and sierra interests, but, like Alfaro, Plaza compiled a rather undistinguished record. After Plaza came three unremarkable leaders, Alfredo Baquerizo Moreno (1916–20), José Luis Tamayo (1920–24), and Gonzalo S. Córdova (1924–25). Overall, the liberal period (1895–1925) gave rise to few real reforms. Indeed, a 1906 law reaffirmed the *legality* of debtors' prisons and various forms of coerced labor, and it was not repealed until 1918. Government in Ecuador continued as before: exclusively by the elite and in the service of its interests. When members of the elite could not agree on policy, they continued to settle matters through violence. Against this generally troubled state of affairs, Ecuador would attempt to craft its relationship with the United States.

## The United States and the Age of Imperialism

At the turn of the nineteenth century, British power in Latin America began a steady retreat and the United States moved in to fill the void. A new day of U.S. assertiveness had arrived. President Grover Cleveland (1885–89, 1893–97) acted to block European imperialists, who, fresh from their successes in Africa, might next turn their efforts to Latin America. As his secretary of state, Richard Olney, announced when the United States intervened in the 1895 Venezuela–British Guiana boundary dispute: "Today the United States is practically sovereign on this continent, and its fiat is law upon the subjects to which it confines its interpositions."[16]

The United States was not the only nation to be concerned about British intentions. President Alfaro issued a call for an August 1896 inter-American conference to be held in Mexico City.[17] Eloy Alfaro sought nothing less than a Latin American version of the Monroe Doctrine, one with real power to stand up to the European use of force against Venezuela. Eloy Alfaro saw the conference as a chance to foster great inter-American cooperation and perhaps to reopen discussion of the re-creation of Gran Colombia. Even more, he sought to organize Latin American support for the Cuban rebels fighting for independence from Spain.

Both Spain and the United States opposed Eloy Alfaro's proposal for a pan-American meeting. The Cleveland administration openly scoffed at the idea, saying that Ecuador lacked adequate status to convene such a congress. Olney found the whole thing rather irritating. The United States was right in the middle of delicate negotiations with Great Britain regarding the Venezuela–British Guiana boundary issue, and Eloy

Alfaro's proposal was only complicating matters, Olney fumed. The United States announced that it could not attend the conference because all the American states would not be there—and then worked hard to make sure that there were plenty of absentees. Venezuela, Bolivia, and Uruguay had previously agreed to attend but now backed out. In the end only Ecuador, Mexico, Guatemala, Honduras, El Salvador, Nicaragua, and Costa Rica showed up for Eloy Alfaro's conference, and the talks never got beyond the most preliminary level. Eloy Alfaro's pan-American dream ended in failure.

But U.S. dreams of empire were just beginning. With its victory in the Spanish-American War in 1898, the United States acquired the island of Puerto Rico and, until 1902, Cuba too. For the United States and for Latin America a new threat came in 1902–1903, when the Germans and the British established a naval blockade in an effort to pressure the Venezuelan government into paying its foreign debts. Argentine Foreign Minister Luis María Drago responded with a plan for pan-Americanizing the Monroe Doctrine—the Drago Doctrine—arguing that no Latin American nation's public debt should be used as an excuse for armed intervention or military occupation by another nation. But U.S. President Theodore Roosevelt (1901–1909) had his own thoughts about how best to deal with the situation, the 1904 Roosevelt Corollary to the Monroe Doctrine: the United States would intervene in order to prevent other nations—European ones—from doing so.

Theodore Roosevelt asserted a leading role for the United States in policing the region. To Roosevelt, "[U.S.] 'intervention to prevent intervention' was justifiable."[18] The Roosevelt Corollary was ultimately used to provide justification for U.S. occupations of the Dominican Republic (1905 and 1916–24) and Haiti (1915–34). In 1913 President Woodrow Wilson (1913–21) pledged not to seek any more territory in Latin America but still declared that the United States had a "civilizing mission," one that would require a U.S. military presence in several Caribbean and Central American nations.[19] "I am going to teach the South American republics to elect good men!" Wilson proclaimed, although he actually applied this edict everywhere in Latin America except South America, his missionary impulse evidently running out south of

Panama.[20] The United States repeatedly intervened to depose leaders in the Caribbean and Central America and set up U.S.-approved governments, which were duly elected in U.S.-supervised elections, although not necessarily more honest for all the attention.

As Peter Smith has noted, it was more than the Monroe Doctrine that led U.S. policy makers to seek to keep Europe out of Latin American affairs. Americans, Smith notes, long harbored an overweening sense of self-confidence in the righteousness of their own ways, most especially their democratic institutions, and viewed Europe as corrupt, flabby, self-interested, even evil. With these notions providing the ideological underpinning, "between 1898 and 1934 the United States launched more than thirty military interventions in Latin America," focusing on regions nearest the U.S. borders, Mexico and the small nations of the Caribbean and Central America, but not South America.[21] Outraged, angry Latin American leaders looked to inter-American meetings of the early twentieth century as an outlet for expressing their deep concerns. Anti-Americanism ran hot.

The several pan-American meetings of the first part of the twentieth century seldom resulted in anything truly meaningful, however, chiefly because the United States effectively blocked any discussion of the complaints against its imperialistic conduct. Ecuador attended the Second International Conference of American States (Mexico City, October 1901), the third (Río de Janeiro, 1906), the fourth (Buenos Aires, 1910), and the fifth (Santiago, Chile, 1923), but these gatherings produced little of substance: trademark agreements, the rules governing the gathering of trade statistics, postal conventions, and the like. The Buenos Aires congress did at least lead to the creation of the Pan-American Union (the forerunner of the Organization of American States), but what emerged was a fully U.S.-controlled body, its permanent chair the U.S. secretary of state and its new building near the White House, its construction underwritten by a donation from Andrew Carnegie.

Latin American resentment of U.S. imperialism had other implications. When the United States entered the Great War in Europe in 1917, the Latin American states proved reluctant allies. As the historian J. Lloyd Mecham put it, they regarded the war as "none of their business."[22] Only eight Latin American nations declared war on Germany, five broke diplomatic relations, and seven Latin American nations remained neutral. Ecuador, initially neutral, broke relations with Germany in 1917. The United States did not enter into any multilateral military arrangements with the nations of Latin America during World War I. During this era Ecuador looked for military aid (navy and army instructors) from Chile, not the United States. In any event, during World War I Ecuador found itself much too preoccupied with putting down a revolt led by Col. Carlos Concha to give much attention to U.S. concerns regarding events in Europe.

During the "age of imperialism" the United States used its newly developed might to aggressively pursue its interests and acquire an empire. In this regard the United States behaved much like the other great powers in the world of that day. Yet Ecuador provided a much different experience for the United States, especially when compared with events in Central America and the Caribbean. In Ecuador the United States did not gain an empire, could not control events when it sought to, and was often frustrated in just trying to wield influence. Nowhere was this made more plain than in the story of the U.S. role in the building of Ecuador's railway.

## The Railroad

Ecuador had a transportation problem: its mountainous terrain made travel within the nation a very difficult proposition.[23] Sending goods down from the highlands to the port of Guayaquil was prohibitively expensive. Shipping a ton of wheat from Quito to Guayaquil cost more than from Australia to Europe.[24] Even within the sierra transportation was generally so primitive that it commonly was too expensive to send agricultural surplus from one valley to the next one over.

A modern railway linking the coast and sierra, it was hoped, would change all this. Nearly everyone in Ecuador believed that this must be true, as Ecuadorians shared an overflowing optimism about what a modern railway could do for the nation. Americans agreed. The rail-

road, the U.S. consul to Ecuador declared, would "eliminate . . . the
political agitator . . . , promote respect for law and liberty . . . , and in
a word prove a blessing to Ecuador in every conceivable respect."[25]
The *Monthly Bulletin of the International Bureau of the American Republics* agreed that completing the railroad would make Ecuador "one of
the most civilized and richest [nations] of the world."[26] U.S. Consul
Perry M. DeLeon asserted confidently that the railroad would create
such prosperity in Ecuador that it would eliminate the "empty pockets and idle brains" that drove "restless spirits into politics."[27] To Ecuadorian President Eloy Alfaro, the railway would be Ecuador's *"obra
redentora,"* redemptive work. Completing the railway would bring Ecuador's economic, political, even spiritual salvation, Alfaro believed.
"My dream . . . my only program is concentrated in this one solemn
word: RAILROAD."[28]

President García Moreno had initiated construction in 1871 on a
short coastal line, an undertaking directed by the U.S. engineer Henry
McClellan. President Caamaño followed up on these efforts, but when
Flores Jijón took office in 1888, all progress stopped. Flores Jijón had
little confidence in the undertaking and in fact saw the whole project
as highly impractical and expensive. He was right, of course: railroads
work very well on flat plains but are spectacularly ill suited to places
with rugged topography, places, that is, like Ecuador. Flores Jijón believed that simple dirt roadways were better suited to Ecuador's needs
and canceled the railway contract in 1890.

But Eloy Alfaro, a railroad true believer, thought he knew better and,
soon after taking office, instructed Ecuador's foreign minister in Washington, D.C., Luis Carbo, to secure U.S. financial support for an Ecuadorian railway project. Fatefully, Carbo found Archer Harman, a Virginia investor and son of a Confederate army officer. Immediately won
over, Harman left for Ecuador at once. He traveled to Quito in March
1897 and by June was on his way home with a signed contract. He incorporated the Guayaquil and Quito Railway Company in Trenton, New
Jersey, on September 7, 1897.

The contract spelled out the details. The work had to be completed
within six years, and Harman's construction company was required

to put up a $500,000 bond; if it failed to finish construction on time, it would forfeit the bond to Ecuador. However, the deadline could be relaxed in the event of natural disaster, foreign invasion, civil war, or an epidemic. Harman's company would own and operate the line for seventy-five years, when it would revert to Ecuador. The cost to Ecuador of building the railway was placed at $17,532,000.

After studying the document, Ecuador's legislature voted to void the contract. Harman returned to Ecuador in November 1898 and signed a supplementary agreement. The revised arrangement fine-tuned some of the bond arrangements and in return gave Harman ten years, instead of the original six, to finish the line.

Before work could begin, however, something had to be done about Ecuador's existing foreign debt. Unserviced and unpaid, this obligation (sometimes called in Ecuador the "English debt") dated from the independence era. Eloy Alfaro had heretofore continued the Ecuadorian practice in this matter, that is, he had failed to make payments. Now Ecuador's principal creditor, the British Council of Foreign Bondholders, had to be satisfied before new Ecuadorian bonds could be taken out for railway construction.

In 1897–98 Archer Harman traveled to London and arranged the matter. Finding that the old bonds had slipped to but 35 percent of their face value, he quietly began to buy them up.[29] He then arranged for the consolidation of the existing debt and the issuing new Ecuadorian bonds to raise money for construction of the railway. The plan was that Ecuador would pay for construction and service the bonds until the railroad was completed. After that Eloy Alfaro expected that Ecuador's share of the railroad profits would allow it to make payments on the new foreign bonds. However, if profits did not cover the cost of servicing the bonds, the government of Ecuador, as guarantor of the loan, promised to make the payments nonetheless.

The new bonds passed through many hands, initially purchased by the U.S.-based Ecuadorian Development Company. However, when construction troubles developed, the bonds then passed to a group of British investors, the Ecuadorian Association. And so, as had been the case with the earlier independence-era debt, the new consolidated debt would be held principally by British investors. The resulting railway funding was convoluted: the British provided most of the money for a U.S. company to build the railway in Ecuador, and if profits fell short, the debt would be serviced by the Ecuadorian government, which had pledged Guayaquil customs revenues in making its payment guarantee.

By June 1899 the initial survey was complete, and on July 10, 1899, Eloy Alfaro cut the ribbon on the railway construction. Trouble commenced at once. Project managers realized that all the existing coastal sections would have to be completely redone. Crossing the fifty miles of tropical jungle from Guayaquil to the foothills of the Andes was a difficult undertaking because the soil was too marshy and soft to support a railroad. New stone beds had to be set into place. Laying the tracks in the sierra, climbing in and out of valley after valley, was even harder. But the toughest part was the thirty-five-mile stretch from the lowlands into the mountains. In one twenty-five-mile section the tracks rose 7,000 feet and, once in the sierra, continue to climb, peaking at Chimborazo Pass at 11,840 feet. Precipitation fell abundantly on the western slopes of the Andes, and engineers found it nearly impossible to locate firm, dry soil upon which to build. Heavy rains in February 1900 produced mud slides that swept away all the work that had been completed on that section of line.

Although the contract specified that no grade would be steeper than 3 percent, the Ecuadorian legislature reluctantly agreed to permit a 5.5 percent grade for the climb up into the Andes. Engineers could see no other solution. The resulting line crossed the Chan Chan River twenty-six times in just twenty-three miles, requiring seventy-two bridges (the iron trestles laid across the Chimbo River were constructed by Eiffel in Paris) and two double switchbacks. Through many travails the mountain ascent was finally completed in 1902 when the line reached Alausí.

Foreigners handled nearly all aspects of building Ecuador's railroad. Harman's construction company relied on imported labor; Ecuadorian workers were not interested. Company officials came to the easy but mistaken conclusion that this was proof of the innate slothfulness of ordinary Ecuadorians. But the impoverished peasants fleeing the sierra had left to find an improvement in their lives, not go looking for even more ruthless exploitation, and word was out about just how dangerous and poorly paid railway work really was. Although formal pay rates might have appeared to be high by Ecuadorian standards, workers learned quickly how little of that money would actually reach their pockets, as unethical labor recruiters skimmed off large sums of the workingmen's wages. About four thousand Jamaicans had to be brought in to work on the project, but as soon as they learned how things were, they too deserted in droves. The drain of labor proved a steady problem for the railway construction.

Foreigners dominated other aspects of construction as well. Col. William Findlay Shunk of Pennsylvania carried out the initial survey. The brother of Archer Harman, Maj. John A. Harman, oversaw construction, assisted by eighty-four U.S. construction engineers and 103 other U.S. personnel. But as other foreigners had learned, it was dangerous to come to Ecuador. Henry Davis, a construction engineer, fell ill and died in 1900, and John Harman followed, probably from yellow fever, in 1907. Day laborers suffered most of all. Overall, about five hundred construction workers, including many of the Jamaicans, died of smallpox and other infectious diseases.[30]

Eloy Alfaro finished his first term in office in 1901 with construction costs soaring out of control. He passed the problem along to incoming president Plaza. Although Plaza feared that he might well be wasting money, he nevertheless saw little choice but to continue the railway construction effort. Plaza resorted to borrowing money from the Banco del Ecuador, raising taxes, and diverting financial resources from other government obligations, all in an ultimately unavailing effort to both keep construction going and make the twice-a-year payments on the foreign-held railway bonds.

With Ecuador constantly short of funding for this massive undertaking, Eloy Alfaro, once he returned to power in 1906, initiated the fiscally unsound practice of just taking the money he was supposed to use to pay the foreign bondholders and giving it to the U.S. construction company. When this money also ran out, Eloy Alfaro kept the project going by borrowing heavily from merchants in Guayaquil. Eloy Alfaro was running his nation deeply into the red, determined to see the line finished, apparently at any cost.

There were yet other problems. Harman was being paid to build a "first-class" railway, but he was not doing this, not even close. In fact, much of the construction was appallingly substandard. The ties were of inferior, less expensive timber. Many bridges were made of wood, not the iron specified in the contract. The section of 5.5 percent grade was supposed to last for only two miles; it went on for twelve. In the sierra Harman's company had laid the tracks right down the middle of the sole existing roadway (the highway built in the García Moreno years). The company promised to build a new highway to replace the old one but never did. The line was supposed to pass through the city of Riobamba but did not (at least not until 1924, when the required spur line was finally added).

By June 14, 1907, the deadline for completion of construction, the line still reached only to Ambato, well short of the Quito finish line that was plainly spelled out in the contract. Harman maintained that the causes of the delay were covered in the contract's article 16, which forgave any delay resulting from domestic war, rebellion, epidemics, and natural catastrophes, all of which had indeed actually taken place. Harman predicted he could finish within a few months. Nonetheless, a clamor arose in Ecuador, with many calling for the outright seizure of the line from Harman's company.

At this the U.S. government could no longer stand apart from the building controversy and now became sucked into the vortex of these swirling contentions. To try to address the matter U.S. President Theodore Roosevelt and Ecuadorian President Eloy Alfaro agreed to appoint arbiters. Ecuador named César Borja, a Guayaquil physician; Williams C. Fox, the U.S. minister to Ecuador, acted on behalf of the United States. Borja met with Fox in Quito on October 5, 1907, and for the moment it appeared they had a resolution. They signed a new accord, granting the U.S. railway construction company a two-year extension to finish. By September 30, 1908, all parties had formally accepted the arbitration settlement.

Work on the railway was completed on June 17, 1908, and Alfaro's daughter, América, proudly drove in the golden spike. Yet, as the fanfare died down, it became painfully obvious that operating this railroad was going to be exceedingly difficult. Even if the utmost care had been taken during construction, one could have expected difficulties in trying to run and maintain this improbable railway into the sky. But the construction methods used—at best, creatively improvised, at worst, slapdash—led to crumbling roadbeds and endless mud slides. The locomotives broke down constantly; the rolling stock was a disgrace. Along remote sections impoverished peasants regarded the railroad as a source of wealth and set to work, prying up spikes, digging out ties, and cutting down and dragging off the telegraph poles, the lines trailing behind. They either sold their bounty or used it in home repair and expansion. Even with the completion of the railroad, the journey from Guayaquil to Quito still took two days, assuming, quite unrealistically as it happened, that there would be no delays. When in 1908 bubonic plague arrived in Ecuador and quickly swept up through each succeeding stop on the line, Ecuadorians began to refer to the railroad as *la bubonica.*

With railway operations—such as they were—now underway, Harman started to take money that was not his, disguising profits and failing to turn over to the Ecuadorian government its fair share of the operating proceeds stipulated in the contract. The agreement had specified that if profits did not match operating costs, the Ecuadorian government had to make up the shortfall. Harman set up a not especially clever shell game, reducing to zero the amount of declared profits from the railroad.[31] Harman falsely inflated construction costs, with his books reflecting little that could be verified with receipts: vast debits bore only the label "miscellaneous." Some items that Harman listed as "railway operating expenses" were clearly inappropriate: Harman's yacht, his personal servants, his beautiful new offices in New York, and his household decorations, to name just a few examples. With good reason, then, Harman refused to allow Ecuadorian officials to inspect the books.

Harman also formed a special freight company, designed ostensibly to handle all rail cargo but functioning actually to deliver more money into his hands. Harman's railway company charged his freight company next to nothing for acquiring the freight rights. The subcontracting freight company took 60 percent of the rail profits before the railway company saw any. Said President Plaza: "So scandalous was this audacious machination that the company was obliged to suspend it, on the energetic intervention of my government."[32]

Because the railway failed to turn a profit—or at least a declared one—it fell to Ecuador as debt guarantor to make the payments due on the bonds. Crying foul, Ecuador refused to pay: Harman was being totally unfair, cheating Ecuador, and, most important of all, the country did not have the money. Ecuador stopped payments in 1910, and the bondholders, principally British but also including a number of Americans, began to complain bitterly to their governments.

There were still other disputes. Beyond the controversy about who should have to make the payments on the bonds, conflict arose regarding who should pay for needed repairs to the railway. Harman and his U.S. company claimed that any problems with the line had been caused by rebel troops during the 1910 civil war. Ecuador's position was that the line had always been faulty and insisted that the U.S. company pay for repairs.

As events unfolded, the U.S. government found itself drawn ever deeper into the dispute. Although the U.S. State Department naturally felt a sense of loyalty to the U.S. firm, in internal memos U.S. officials wondered whether Ecuador's complaints might well be justified. As the U.S. chargé d'affaires in Quito, Rutherfurd Bingham, explained, "It cannot be denied that the Government of Ecuador has many just grounds for complaint against the railway."[33] Nevertheless, the railway company was a U.S. one, and so despite the reservations of some officials, the U.S. government took the side of the railroad company in the dispute. In April 1912 State Department officials met with railway management in Washington, D.C. After the meeting the U.S. government directed its representative in Quito to warn Ecuador that it must meet its legal obligations with no further delay.[34] The State Department's view was the same as that of the railroad company's management: Ecuador had to pay the bondholders now.

That year the two governments again agreed to appoint arbiters; the United States named Henry L. Janes, of the U.S. Diplomatic Service, and Ecuador selected the president of the Senate, Dr. Alfred Baquerizo Moreno.[35] But discussions began poorly, the two men having trouble even finding a meeting time. Janes arrived in Guayaquil in early 1913 and swiftly made his way up to Quito, but Baquerizo Moreno did not get to the capital until five weeks later. The Ecuadorian Ministry of Foreign Affairs then requested that Janes be removed, alleging that he was biased in favor of the U.S. company. Ecuador was obviously stalling, but the United States recalled Janes anyway, in April 1913.

The next month the United States named Judge A. L. Miller to serve as its new arbitrator. But problems continued, as Ecuador now insisted that the only basis for resolving the matter must be the strict application of existing Ecuadorian law. Miller had thought he would enjoy something of a freer hand, using international law or even just common sense. Frustrated and rebuffed, Miller packed up and left in February 1914. There would be no agreement. As President Plaza put it, relations with the U.S. railroad company were "a semi-permanent and vexatious misunderstanding."[36]

With talks broken off Ecuador settled on a new strategy: it would seek a large foreign loan and then use some of the money to pay off the bonds, even though Ecuador still believed that the debt was not really its responsibility. Ecuador claimed that it had no money to pay the bond debt, or anything else, but this was not really accurate. Internal civil war in 1912 and the trade disruptions of World War I had indeed flattened cacao sales, but Ecuador still had enough money on hand to pay the debt. The government just preferred to use it to buy other things, especially munitions. Ecuador earned about $10 million per year in customs receipts, and the amount due bondholders was only about $850,000 a year.

In any case, Ecuador held that it was inappropriate for the U.S. government to try to push its way into a dispute between Ecuador and a private company operating within Ecuador's sovereign borders. That the U.S. government was behaving in this way was a pity, for until now Ecuador had never really had any trouble with the U.S. government, Ecuador's foreign affairs minister, R. H. Elizalde, told the U.S. ambassador.[37]

By this time Ecuadorians were completely disillusioned with their new railway. Modesto A. Peñaherrera, the minister of the interior, noted that "it [was] beyond all doubt how irregular and damaging is the present administration of the railway."[38] Ecuador had made considerable financial outlays for construction but had realized no profit from the railway. In 1915 Ecuador's legislature began considering a lawsuit against the U.S.-owned railway, freezing company assets and moving toward nationalization. When the U.S. minister to Ecuador, Charles Hartman, learned what the Ecuadorian legislature intended, he made a personal visit to President Plaza and lodged a vigorous protest. The congress approved the resolution anyway, on October 8, 1915.

The United States tried a temporary shift in course, signaling that it would be willing to help Ecuador get a loan of $10 million from a U.S. bank. However, in return for this favor Ecuador would have to start using daily proceeds from its customhouse to pay the railroad bondholders and would have to accept arbitration of the overall dispute. If Ecuador did not commence paying the bondholders (something it had not done since the line was completed in 1908), wrote U.S. Secretary of State Robert Lansing in a 1917 internal memo, then the U.S. government would "be forced to give consideration to the question of taking such action as may be necessary properly to protect these American interests [and that] . . . in no case . . . [would] the Department give its approval to any loan by American bankers to Ecuador until interest . . . [is] paid and daily deposits resumed."[39] Ecuador indignantly rejected the conditions and as a result got no loan. When Ecuador tried to arrange loans from other nations, the United States maneuvered behind the scenes to quash them. Washington continued to hold to the railway management's view that the U.S. company did not have the profits to pay the bondholders, that the obligation then fell to the government of Ecuador, and that Ecuador did in fact have the money to pay.

The situation changed with the coming of World War I. The conflict brought a major shift in the structure of the world economy as large industrial nations reoriented their economies to the exigencies of war, a development that had far-reaching implications for Ecuador. The reordered economic priorities of leading European nations led them to stop buying cacao, leaving only the United States to purchase Ecuador's key export. However, in 1918 the newly created U.S. Shipping Board and the U.S. War Trade Board began to drastically reduce the number of licenses granted for cacao and other imports deemed nonessential to the U.S. war effort. The sole remaining purchaser of Ecuador's cacao was buying ever less.

That this changed economic circumstance gave the United States considerably more leverage in dealing with Ecuador was not lost on the State Department. Washington now had the weapon it needed to force Ecuador to pay the interest due on the railway bonds. Although President Baquerizo Moreno (1916–20) had promised to make deposits into the account of the Guayaquil and Quito Railway in Guayaquil banks beginning on January 1, 1917, he had not actually done so. Therefore, Lansing warned the Ecuadorian Ministry of Foreign Relations that "the interests due . . . must be paid in order to avoid more serious restrictions being placed by the War Trade Board on the import of cacao in the United States."[40] In response, the Ecuadorian representative to the United States informed the State Department: "I would rather burn all the cacao of Ecuador than accept this U.S. imposition."[41] By June 1918 the War Trade Board was considering blocking all Ecuadorian cacao shipments "in order to save tonnage for important war purposes."[42] The United States was also considering restricting imports of tagua and Ecuadorian-made panama hats.

Ecuador could not understand why the United States was delivering ultimatums when Ecuador clearly could not pay, when the railway company was obviously in the wrong and should pay, and when Ecuador had proved that it was the true friend of the United States by breaking relations with Germany during World War I. But the U.S. economic threats had the desired effect. Ecuador caved in completely, promising in July 1918 to make daily deposits from customs receipts to service the bonds. Washington informed Ecuador that it could continue to send cacao to the United States.

A month later Ecuador had still failed to make any of the promised daily deposits, and so the U.S. War Trade Board at last delivered on the threat, withdrawing all Ecuadorian licenses for cacao shipments to the United States. Trade immediately halted in Guayaquil; dockworkers stopped loading all cacao on the ships at the wharf. Confronted with

U.S. pressure, Ecuador relented and commenced daily bank deposits to service the debt. Utterly humiliated, Ecuador had to submit the paperwork for the daily customs receipts to the U.S. consul in Guayaquil so that he could verify that the deposits were being made. In November 1918 the War Trade Board lifted the ban and approved Ecuador's request that fourteen thousand tons of cacao in storage be shipped to the United States, with tax receipts from sale of the cacao going toward retiring the debt owed the bondholders.

By World War I Ecuador was producing about 45,000 tons of cacao a year, 15 percent of the world total. However, the U.S. War Trade Board in 1918 limited Ecuador to the sale of 14,400 tons a year. By June 1919, with another Ecuadorian harvest on the way, Ecuador would soon have about 42,000 tons of cacao awaiting sale. The cacao could not keep forever—only about nine months if stored in tropical Guayaquil, perhaps two years if it could be kept in a temperate zone.

By May 1919 Ecuador had sold its allotment of 14,000 tons of cacao and shipped it to New York City but had still failed to deliver on its commitment to use the proceeds to pay all $859,740 due railway bondholders. Ecuadorian officials claimed that there had been a misunderstanding, maintaining that the "800,000" that they had promised to pay was sucres, not dollars (or only about $300,000). In any case, the cacao that had been sold was not the property of the Ecuadorian government but that of private merchants. Ecuador had promised only to use export tax receipts from the sale, not the entire sum earned from the cacao sales, toward the outstanding government debt. Meanwhile British and U.S. railway bondholders now calculated the amount owed them at nearly $5 million. But with the end of World War I in 1919, the United States closed down its wartime bureaucracies, thereby surrendering the only mechanisms, the War Trade Board and the Shipping Board, that had managed to compel Ecuador to pay on the railway bond debt. At first Ecuador just slowed down its payments but soon stopped paying altogether.

This was a problem that would not go away. As the State Department informed the U.S. minister to Ecuador in 1920: "The Department desires you to obtain an interview with President Tamayo and inform him that the failure of the Government of Ecuador to remit to London the sums due for the service of the Guayaquil and Quito Railroad bonds is causing this Government considerable concern."[43] Ecuador continued to use for other purposes the money that was supposed to go to service the bonds. Ecuador typically dedicated about 40 percent of its customs receipts to pay the army. All its revenue from customs receipts did not cover the Ecuadorian government's ordinary operating expenses, let alone enough to pay off foreign creditors. And the debt just kept growing. By 1923 the sum owed to bondholders had reached $7.6 million.

Ecuador's railway had not worked out the way Eloy Alfaro and others had planned. The British consul to Ecuador, writing in 1923, noted that the railway was "a standing disgrace to the owners of it (the Americans) who have done nothing but exploit this country since President Alfaro was foolish enough to entrust Mr. Harman with the construction of the line. . . . The Guayaquil and Quito Railway is . . . the most miserable apology for a railway that exists, either in South or Central America, and that is saying a good deal."[44] As President Plaza put it, the railway had turned out to be "an immense dump for gold with no profit to any of the interested parties except the gentlemen who manage the company according to their own sovereign will."[45] Concluded the railway historian Eva Maria Loewenfeld : "It . . . appears fairly certain that Harman and his associates personally did not suffer any financial loss in the enterprise, no matter how much the stockholders of the company or subsidiary construction companies might have lost."[46] And Clark adds: "The Guayaquil-Quito Railway turned out to be one of the most expensive railways in the world."[47] In the end the U.S. railway company decided that trying to do business in Ecuador was not worth all the hassles. On May 22, 1925, the company sold out to Ecuador, handing over the stock in exchange for long-term bonds. Henceforth the search for profits, the debt obligations, and the headaches would be Ecuador's alone.

## The Galápagos Islands

Contention with the United States regarding the railway set the larger context for other controversies that arose between the two nations in the first two decades of the twenieth century. Ecuadorian leaders in this period, like those before them, saw the Galápagos Islands as an asset that might be used to obtain large sums of money. But as before, serious disputes developed in regard to Ecuador's plans to sell the islands to the United States.[48]

The Galápagos (in Spanish, "big tortoise") Islands had a history apart from the rest of Ecuador. The archipelago numbers sixteen major islands, covering a total of twenty-four hundred square miles (about the size of Delaware). Distant (more than five hundred miles from the mainland) and devoid of freshwater, the Galápagos never attracted much of a population. Even as late as the 1940s only two islands, Isabela and San Cristóbal, were inhabited (although today a few people live on Santa Cruz Island too). During the colonial period pirates and whalers used the islands as staging areas, and by the early 1800s U.S. vessels, whalers or cargo ships traveling to China, stopped in to take on provisions, capturing island tortoises by the thousands. Stacked alive beneath the deck, the tortoises provided a steady supply of fresh meat for long ocean voyages.

Ecuador took formal control of the island group in 1832, establishing a tiny penal colony on Charles Island. There followed numerous colonization attempts—1850, 1874, 1884, 1893, 1922, and beyond—involving Norwegians, Germans, Estonians, and others, but all these efforts failed. One angry, departing, would-be immigrant declared that the islands were clearly "'one of those places on earth' where human beings were 'not tolerated.'"[49] The islands are, of course, most famous for the visit of Charles Darwin in 1835.

At the close of the nineteenth century President Eloy Alfaro reinitiated Ecuador's earlier efforts to make some money from the Galápagos, offering a lease of the islands to the United States in exchange for cash and the warship *Detroit*. Eloy Alfaro thought the Americans might use the islands as a coaling station, but when the U.S. Department of the Navy announced it did not need a Galápagos base and the French sold Ecuador a warship, Alfaro shelved his lease idea.

He was soon back with a new proposal. Recognizing that Ecuador did not have the navy to defend the Galápagos, and fearful that a European nation or Peru might seize them, Eloy Alfaro offered to give one of the islands to the United States in exchange for a guarantee of protection and, of course, money. But because public opinion in Ecuador would never accept any plan that surrendered territory, Alfaro insisted that any arrangement with the Americans be kept secret, at least until he left office. He need not have worried; the United States remained uninterested.

The situation changed, however, with the 1903 U.S. acquisition of canal construction rights in Panama. This development came at a time, moreover, of growing U.S. concern that the French or Germans might have ideas about acquiring the islands. (There was some truth to this. Great Britain had offered to buy the Galápagos Islands in 1895, and in 1898 France had attempted to rent them.) Ecuadorian President Plaza, for his part, worried that with the United States now in Panama, its next move might be to take the Galápagos. As Plaza warned, "What occurred in Panama a few months ago is, in my judgement, an awful lesson by which we should profit."[50] When Eloy Alfaro returned to office in 1906, he reinitiated his efforts to sell or lease the islands to the United States.

The United States was not particularly interested in the islands. The U.S. Navy was changing its ship resupply practices, beginning to recoal vessels at sea, thereby eliminating the need for coaling stations. But in keeping with the Monroe Doctrine, U.S. officials certainly opposed the intrusion of any nonhemispheric power there. As one State Department official, Alvey A. Adee, summed up the U.S. position: "We don't want them for ourselves and won't allow any European (or extra-American) power to acquire control of them."[51] When rumors again reached the State Department in 1908 that a German, French, or Chilean purchase of the islands might be in the offing, Washington took notice. Secretary of State Elihu Root (1905–9) informed the Ecuadorian government that the United States would object to the sale to a European state but not to a transfer to Chile.

When a war scare with Peru developed in July 1910, Eloy Alfaro began to explore ways of using the Galápagos Islands to raise money to purchase arms. The Ecuadorian congress gave the president permission to look into renting the Galápagos to the United States in exchange for money to buy weapons. Using Archer Harman (a personal friend of Eloy Alfaro's) as liaison, in November 1910 Secretary of State Philander Knox (1909–13) offered to lease the islands for ninety-nine years for $15 million in gold. However, Knox insisted that Ecuador use the money for the sanitation of Guayaquil under close U.S. direction and not for making war on Peru. Eloy Alfaro angrily denounced what to him was blackmail but quickly made a counterproposal: Ecuador would spend $8 million of the money on the sanitation of Guayaquil and $7 million for new railway construction. The United States agreed in December 1910 but attached conditions: the United States could not promise to defend the Galápagos, and the Guayaquil sanitation plan would have to be approved by U.S. authorities. Eloy Alfaro rejected these conditions and withdrew from further discussions. When, inevitably, the story became public, other Latin American nations lodged strong objections and Ecuadorians protested. Backpedaling furiously, Eloy Alfaro publicly renounced all lease or sale plans by January 1911. Fear of war with Peru had receded anyway, and popular opposition to alienation of Ecuadorian territory was much too strong.

Despite his denials, Eloy Alfaro continued to quietly explore the possibility of leasing the islands, this time to Chile. When word of this new scheme leaked out, four hundred angry Guayaquil students gathered outside the offices of the progovernment newspaper *El tiempo* (where they thought Eloy Alfaro might be) and at the home of president-elect Emilio Estrada. "Down with the government!" the crowd shouted. "Down with Alfaro!" The U.S. consul in Guayaquil reported that other protesters were shouting, variously, "Death to Alfaro!" "Down with Harman!" "Death to Harman!" "Down with the Americans!" "Death to the Americans!"[52] When the students tried to smash their way into the newspaper's offices, mounted police charged in and sent everyone running. Further consideration of transferring land to the Americans or anyone else had to be tabled. In 1916 the Ecuadorian Ministry of Foreign Relations instructed its legation in Washington, D.C., to entertain no further discussions of selling or renting or in any way compromising Ecuador's sovereignty over the islands. That effectively ended any effort to alienate the Galápagos, at least for the time.

## The Sanitation of Guayaquil

In the discussions about leasing the Galápagos, the United States had had good reason to insist that Ecuador use some of the rent money to improve public health conditions in Guayaquil, which continued to be plagued by deadly diseases: yellow fever, malaria, bubonic plague, cholera, typhoid fever, smallpox, measles, tuberculosis and an array of other fatal respiratory and digestive infections. Guayaquil was a dangerous place even for lifetime residents, but it posed special hazards for the many newcomers from the sierra who had not acquired immunities to the many afflictions found there. That internal migrants kept coming suggests that people either learned too late of the dangers or that they were willing to risk death to get away from the desperate and oppressive conditions of the sierra. The pestilential conditions in Guayaquil certainly discouraged U.S. visitors, or at least those who took the time to learn about the health risks and were prudent enough to heed the strong warnings to stay away.

U.S. involvement in the sanitation of Guayaquil actually stemmed from its concern about the health conditions in Panama. There, Col. William C. Gorgas and others directed a highly effective sanitation campaign, greatly reducing the risk of malaria and eradicating yellow fever in the U.S. canal zone. The success of this sanitation effort had been essential for building and operating the canal, and U.S. officials well understood the precarious nature of their achievement. The canal zone could easily become reinfected, and ships making the two days' journey from nearby Guayaquil were a particular concern as potential carriers of yellow fever and other infectious killers.

In 1906 Ecuadorian President Eloy Alfaro requested U.S. help in carrying out the clean-up of Guayaquil. Alfaro had to proceed with some caution; he understood that Guayaquil officials would resent any usurpation of local authority, especially by foreigners. But when bubonic plague struck Guayaquil two years later, raising the threat of international quarantine, Eloy Alfaro could see no other option than to seek U.S. assistance. Two U.S. doctors, J. S. Perry and Bolivar C. Lloyd, arrived to organize and direct a special sanitation campaign for the entire city. However, local authorities objected so fiercely that Eloy Alfaro felt compelled to ask the Americans to leave. Perry and Lloyd departed, but because local health officials lacked the resources to do the job themselves, conditions in Guayaquil continued to be awful.

When civil war erupted in 1912, health conditions in Guayaquil reached a new low.[53] During the conflict rebels blew up a wooden railway trestle near Alausí and threatened to seize the assets of the U.S. railway. The railroad company was frantic, pleading with the U.S. State Department to send help. In response Washington ordered the warship *Yorktown* down from Panama to protect U.S. property in Ecuador. The vessel arrived in January 1912, but before Cmdr. L. C. Bertolette could do anything, he contracted yellow fever and died. Soon two more deaths and eight additional cases of yellow fever were reported aboard the *Yorktown*. Given the continuing risk to the crew, the *Yorktown* withdrew from Guayaquil. Two other U.S. vessels, the *Maryland* and the *Prometheus,* were intercepted en route and diverted.

In 1914, during the next Ecuadorian civil war, U.S. officials again requested that the Navy Department send warships to Ecuadorian waters. With the northern port city of Esmeraldas under bombardment and ablaze, the U.S. minister to Ecuador wrote the State Department in a panic: "I think [a] cruiser should be sent . . . immediately."[54] The secretary of state wrote back that "on account of yellow fever and the unfortunate deaths of Captain Bertolette and two seamen . . . , Department does not desire to send ship unless absolutely necessary."[55]

The deaths of Bertolette and the two navy crewmen stimulated a heightened U.S. interest in effecting the sanitation of Guayaquil. Washington began to apply steady pressure on Ecuador to accept a U.S.-directed clean-up campaign for the city. Responding, President Plaza labored to craft an arrangement that would secure U.S. assistance while assuaging regional sensibilities: the United States would supply all the doctors, assistants, and foremen for the work crews, write all the regulations, and build two quarantine hospitals (one for yellow fever and one for plague), but local authorities would retain total control of all public works, potable water, paving, and sewers, as well as administration of all matters pertaining to other diseases.

Col. William C. Gorgas, fresh from his success in Panama (and following his earlier public health achievements in Havana), arrived in December 1912 to conduct a feasibility study for the sanitation of Guayaquil. Gorgas reported that he could definitely do the job, adding that the earlier effort led by Doctors Lloyd and Perry had failed only because of the lack of cooperation from local authorities in Guayaquil.

At about the same time Ecuador awarded a large construction contract to the British firm J. G. White for building Guayaquil's new water lines and sewers. This decision deeply angered U.S. authorities and not just because a U.S. firm did not get the job. U.S. officials believed that the tax revenues that Ecuador had pledged to the British to pay for the project—the customs receipts—had already been designated for paying off the railway debt. The U.S. minister to Ecuador met with President Plaza and warned that the United States "might, on occasion, be compelled, however reluctantly, to exclude from passage through the canal vessels touching at ports infected with contagious diseases."[56] Ecuador granted the contract to the British anyway, pledging customs taxes to pay for the work, no matter what other encumbrances these port duties may have already carried.

In 1916 the Ecuadorian Ministry of Foreign Relations proudly declared that "while there have been contagious diseases in Guayaquil in the past, for the most part this is no longer the case."[57] This claim was simply not true, as Guayaquil's own public health records show. In 1916 in Guayaquil, a city of about 85,000, 358 people died of malaria, 345 of bubonic plague, and 166 of yellow fever.[58] In July 1916 Gorgas returned to Guayaquil, this time at the behest of the International Health Board of the Rockefeller Foundation, and conducted a reinspection of the city. Gorgas issued a report that strongly criticized the handling of public health in Guayaquil; city residents responded by burning Gorgas in effigy. But Gorgas was right—Guayaquil's health conditions were a disgrace. Steamship companies avoided Guayaquil. In Panama the United States enforced a quarantine on any ships proceeding from Ecuador.

Gradually, the efforts to clean up Guayaquil brought some success. One step in the right direction was the completion in 1918 of the public works construction project by the J. G. White company. This greatly increased the available supply of potable water and provided modern sewage disposal. In 1919 the International Health Board of the Rockefeller Foundation tried again, reaching an agreement with local authorities to launch a program to rid Guayaquil of yellow fever. U.S. physician Michael E. Conner headed the effort, but the team of international health experts and he worked under the supervision of local officials. The efforts of the Rockefeller Foundation, which generously contributed more than $100,000 toward the sanitation of the city, eliminated the scourge of yellow fever in Guayaquil in 1919. It was the last city in South America to complete the eradication of this disease.

## Conclusions

In the period 1895–1925 Ecuador became more dependent on the United States. The United States was now the leading buyer of Ecuador's exports and the leading supplier of imports, the trade carried almost entirely in U.S. vessels. Ecuador relied on the United States for purchases of military hardware and for desperately needed loans. Ecuador found itself at an ever-increasing economic and political disadvantage with respect to the United States. Policy makers in Washington understood this and sought to use their power advantage to advance U.S. interests in Ecuador, from payment to the railroad bondholders, the defense of U.S. investments, to the sanitation of the port of Guayaquil to protect the Panama Canal from reinfection with yellow fever.

Yet despite the great asymmetries in power between the United States and Ecuador, it is remarkable how unsuccessful the United States was in getting what it wanted and how remarkably unpowerful the instruments at its disposal really were. Ecuador was painfully slow to yield to U.S. demands for a U.S.-directed Guayaquil sanitation campaign and gave in only when local authorities retained significant control of the process, one undertaken by private experts sent by the Rockefeller Foundation, not by the U.S. government. Even though Washington cared a great deal about this matter—more to protect the economic viability of the Panama Canal than to protect Ecuadorian lives—all U.S. attempts to compel the sanitation of Guayaquil under U.S. direction failed. Nothing the United States tried got Ecuador to budge.

Sometimes the United States looked completely powerless in exchanges between the two nations. When rebels blew up parts of the U.S.-owned railway, the U.S. warship on the scene fled epidemic-ravaged Guayaquil rather than stay and protect U.S. investments. After the deaths of U.S. crewmen from yellow fever, the U.S. Navy subsequently refused to come back, no matter how much U.S. officials pleaded. It was just too dangerous, and the navy would not do it.

But most significant of all was the case of the railway bondholders. Despite the deep U.S. concern and application of continuing and considerable pressure, in the end the railway bondholders got nearly nothing. Ecuador did not want to pay, and so, except briefly during World War I, no matter what Washington tried, no matter how much it threatened, Ecuador would not pay. Despite all the great power advantages of the United States, it could not force its will upon Ecuador. In each of the exchanges between the two nations in these years, Ecuador proved that it could frustrate even the most determined U.S. efforts.

# 4    Economic Collapse and War: The 1920s to the 1940s

The 1920s through the 1940s were perhaps Ecuador's most difficult years, a time of deep economic, political, and foreign policy crises. World market conditions shifted, destroying Ecuador's once-prosperous cacao economy, and the sharp decline in commerce contributed generously to a state of continual political chaos. It was also a time of extraordinarily poor leaders, men who foolishly steered Ecuador into a disastrous conflict with Peru. When the war was over, Ecuador had surrendered half its national territory.

In these years the United States came to be more involved with Ecuador than ever before. Washington now wanted more from Ecuador—debt payment, cooperation in the Allied effort in World War II, and, above all, military bases. But though Ecuador was a weak and divided nation, Washington nonetheless had great difficulty in enforcing its will. The United States sometimes got what it wanted but usually only when its goals coincided with those of Ecuador.

## The Collapse of the Cacao Export Economy

International economic competition can be a fierce and volatile process, especially for raw material exporters like Ecuador.[1] When any poor nation finds a primary product it can sell profitably on the world market, inevitably other nations will scramble to emulate this success. The pattern is a familiar one: new producers appear, supplies increase, and prices fall. This is what happened with Ecuador's cacao exports. African competitors in the 1910s and 1920s followed Ecuador's lead, developed their own cacao exports, glutted the market, and prices tumbled. In 1920 the price for cacao dropped from $26 to $6 a quintal (a measure equaling

93

220 pounds). The value of Ecuador's cacao sales fell two-thirds from 1914 to 1929, hitting their lowest level since the mid-1800s. Ecuador's cacao production dropped by half from 1917 to 1926, in part because of plant disease but mainly because growers were getting out of cacao. In 1915 cacao had made up three-quarters of Ecuadorian exports. By 1925 it comprised less than half, and by the Depression years of the 1930s less than one-fifth.

At first some Ecuador planters clung to the hope that they might be able to revive the cacao export industry. In 1929 the Ecuadorian government brought in U.S. agricultural experts to give advice on how to cure the diseases afflicting cacao. But it was no use; it was over. Some cacao growers converted their plantations to sugar, rice, or coffee, but most simply abandoned their estates, the vacant land taken over by squatters. All over the coast during the 1930s and 1940s free land was available for the taking. Balsa wood, rubber, and panama hats replaced cacao as Ecuador's leading trade items, although their combined totals did not approach the value of exports shipped during the cacao boom years.

Ecuador's changed economic situation brought important modifications to the social and political context. While the overall population of Ecuador continued to grow in these years, rising from two million in 1930 to three million in 1942, urbanization slowed as the economy slumped. The two largest cities of Ecuador grew only modestly in population, Guayaquil to 130,000 and Quito to about 110,000 by 1933.[2] The population distribution also shifted. Now about a third of the nation's population lived on the coast, the other two-thirds in the sierra. In the highlands, indigenous people locked in servile and impoverished conditions continued to make up the bulk of the population.

The political rights of ordinary Ecuadorians reflected their lack of economic power: most people did not have the right to vote. Literacy was a requirement for suffrage, and only one in five Ecuadorians could read and write. (Although literate women gained the right to vote in 1929, few were literate and even fewer voted.) Other restrictions—voter registration fees, the requirement that one return to one's hometown to cast a ballot—excluded most other potential voters. In 1931 and 1933 only 3 percent of the population voted; in 1948 only 9 percent did.

But change was coming, and in the 1920s and 1930s the political power of Ecuador's old elite commenced its long decline, even if the oligarchy never reached total powerlessness. As the economy changed and matured during the twentieth century, the Ecuadorian elite grew increasingly complex as a class, which came to include elements beyond its traditional land-based roots. At the same time the nascent emergence of urban mass society created a more restive population, one far less imbued with old colonial-style habits of deference and fatalism. Some worker organizations appeared and soon formed into two national labor federations, the conservative Confederación Ecuatoriana de Obreros Católicos (the Ecuadorian Confederation of Catholic Workers) in 1938, and the socialist/communist-oriented Confederación de Trabajadores del Ecuador (the Confederation of Ecuadorian Workers) in 1944. While Ecuador's old elite still sought to run the nation by and for itself, doing so was becoming increasingly complicated. The elite now had many more popular organizations and trade unions to contend with.

The twentieth century was therefore a time of political challenge for Ecuador's elites, of attempting to fend off demands for political inclusion from new groups. In a society so riven by great inequalities and vast injustices, elites instinctively distrusted the masses. What would stop them from simply using their votes to take the elite's wealth? In the ensuing struggles the incorporation of popular elements into the political process was haphazard and incomplete. As Ecuador moved through the twentieth century, concessions to democratic change came slowly and grudgingly, but they came.[3]

The most salient feature of Ecuadorian politics from the 1920s into the 1940s was its instability and uncertainty. From 1925 to 1947, twenty-three different presidents attempted to govern the nation. Each lasted about a year, and not one finished his legal term of office. From August 15 to October 30, 1933, Ecuador had *twelve* foreign ministers. The congress, the stronghold of regional interests, used its power to block nearly all legislative initiatives offered by the many presidents. As the historian Linda

Alexander Rodríguez has noted, "None of the presidents . . . could govern while the congress was in session."[4] Most presidents saw no choice but to assume dictatorial powers, a move that typically led one group of elites or another to beg the military to oust the tyrant in the name of restoring "constitutional" authority. As Ecuador's representative in the United States, Romero Viteri L., concluded, the ceaseless, pointless cycle of "revolutions" left Ecuador in a perpetual state of "spasmodic convulsions."[5] This chaotic situation had major implications for the construction of a foreign policy.

On July 9, 1925, a coup (known to Ecuadorians as the *juliano*) led by a group of junior officers from the sierra, the Liga Militar (Military League), removed President Gonzalo S. Córdova from office. The Liga Militar, filled with the hope and energy of youth, promised to initiate a new era of clean government, honest elections, and economic renewal. Instead, the coup inaugurated an extraordinary period of political instability, even by Ecuadorian standards. Although to some scholars the *juliano* represented the end to corrupt bank rule, the plutocracy, or coastal dominance, such interpretations greatly overstate the case.[6] What the *juliano* really represented was another adjustment in the distribution of power between regionally based elites. Now that the cacao economy had collapsed, the coastal export elites were no longer so preeminent, and power shifted back toward the sierra. However, the coastal interests had only been weakened; they had not been eliminated.

In the wake of the *juliano* the military governed until April 1926. One of the military's first actions was to close four coastal banks, seizing all their assets. Leading bank officials, including the spectacularly opulent Francisco Urvina Jado of the Banco Comercial y Agrícola, were arrested and sent into exile, as was former president Leonidas Plaza. In 1926 the military designated a forty-seven-year-old sierra intellectual and Quito obstetrician, Isidro Ayora Cueva, as Ecuador's next president. He swiftly converted his position to dictator. Disdainful of the obvious illegality of Ayora's power grab, the United States withheld formal diplomatic recognition of the new regime until August 1928. The three-year span was the longest period in which the United States withheld recognition for any Ecuadorian government.

## The Kemmerer Mission

In one of his first actions, Ayora invited the U.S. financial expert Dr. Edwin Walter Kemmerer to Ecuador. A professor of economics at Princeton University, Kemmerer enjoyed an international reputation as a financial wizard and economic problem solver. He helped restructure the U.S. monetary system, including the creation of the Federal Reserve System in 1913, and from 1923 to 1931 led a team of experts on economic reform missions all over the world—Mexico, Guatemala, Colombia, Peru, Bolivia, Chile, Germany, Poland, Turkey, South Africa, China, and, in 1926–27, Ecuador.

After the dramatic drop in cacao exports in 1922, Ecuador desperately needed to borrow money but could only look on with envy as other Latin American nations lined up to receive large loans from U.S. banks. Ecuador's record as a defaulting debtor—seventy-two times from 1834 to 1927—meant that its bonds carried the lowest rating of any South American nation's.[7] Ayora needed to reorganize Ecuador's finances, and he began by targeting coastal banks. Because the coastal cacao oligarchy had led the earlier economic advance, most Ecuadorians now blamed its financial institutions, the coastal banks, for the economic disaster. Seeking to punish the coast and favor the sierra, Ayora called for closing the leading Guayaquil banks and creating a national bank in Quito. Ecuador began to implement a financial reform package modeled after the program being followed in Colombia and Chile. Kemmerer had drawn up both programs.

Bringing Kemmerer to Ecuador was a safe bet. No matter what the question, he always had the same answer. Wherever he went, as the Kemmerer historian Paul Drake notes, "hardly a word [of his proposals] . . . varied from Poland to Bolivia."[8] Not a free thinker, Kemmerer unfailingly called for rigorous implementation of the economic orthodoxies of his age. One thing was absolutely certain: he would recommend the creation of a national bank in the capital; he always did. So Ayora called on Kemmerer, as Drake notes, to "help . . . local elites burnish and legitimize proposals they already expected, favored, and, . . . had initiated on their own."[9] Kemmerer's stamp of approval could help

bring foreign loans to Ecuador. The economic rules that Kemmerer recommended were those found in the United States, something likely to
make U.S. investors feel more comfortable about putting their money
into Ecuador.

Kemmerer and his team arrived in Ecuador in October 1926 and remained until February 1927, completing its work with tremendous dis-
patch, if not always great care. Vast sections of the mission's report were
borrowed from recommendations drawn up for other countries. Robert
Vorfeld, who wrote Ecuador's new customs code, "simply copied his
previous work in Paraguay. Since external commerce moved on an international river there, this . . . inadvertently led to the application of
customs regulations to Ecuador's internal waterway traffic, thus inhib-
iting domestic commerce."[10] Such errors notwithstanding, Ayora was
quite pleased overall, and his dictatorship swiftly made into law all two
thousand pages of Kemmerer's recommendations. Kemmerer's reforms
served to create "exchange stability, modern banking, fiscal order, more
efficient customs administration, punctual debt payments, Anglo-Saxon
commercial practices, and equal rights for foreign capitalists."[11] Crown-
ing these achievements was the founding in 1927 of the new Banco Central de Ecuador, headquartered in a handsome building located, to no
one's surprise, in the capital city of Quito.

After Colombia put its Kemmerer program in place, it had immediately started borrowing money from overseas banks, increasing its
foreign debt ten times over from 1923 to 1930. Peru, looking to start
borrowing money too, adopted Kemmerer's plan in just one day, with
its legislature dispensing with the formality of reading the detailed
package of reforms. Working from these examples, Ecuador began to
push for its U.S. loans even before Kemmerer left town. But despite
Ecuador's financial overhaul, U.S. investors still did not find much of
interest. The hoped-for foreign loans did not materialize. In the end the
only loan that Ecuador received was a small advance from the Swedish
Match Company, in exchange for monopoly rights to sell matches in
Ecuador for twenty-five years. Meanwhile the rest of Latin America got
a lot of money, taking out in the 1920s more U.S. loans than at any time
until the 1970s.

Ecuador failed to attract foreign loans for several reasons. Certainly, the U.S. government's refusal to recognize the Ayora dictatorship complicated discussions with foreign banks. But worse, disgruntled foreign railway bondholders lobbied furiously in Washington to keep Ecuador from getting a new loan unless they got paid first. The bondholders had legitimate grievances. In 1926 the Ayora dictatorship had authorized the use of customs receipts to help pay some of the costs of the bank consolidation and reorganization, a clear violation of the agreement with the foreign bondholders who had been promised the same monies. Ecuador started making token payments on the railway debt to the bondholders in 1927, but these disbursements halted with the Great Depression. Of course, Ecuador was hardly alone in this: when the depression hit, all the nations in Latin America except Argentina, Haiti, and the Dominican Republic stopped servicing their foreign debt. Ecuador ultimately reached a new arrangement with foreign bondholders and resumed partial payments in 1936, but Ecuador never did pay off the railway bonds in full.

Along with the loans from international sources, in the 1920s U.S. capital poured into Latin America in the form of direct investment, but little came to Ecuador. U.S. investors saw Ecuador as a bad risk. Ecuador claimed only 0.3 percent of the total U.S. direct investment in Latin America in the 1920s. Neighboring Peru had nineteen times more direct U.S. investment than did Ecuador. After Ecuador nationalized the railroad in 1925, the only significant U.S. holding in the nation was the Guayaquil electrical power plant. The U.S.-based South American Development Company came to the province of El Oro (in the extreme south of Ecuador) and set up a small gold-mining operation but found little.

When Kemmerer departed in 1927, he left behind four U.S. experts to oversee the implementation of his reforms and run Ecuador's finances. For three years the reforms worked: Ecuador increased its tax receipts, turned government deficits into surpluses, and dramatically reduced its internal debt. But with the coming of the Great Depression the deficits and debt returned, private banks folded, and Ecuador went off the gold standard. Ecuador sent the Kemmerer foreign financial advisers packing; they had run afoul of local sensibilities and, more seriously, could find little support for continued economic orthodoxy (policies not unlike modern-day International Monetary Fund recommendations), given the harsh realities of the Great Depression. Disillusioned with the results of the Kemmerer policies, Ecuador eventually abandoned the whole project. Foreign investors were not coming to Ecuador anyway. The government kept the central bank but not much more.

## Depression

The Ecuadorian economy, already in steep decline from the catastrophic drop in cacao prices, went into free fall during the worldwide Great Depression of the 1930s. Cacao sales had collapsed and what remained of Ecuador's exports fell by two-thirds from 1928 to 1932, dropping in value from $15 million to less than $5 million. Imports fell from $17 million to $6 million in the same period. Ecuador's trade orientation remained unchanged; it still was focused on the United States. Of Ecuador's $17 million in imports in 1929, 41 percent ($7 million) came from the United States. Of Ecuador's $17 million in exports in 1929, 47 percent ($8 million) went to the United States. But the overall trend was down. By the 1930s Ecuador had fallen behind nearly every Latin American nation in per-capita export value, performing worse than even landlocked Bolivia and Paraguay. Prices for Ecuador's few exports—coffee, sugar, and rice—fell sharply into the 1930s.[12]

Ever hopeful of finding some niche in the U.S. market, some Ecuadorians reasoned that the end of Prohibition in the United States in 1933 might allow them to bring the economy back to life by exporting locally produced spirits. The Ecuadorian legation in the United States certainly thought so, suggesting that "there appeared to exist the opportunity to sell better quality Ecuadoran aguardientes" (an anise-flavored liquor distilled from sugar cane) in the United States.[13] But U.S. consumers had little desire for *aguardiente*, Ecuadorian or otherwise. The few Americans who had tried *aguardiente* usually found it to be overly sweet and not especially pleasant tasting, even if it was easily affordable and very strong. Indeed, most Ecuadorians, or at least those who could afford it, preferred

U.S.-made spirits. Liquor imports from the United States always greatly exceeded Ecuadorian exports of alcoholic beverages in these years.

As the importation of manufactures fell off, the Ecuadorian sierra's textile shops recovered modestly, especially after the adoption of a mildly protective tariff in 1925. Otherwise, Ecuador developed scant industry. This was particularly frustrating because other Latin American nations were developing significant industrialization in the 1920s and 1930s. The Great Depression sharply reduced Latin American industrial imports from the developed world, and in some Latin American nations, notably Mexico and Brazil, this helped stimulate domestic industrialization to make locally what had previously been imported. But Ecuador lacked nearly all the preconditions necessary for industrialization. Transportation remained a major obstacle. In 1940 the nation had only 640 miles of rail line, a virtually nonexistent road system, and only about four thousand automobiles. Potential internal markets remained scattered and inaccessible. Even more serious was that Ecuador's markets were just too small, its middle class too minuscule to constitute anything approaching an adequate base of consumers. Even by the 1940s Ecuador's few industries—refined sugar, shoes, beer, matches, tanning—were the same ones it had at the turn of the century. The rule for industry in Ecuador continued: if a product could be imported, it was.

The Great Depression brought further economic havoc for Ecuador. As the economy shut down, the income of the national government fell from $13 million in 1927 to $4 million in 1934. The government borrowed to make up the shortfall, triggering runaway inflation; Ecuador had one of the highest inflation rates in Latin America in these years. The value of Ecuador's currency plummeted, losing two-thirds of its value from 1930 to 1942. Ecuador stopped servicing the public domestic debt (it had long since stopped paying on its foreign obligations), leading to a string of bank failures. Overall, the cost of living quadrupled from 1938 to 1944.

## Depression and Political Chaos

The political picture was as troubled as the economic one. The Great Depression triggered increased unemployment and inflation, and popular revolts followed. The military turned on the Ayora dictator-ship, ousting him in August 1931. A botched election, four caretaker presidencies, and civil war followed. Neftalí Bonifaz Ascázubi, the con-servative candidate, won the 1931 contest, but when an array of regional interests in the legislature united to block Bonifaz's assumption of office, a bitter military clash ensued. In August and September 1932 fighting erupted in and around Quito, with the people of the capital city suffer-ing through four days and nights of heavy combat. Fierce battles raged from house to house, with exchanges of artillery fire in high-density res-idential neighborhoods. The anti-Bonifaz provincial units prevailed but only after at least a thousand people, mostly civilians, had been killed.

The next year the coastal liberals rigged the election of Juan de Dios Martínez Mera (1932–33), an enormously unpopular Guayaquil rob-ber baron. After another coup and another brief caretaker government, fresh elections in 1934 placed José María Velasco Ibarra in power for the first of his five turns in the presidency (1934–35, 1944–47, 1952–56, 1960–61, 1968–72). When in 1935 Velasco Ibarra dissolved the legisla-ture and jailed opposition lawmakers, the military overthrew him and set up another caretaker government. The military placed in power Federico Páez, who established a highly repressive—some say cryp-tofascist—dictatorship (1935–37). His ouster, spearheaded by Gen. Al-berto Enríquez Gallo (1937–38), brought a brief effort at social and po-litical reform. Under Enríquez, Ecuador enacted a labor code (1937) and permitted unions and progressive political parties to reopen. But after Enríquez was removed from office, Ecuador got another caretaker gov-ernment, that of the authoritarian and highly repressive Aurelio Mos-quera Narváez (1938–39), which rolled backed the reforms. Mosquera shut down the legislature before closing the nation's colleges and even its high schools. Beleaguered and physically weak, the dictator commit-ted suicide (some say he died of a physical illness) in November 1939.

The head of the senate, Carlos Alberto Arroyo del Río, filled the lead-ership void, running Ecuador from 1939 to 1944. After taking power extralegally in 1939, Arroyo del Río resigned briefly so that he might be a legal candidate in the 1940 election and thereby legitimize his rule. The plan did not work. Arroyo del Río trailed badly in the voting and could think of no alternative than to steal the election. The leading vote getter, former president Velasco Ibarra, vigorously protested the fraud, triggering serious unrest in the streets of Guayaquil. Arroyo del Río sent Velasco Ibarra into exile. But even in defeat Velasco Ibarra had accomplished something important. By carrying his electoral campaign directly to the ordinary people of Ecuador, both those who had the right to vote and even those who did not, he had begun to propel Ecuador into the modern age of mass politics, furthering the process of political incorporation and democratization. But the achievement of democracy still stood far in the future. The political reality in Ecuador was one of all-consuming internal conflict.

## Ecuador and the United States in the Prewar Period

The economic and political context of these years—a shattered economy and chaotic political scene—severely weakened Ecuador's ability to respond effectively to foreign policy challenges and defend its national interests. This became painfully apparent in the 1920s and 1930s as Colombia and Peru squared off in a conflict about control of Amazonian territory, lands to which Ecuador had long-standing and legitimate claims. Rather than enter into an alliance with either nation, Ecuador chose to remain neutral. From Ecuador's perspective, Colombia could never be counted on, and Ecuador still blamed it for failing to honor its treaty agreements and come to Ecuador's aid in the border conflicts of 1859 and 1910. Peru was too much of an enemy to ever be considered as a potential Ecuadorian ally. In any event, Ecuador lacked the firepower to get into a war against either nation.

With Ecuador unwilling to pick sides, neither Colombia nor Peru saw any advantage in inviting Ecuador to talks on the disposition of the disputed territory. Colombia and Peru reached an accord in 1922, the Salomón-Lozano Treaty. Colombia gained access to the Amazon River at Leticia and in exchange conceded to Peru vast stretches of Amazonian territory that Ecuador thought it owned. Ecuador tried to get a hearing on the matter before the League of Nations, but the organization refused to listen because Ecuador was not a member. It had never joined. In its endless changes of government, Ecuador had let lapse nearly all its diplomatic postings, maintaining only minimal representation in Peru, Colombia, and the United States. Seeing now that Ecuador's lack of membership in the League of Nations had harmed his country's interests, President Velasco Ibarra entered Ecuador into the League of Nations in 1935, although it was too late to do any good in this case.

Ecuador did at least gather the resources to send delegates to the series of inter-American conferences held in the 1920s and 1930s, although it played only a supporting role at the meetings. At the 1928 Sixth Pan-American Conference, held in Havana, the Latin American nations gave voice to their strong opposition to U.S. military interventionism in Haiti, the Dominican Republic, and Nicaragua. Although the United States attempted to silence any discussion of these actions, the Latin American delegates issued, as the historian Dick Steward puts it, "a collective indictment of United States policy."[14] Secretary of State Charles Evans Hughes (1921–25) offered the view that U.S. military intervention in Latin American nations did not constitute an act of aggression. But Latin American critics believed that the United States was using the Monroe Doctrine to keep European powers out of the hemisphere so it could take Latin American territory for itself.

This Latin American rebuke to the United States came at a time when many U.S. policy makers and the U.S. public were themselves beginning to reassess the wisdom of military interventionism in Latin America. Not all Americans had been supportive of the imperialistic actions that the United States had taken in the Caribbean and Central America. The United States lost more than one hundred soldiers in Nicaragua from 1927 to 1932, and few Americans could see what had been gained from this sacrifice. And once the United States was plunged into the Great Depression, many concluded that the United States could no longer afford a policy of interventionism. In the words of the historian Bryce Wood, the United States was coming to see military interventionism in Latin America as "troublesome, embarrassing, and costly."[15]

Although President Franklin D. Roosevelt (1933–45) usually gets credit for the "Good Neighbor" policy, or the end to the era of direct U.S.

military interventionism in Latin America, the phrase actually belongs to his predecessor, Herbert Hoover (1929–33). As president-elect in 1928 Hoover toured Latin America, the first U.S. leader to do so. As he traveled, Hoover proclaimed that the United States and Latin America had to become good neighbors.[16] The president-elect made a stop in Guayaquil, and his one-day visit with President Ayora went well, even if Ecuadorian officials seemed mostly interested in extracting a promise that Hoover would not spend any more time in Peru than he had in Ecuador.

In 1930 Hoover's undersecretary of state, J. Reuben Clark, wrote a formal repudiation of the Roosevelt Corollary, but the document failed to cede the United States' self-proclaimed right to intervene in Latin America. President Hoover subsequently took a more concrete step toward a new U.S. policy direction for Latin America, ordering U.S. forces out of Nicaragua in January 1933. His successor, Franklin Roosevelt, was an outspoken critic of U.S. interventionism in Latin America and built on this from the beginning, announcing his Good Neighbor policy in his inaugural address on March 4, 1933. This was at last a full and formal renunciation of intervention. Franklin Roosevelt pledged that henceforth the United States would not interfere in the domestic affairs of other American states. Under FDR the United States withdrew its remaining troops from Haiti and renounced the Platt Amendment, which had asserted a right to intervene in Cuba's domestic affairs. FDR traveled to Montevideo, Uruguay, in December 1933 to attend the Seventh Pan-American Conference and spoke to the Latin American delegates, strongly reaffirming the principle of nonintervention. The Montevideo meetings also led to a call for a gradual mutual lowering of all trade barriers. This was a U.S. initiative; Ecuador and Chile joined in arguing for some preferential tariffs for Latin American nations. Ecuador pushed for protective tariffs for nascent Latin American industries and called for a Latin American common market.

At the Conference for the Maintenance of Peace, held in Buenos Aires in 1936, the United States reaffirmed unconditionally its renunciation of the unilateral use of force in Latin America. Yet this declaration amounted to less than it might at first seem. Pressure by Sumner Welles, the U.S. undersecretary of state, had nearly led to the use of U.S. forces in

Cuba in 1934, as Washington sought to shape political outcomes there. In some ways military intervention was no longer really necessary for the United States. Given that so many places in Latin America had been subjected to invasions in the past, just threatening the use of force probably was enough to get the desired effect. As Drake has noted, "A great power does not need to invade everywhere in its domain; a hegemon only has to punish a few of its underlings to extract obedience from the rest."[17] Of course, when threats were not enough, the United States could always use its great economic leverage over Latin America. But contemplation of whether the Good Neighbor would really represent a significant shift in U.S. policy soon was overshadowed in importance by increasingly urgent events: the building threat of war.

## The Coming War and the Pan-American Meetings

In the years leading up to 1941 the United States and Ecuador both sought to deal with the growing likelihood of a terrible war—one for Ecuador, another for much of the rest of the world. These disparate concerns were evident at the special inter-American congress in Buenos Aires in 1936. FDR had called the meeting to arrange a collective American response to Italian aggression in Ethiopia, the Japanese invasion of China, and German rearmament under the Nazis. Addressing the gathering, Franklin Roosevelt called for making the Monroe Doctrine a shared American policy. The meetings resulted in the Consultative Pact, an agreement to meet and talk in the event of an outside attack on the Americas. Ecuadorian diplomats, something less than fully convinced by Washington's commitment to be a good neighbor, pushed for "U.S. adoption of a non-aggression formula . . . prohibiting the dispatching of armed forces beyond . . . national boundaries."[18] The words held double meaning for Ecuador, which was seeking to address its own concerns in pressing for a "doctrine of non-recognition of territory gained by force of arms."[19] What Ecuador was thinking about was Peru, not Germany, Japan, or Italy. Ecuador called for the creation of a Latin American League of Nations to assure compliance, although little came of its proposal.

War was growing closer as the Eighth International Conference of American States met in Lima in December 1938. Responding to Franklin Roosevelt's appeals, the conference issued the Declaration of Lima, moving a step beyond the Buenos Aires Consultative Pact of 1936 by calling for a military aspect to inter-American defensive cooperation. In the end, however, the Declaration of Lima still left it up to each state to decide how it might respond to any outside threat. Ecuador, however, sought to use the discussions to advance its own agenda. At both the Buenos Aires and Lima meetings Ecuador focused on attempting to get Peru back to the negotiation table to settle their boundary dispute.

After Germany attacked Poland in September 1939, the United States called for an immediate consultative meeting of the ministers of foreign relations, and it was held in Panama in September and October 1939. The Declaration of Panama, which resulted from the meetings, announced a hemispheric three-hundred-mile zone of exclusion for all belligerents. But as with the earlier meetings, Ecuador had its own goals: the Ecuadorian delegation wanted to talk about Peru and the boundary dispute. When other delegates spoke of Poland, Belgium, and the Nazis, Ecuador thought of Peru.

In response to the lightning attacks by the Germans on the neutral Low Countries, Washington brought together the American foreign ministers for a special session in Havana in July 1940. Ecuador supported each measure passed at the meeting, pushing hardest for resolutions against warfare among the American states and for the peaceful resolution of inter-American differences. But the focus of the meetings was on potential aggression in the Americas by extrahemispheric forces. The conference concluded with the Act of Havana, which reaffirmed united Latin American endorsement of the "no transfer" principle, opposing the transfer of any European colonial territory in the Americas to any nonhemispheric power. For Washington the purpose of these pre–World War II inter-American meetings had been to arrange hemispheric solidarity against the growing fascist threat. For Ecuador the meetings were a forum to talk about Peru. Ecuador borrowed the language of the Americans—outrage against naked aggression, denunciation of a strong nation's seizing territory from the weak—but used these words as a way of legitimizing its concerns about Peru.

## War

The source of the trouble between Ecuador and Peru was their un-settled boundary line. The border ran somewhere through the trackless reaches of the Amazon tropical rainforest, but its precise location had been in dispute since even before the founding of the two nations.[20] During the colonial period the Audiencia of Quito had comprised the territory that, more or less, makes up Ecuador today. However, the Span-ish never bothered to establish exact boundaries between the *audiencias*. The border zones were largely devoid of Spanish population, and all the areas belonged to the king anyway, so determining where one jurisdic-tion ended and another began was just not important to Spain.

In 1827 Peru requested U.S. mediation to determine the boundary, but the U.S. envoy arrived well after hostilities had already commenced be-tween Ecuador and Peru—the 1829 Battle of Tarqui, which was won by Ecuador. The issue continued to fester. Ecuador thought it had an agree-ment in 1890, the García-Herrera Treaty, but Peru ultimately backed out of the deal. In 1895 King Alfonso XIII of Spain agreed to arbitrate the dispute, but in 1910, just before he was ready to issue his ruling, Ecuador somehow learned in advance what he was going to say and abruptly withdrew from the arbitration agreement.

U.S. officials sought again to help resolve the lingering dispute, but they accomplished little. The United States tried in 1924 (under the aus-pices of the Ponce-Castro Oyanguren protocol), hosting talks in Wash-ington. Invited to do so by both Ecuador and Peru, FDR announced on February 6, 1934, that he would arbitrate the boundary dispute. How-ever, the Peruvian negotiators did not even arrive in Washington until July 1936, and once there they showed little interest in the discussions. When Franklin Roosevelt finally opened the talks on September 30, 1936, squabbling about minor points quickly dominated the discussions. The two sides could agree on nothing. Peru tried to pin the blame for the impasse on Ecuador, and the talks collapsed in 1938.

What Ecuador sought most was territory along the north bank of the Marañón River, a wide, navigable tributary of the Amazon. Access to this river would assure Ecuador an outlet to both oceans. Ecuador would not compromise on this point; it believed it had already conceded too much. The nation had surrendered Amazonian territory to Brazil in 1904; to Colombia in 1916; and to Colombia and Peru in 1920 and again in 1935, when Colombia turned over to Peru land claimed by Ecuador.

Peru was equally unmovable. Peru had already lost territory to Chile in the War of the Pacific (1879–83) and to Colombia in the Leticia dispute (1932–33). These conflicts settled Peru's boundaries with these two neighbors although hardly to Peru's satisfaction. Only Peru's border with Ecuador remained to be firmly fixed, and Peru did not care to lose again. By the late 1930s and into the 1940s Peruvian settlers were spilling into disputed territory, followed in short order by the Peruvian military. Bit by bit Peru was encroaching on what Ecuador regarded as its sovereign territory.

Both nations were receiving foreign military assistance, although Peru took much more than Ecuador. Ecuador brought in a small number of Italian military trainers beginning in 1922, but this mission offered scant instruction, instead serving principally as a conduit for fascist propaganda. The mission probably influenced Ecuador's decision to lift its economic sanctions, which had been imposed on Italy in 1936–39 by the League of Nations as punishment for the Italian attack on Ethiopia. After the Ethiopia campaign Ecuador bought some surplus Italian arms, but most were obsolete and in poor working order. Relations with Italy soured when Ecuador stopped payments for the damaged goods. Meanwhile from 1931 to 1941 Peru greatly strengthened its military, more than doubling its army from 8,000 to 16,705 soldiers, and purchased significant new armaments, including fighters, bombers, and navy destroyers.[21] Peru also hosted a military mission from fascist Italy from 1937 to 1941. Many Ecuadorians believed that the Peruvians were using the Italians to obtain the details of Ecuadorian military planning.

Ecuador did almost nothing in response to Peru's military buildup. The Ecuadorian military remained one of very limited strength, equal perhaps to the task of putting down small internal uprisings of unarmed Indian peasants but not much more. Ecuador's armed forces included only eight thousand soldiers, a few patrol boats and transports, and six unarmed trainer planes but no tanks, no warships, and no antiaircraft guns. The Ecuadorian military was poorly led: all Ecuadorian generals were patronage appointees.

Amazingly, Ecuador's military weakness did not lead to circumspection in its Peru policy. From 1937 to 1938 Ecuador moved troops in along the border and in 1939 advanced three battalions (about fifteen hundred men) into the disputed zone. In early 1941 Ecuador transferred soldiers into border regions along the Pacific coast, especially around Zarumilla (see map 2). With this action Ecuador was challenging Peruvian ownership not of remote jungle regions somewhere out in the distant Amazonian wilderness but of rich and heavily populated farmlands along Peru's northwest border with Ecuador. This was an area that Peru had plainly controlled since it achieved nationhood. Nevertheless, Ecuadorian leaders, backed by popular sentiment that had been whipped into a froth by the press, relentlessly pushed unrealistic and extreme positions on the boundary question, exaggerated claims that Ecuador was in no position to back with force of arms.

On May 8, 1941, the United States, Argentina, and Chile sent a joint letter to Peru and Ecuador, urging an end to the dispute. Ecuador immediately accepted their friendly services, but Peru refused. Instead, Peruvian President Manuel Prado quickened his military buildup along the border. The U.S. undersecretary of state, Sumner Welles, speaking with the Peruvian ambassador, expressed Washington's fears that war between Peru and Ecuador might open a way for Axis penetration of South America.

Peru, in fact, wanted war, for it was seeking something more important than territory: redemption. Thoroughly humiliated by Chile in the War of the Pacific, the Peruvian military wanted to restore its honor. And after being so seriously outmaneuvered by Colombia in the Leticia dispute, Peruvian civil authorities now sought to rehabilitate their image. Given Washington's preoccupation with Japanese and German aggression, Peruvian officials reasoned that the time was right. And so the advances led by Ecuadorian field commanders into the disputed territory—some authorized, some not—provided Peru with all the excuse it needed to launch its long-planned invasion. On July 5, 1941, some Peruvian civilians—farmers—inadvertently crossed into Ecuadorian

Map 2. Ecuador-Peru Conflict, 1941–42. Source: Bryce Wood, *The United States and Latin America Wars, 1932–1942* (New York: Columbia University Press, 1966), map 3. Modified by Tiffany Henley.

territory, and Ecuadorian troops opened fire. Border patrols on both sides exchanged shots. The following day Peru dramatically deepened the conflict, sending in its bombers and launching an artillery attack.

The war lasted three weeks. It was a very uneven match. Peru's population stood at 7.2 million, Ecuador's at 3.1 million. Peru's national budget totaled about $39 million a year, Ecuador's $9 million. Ecuador's military budget was one-twelfth the size of Peru's. Peru invaded with 13,000 soldiers; Ecuador defended with at most 2,000. Moreover, as one historian of the conflict, David Zook, notes, Ecuadorian troops "were in miserable condition and poorly supplied."[22] On July 22, 1941, Peru's massed troops poured across the border into Ecuador's El Oro province, quickly overrunning all Ecuadorian positions. By July 23–26 Peruvian forces were beginning to bear down on the southern coastal cities of Machala and Puerto Bolívar. Peru supported its advance with air assaults, using newly purchased Italian and U.S. fighters and bombers, and a parachute drop. The Peruvian navy shelled Puerto Bolívar and blockaded the port of Guayaquil.

In Guayaquil troops slated to reinforce the frontier mutinied. President Carlos Alberto Arroyo del Río might have considered arming the masses to repel the Peruvian advance, but he had few weapons to offer. Moreover, Arroyo del Río was so despised by the populous that he had every reason to fear that any arms he supplied would instead be turned against his dictatorship. In El Oro the local population did nearly nothing to assist the war effort, looking on with indifference as foreign troops invaded. Ecuador's best fighting force, the Cuerpo de Carabineros (Rifle Corps), never made it to the front, because Arroyo del Río was holding the riflemen back in the capital to defend his unpopular regime. In the end, as Zook notes, Peru "really did not encounter the Ecuadorian Army per se, but only feeble detachments from it. The bulk of the regulars remained in garrison duty throughout the Republic."[23] By July 26, 1941, the Ecuadorian military had been convincingly defeated, swept from the field in disarray, and was openly deserting. Eighty to one hundred Peruvians died in the fighting, but at least five hundred Ecuadorians had been killed.

The United States responded to the crisis by opening up talks with Argentine and Brazilian diplomats in Washington, D.C. Together, these nations called on Peru and Ecuador to pull their troops away from the border. Ecuador and Peru agreed on July 26, 1941, to a cease-fire, although Peruvian troops continued their advance for several more days. Peruvian officers smelled blood, and Gen. Eloy Ureta, the field commander, pressured Lima for the authority to advance into Guayaquil. Some in Peru began to talk of taking all of Ecuador. The mediating nations proposed a troop pullback on August 2, 1941, which Ecuador accepted at once. Peru did not reply. At length a buffer zone was created, with the Peruvian army continuing to hold its most forward positions while Ecuadorian forces pulled farther back to establish a neutral zone. By this time Peru had captured nearly four hundred square miles of Ecuadorian territory. On September 15, 1941, Peru demanded that Ecuador cede control of these newly occupied territories. The Peruvian army was ready to press on to Guayaquil; nothing stood in its way. Seeking to avoid further losses, Ecuador requested an armistice. Despite some calls to press its advantage, Lima decided it had won enough and accepted. On October 2, 1941, the fighting stopped. In December 1941 the mediating nations suggested a withdrawal to the prewar 1936 line: Ecuador immediately accepted; Peru refused.

At the same time as these events the leading diplomatic authorities of the Americas gathered in Río de Janeiro in January 1942 for the Third Consultative Meeting of the Ministers of Foreign Affairs of the American Republics. After the Japanese attack on Pearl Harbor, the United States had called the Río conference to line up Latin American support for the Allied war effort. Ecuador sought to have the Peru-Ecuador boundary question put on the agenda but found no support from any quarter. Ecuador was on its own. At the conference the delegates decried acts of aggression, but they referred only to Japanese aggression, not Peruvian. All the delegates—except those from Ecuador—saw the Peru-Ecuador war as a distraction; the United States was infinitely more concerned with the exigencies of World War II than Ecuador's problem with Peru. Peru understood this; indeed, Peru had invaded Ecuador because of what was happening internationally, calculating, correctly as it turned out, that no nation, and least of all the United States, would come to Ecuador's defense, given the more urgent concern of dealing with the Axis.

So the problem for Ecuador was clear. Peru was not going to leave the southern coastal province of El Oro until it had secured a favorable boundary settlement. The Ecuadorian delegation tried to hold out for an outlet to the Amazon by way of the Marañón, but Peru refused to even consider it. Instead, Peru now insisted on territory that it had not even controlled before the war, plus reparations. Peru gave Ecuador a six-month deadline to capitulate or else. In the meantime Peruvian troops continued to occupy El Oro.

The Ecuadorian government had no choice but to relent. If it had not given in, Peru would probably have pressed its military advantage and taken much more territory. U.S. officials, sympathetic to Ecuador's plight and certainly reluctant to endorse the practice of seizing land by force of arms, were, however, much more intent on seeing an end to the Peru-Ecuador matter so that full attention could be given to the rather more important business of securing inter-American support for the Allies. Ecuador tried everything it could think of to win U.S. backing. Ecuador broke relations with the Axis and sent its leading diplomatic representatives to Washington to plead for help. But it was no use. Deep into its own problems, the United States had no attention to spare for Ecuador's. Sumner Welles promised Ecuador that the United States would assist financially with the rebuilding of El Oro, but that was all the help it could offer.

Ecuadorian Foreign Minister Julio Tobar Donoso, the leader of the Conservative Party, signed the Protocol of Peace, Friendship, and Boundaries at Río de Janeiro on January 29, 1942. The United States, Chile, Brazil, and Argentina all promised to serve as guarantors of the protocol. The agreement, the Río Protocol, was a bad deal for Ecuador, although it is worth noting that Ecuador did not give up any territory upon which its citizens actually lived. What Ecuador did give up was its claims to about 100,000 square miles of territory. Ecuador was left with only those parts of the rainforest that were not accessible by major navigable waterways, hundreds of miles from the Amazon River. Peru began pulling its troops out of El Oro on February 11, 1942, and ratified the Río Protocol on February 26, 1942. Ecuador followed, ratifying on February 27, 1942. The nations exchanged ratifications at Río de Janeiro on March 31, 1942.

Washington avoided taking sides throughout the entire conflict. Before the war Ecuador had asked that the United States send a warship to Ecuadorian waters as a warning to Peru, but U.S. officials never even considered it. During the war Ecuador asked the United States to provide forty million rounds of ammunition, but Washington denied the request. Maintaining a stance of neutrality, U.S. authorities also seized eighteen modern bombers that Peru had purchased in Canada from Norway and that were passing through U.S. territory on the way to Peru. U.S. authorities also blocked arms sales from Bolivia to Peru.

The United States might have done more to help Ecuador while still maintaining its neutrality in the conflict. But Washington did not even attempt to make a case against the Peruvian aggression. It said nothing about Peruvian bombing runs on Ecuadorian civilian populations. When Peruvian advances in the Amazon violated the cease-fire, the United States did not attempt to pressure Peru. Although Peruvian air attacks damaged some U.S. property in El Oro, the mining operations of the South American Development Company, and the Tenguel banana estate, Washington filed only a mild protest with Peru.

The leading reason for this inaction was that United States did not want to alienate Peru in the struggle against the Axis. Moreover, U.S. authorities reasoned that their protests would do little to stop Peru. Certainly Washington was not willing to commit troops to the Ecuador-Peru war. The principal U.S. concern lay with maintaining hemispheric solidarity against the Axis and the flow of raw materials from Latin America to the United States. In the end the United States did not care what happened to Ecuador and did not care where the boundary might be put. The United States had its own problems, and this was not one of them.

Peruvians were ecstatic at their victory; Ecuador hit bottom. This punishing defeat cut deeply into Ecuador's self-confidence, leaving the nation with a profound sense of frustration and victimization for many years to come. Circumstances surrounding the signing of the Río Protocol also created a good deal of bitterness toward the United States. As Robert M. Scotten, the U.S. ambassador to Ecuador, noted later, the Río Protocol was "extremely unpopular in Ecuador. Both the United States and President Arroyo are, rightly or wrongly, blamed for allegedly hav[ing] forced this Protocol upon Ecuador."[24]

Seeking to improve its standing with Ecuador, while still underscoring U.S. evenhandedness in the conflict, the United States invited the leaders of both nations to come—separately—for state visits to Washington. In May 1942 FDR had Peruvian President Manuel Prado to the White House for dinner. Prado also addressed the U.S. Congress. After Prado left, Ecuador's Arroyo del Río visited the United States for ten days in November 1942. President Roosevelt and Vice President Henry A. Wallace even came out to the airport to greet Arroyo del Río in person. Arroyo del Río, like Prado before him, was feted with a banquet at the White House and addressed Congress. He then received honorary degrees from Columbia and George Washington universities.

Arroyo del Río's trip to the United States, the first by a sitting Ecuadorian president, was loudly celebrated by the obsequious Ecuadorian press.[25] But the admiring coverage aside, Arroyo del Río was no hero at home. Ecuador's humiliating rout in the war with Peru had provided sufficient proof to most ordinary Ecuadorians that the oligarchy did not deserve to govern their nation. Undaunted, Arroyo del Río clung to power, using vigorous and not especially selective repression against all political opponents, real and imagined. In May 1943 a popular revolt against the dictator climaxed in an armed assault on the Presidential Palace in Quito. The Carabineros (Arroyo del Río's palace guard) managed to beat back this and other armed opposition until 1944. Then, as new elections approached, Arroyo del Río made plain his intention to handpick his successor. On May 28, 1944, elements of the Guayaquil military staged a successful uprising, joined by thousands of ordinary people who attacked the barracks of the hated Carabineros, burning it to the ground. Hundreds died in ugly street fighting in Guayaquil, and the revolt swiftly spread to other cities. The big concern for U.S. Ambassador Scotten, who was close to the situation but far from understanding it, was whether the uprising might be part of a Nazi plot.[26] The proximate cause of the uprising was the surrender of more territory in setting the new border with Peru, in particular Arroyo del Río's decision to cede the Isla de Matapalo. The uprising (which Ecuadorians refer to as *la gloriosa*) may be rightly viewed as a glorious effort by the Ecuadorian people to try to reclaim their national dignity, their pride in being Ecuadorian. The popular uprising brought Velasco Ibarra out of exile in Chile and to power again, for the second of his five tours of duty. In bringing vast numbers of people into open protest against political corruption and election fraud, *la gloriosa* may also be read as another important step toward democracy. Arroyo del Río fled to exile in the United States in disgrace.

## Ecuador and the Coming of World War II

While Ecuador was absorbed in trying to deal with its own problems—economic decline, political turmoil, and then war with Peru—the U.S. government was increasingly concerned with a perceived German and Japanese threat to U.S. strategic, economic, and even cultural interests in the Americas. By the 1930s Germany had established military training missions in more than half of the Latin American nations and had also strengthened its commercial ties. On the eve of World War II Nazi Germany was supplying more imports to Latin America than even Great Britain and was second only to the United States. German imports from 1929 to 1936 rose from 12 percent to 21 percent of Ecuador's total, with the U.S. share falling from 40 percent to 27 percent.

Washington addressed this challenge in several ways. Seeking to improve its economic relations with Latin America, the United States arranged new commercial treaties with eleven Latin American nations, including Ecuador, by 1939, reducing tariffs on key imports. The United States also won Latin American backing for the removal of all Nazi military missions from the region. In their place came an increased U.S. military presence, with the United States adding significantly to the number of military attachés it assigned to Latin America. In December

1940 Ecuador signed an agreement with the United States, and Washington sent a naval attaché to Ecuador (although he was initially stationed in Quito, miles from the ocean).[27]

Efforts to influence Latin American attitudes toward the United States also increased in the prewar years. The Nazis had been trying to woo Latin America, offering lavish cultural exchange programs, so the United States responded in kind. Heretofore the U.S. government had few cultural exchanges with Latin America, but in 1938 the United States created the Division of Cultural Relations at the Department of State and in 1940 opened the Office for the Coordination of Commercial and Cultural Relations, later called the Office of the Coordinator of Inter-American Affairs (OCIAA). Headed by Nelson Rockefeller, the OCIAA's main mission was to counter Nazi propaganda. Even as Axis aggression advanced, many Latin American nations continued to view the United States as the more serious threat to their safety and to doubt the sincerity of the Good Neighbor policy. The OCIAA's charge was to encourage a friendlier image of the United States. Rockefeller started an exchange program for professors and students and promoted the arts, but he spent the greatest share of his budget on making U.S. movies available for Latin American audiences.

Partly as a result of these efforts, Ecuador began to cooperate with U.S. wartime initiatives. One area of U.S. concern was the Germans who lived in the Americas. The Federal Bureau of Investigation provided Ecuador with information regarding Germans who had been expelled from the United States and who were seeking entry into Ecuador. Ecuador jailed or deported Axis nationals living in Ecuador, freezing their bank accounts and seizing their business assets. An even more significant area of wartime cooperation with the United States came in the closing down of the German-owned airline Sedta (Sociedad Ecuatoriana de Transportes Aéreos, or Ecuadorian Air Transport Society).

U.S. war planners feared that Germany was planning to build an air base in the Amazon and use it to launch an attack on the Panama Canal. This concern was what drew U.S. attention to Sedta, which was run by German-controlled Lufthansa Airlines. Sedta, operating in Ecuador since 1938, was the first, and at the time the sole, commercial aviation company in the nation. In April 1940 U.S. officials sought to close Sedta, but Ecuador wanted assurances that the United States would provide replacement air service. Within a month the two nations had a sketched the outlines of an agreement. The U.S.-based Latin American airline Panagra would replace Sedta and promised not to reduce the number of flights.

Seeking to respond to the challenge, Sedta expanded its service and slashed fares. But by May 1941 the United States had arranged with the Canadian-based International Petroleum Company in Peru to cut off the sale of aviation fuel to Sedta. Sedta had no choice but to begin mixing gasoline with aviation fuel in a last-ditch effort to keep the airline up and running. In August 1941 Ecuadorian President Arroyo del Río finally shut down Sedta, charging that its fueling practices were unsafe. On October 2, 1941, the United States and Ecuador finalized the Panagra takeover of Sedta, removing German aviation from Latin America.

## Latin America, Ecuador, and World War II

When World War II began, Ecuador had followed the lead of the other Latin American nations and issued a declaration of neutrality on September 4, 1939. After the Soviet invasion of Finland that December, Ecuador joined the majority in the League of Nations in voting to expel the Soviet Union. In November 1941 Ecuador suspended its relations with Vichy France. And in early January 1942 Ecuador was one of the first Latin American nations to sever relations with Germany, Italy, and Japan.[28] Some Latin American nations declared war on the Axis, including all the nations of Central America and the Caribbean, along with Mexico, Brazil, Bolivia, and Colombia, but not Ecuador. While Washington strongly approved of diplomatic measures against the Axis, it did not generally encourage Latin America's active participation in the Allied war effort. The United States feared that this might actually provoke a direct Axis attack on Latin America, something neither Latin America nor the United States was adequately prepared to defend against. Only Mexico and Brazil took an active combat role in the war. In the end what was most vital to the United States was a continuing and unequivocal Latin American commitment to the Allied cause.

Helping to cement this relationship was the revival of U.S. importation of Latin American products, as the U.S. economy, spurred by wartime spending, pulled out of the Great Depression. At the same time World War II led to the loss of most European markets for Latin American exports. The Allied blockade closed German markets, and Great Britain's reordered wartime spending priorities eliminated purchases of many Latin American goods. These developments left the United States with a virtual monopsony for the purchase of Ecuadorian and Latin American goods, and the United States stood ready to buy more than ever before. After the Japanese seized control of traditional rice-producing zones, Ecuador stepped in and became a leading supplier for the U.S. market. Rice quickly emerged as Ecuador's number one export, accounting for half of all sales abroad during the war years. Shipments of straw hats made up another quarter of exports, and Ecuador shipped important quantities of balsa wood, chinchona bark (for quinine), and rubber to the United States. Ecuadorian exports rose from $7.5 million in 1939 to $22.8 million in 1945 ($28.6 million in 1944). Ecuadorian imports increased from $11.2 million in 1939 to $24 million in 1945. If in 1938 only about a third of Ecuador's imports came from the United States, by 1942 nearly three-quarters did. The war profited Ecuador but in the process bound its economy closer to that of the United States.

Ecuador also benefited modestly from several U.S. wartime initiatives, including Lend-Lease, the $42 billion economic and military assistance program provided initially for Great Britain and the USSR but later extended to Latin America. The relatively small amount of U.S. assistance to Latin America—$459 million—one percent of the total amount of Lend-Lease aid—reflected in part the judgment that by mid-1942 the western hemisphere no longer required defense from a full-scale overseas assault, although German U-boat activity in the Caribbean and Gulf of Mexico remained a threat until well into 1943. By 1944 U.S. Lend-Lease assistance for Latin America was going to the two nations actively at war against the Axis (that is, sending troops), Mexico and Brazil. Overall, Ecuador received less than 2 percent ($8 million) of the allocation for Latin America. Neither Ecuador nor Peru received Lend-Lease aid while they were at war with one another.

Beyond Lend-Lease the United States also provided direct economic support to Latin America and Ecuador by altering the mission of the Export-Import Bank of the United States, which had been founded in 1934 to provide financial support to U.S. exporters during the Depression; now it permitted loans to Latin American governments for development projects. In June 1940 Jesse H. Jones, the bank's president, approved an Export-Import Bank (Ex-Im Bank) loan to Ecuador for $1.15 million: $900,000 to buy U.S. goods and hire U.S. contractors to work on the Ecuadorian portion of the Pan-American Highway in the southern sierra; $200,000 for U.S. locomotives and railway cars; and $50,000 to help conduct research to develop disease-resistant cacao. However, the money came with special conditions; Ecuador was on a short leash. "The highways to be constructed," the contract stipulated, "[were to be] approved by Eximbank. . . . Ecuador agrees to carry through the . . . programs in accordance with recommendations and under the supervision of the United States Department of Agriculture."[29] All goods had to be transported in U.S. vessels.

The first significant government-to-government social and economic aid—grants, not loans—for Latin America from the United States came under auspices of the Institute for Inter-American Affairs. For Ecuador the program lasted from 1942 to 1946 and sought to bring progress in sanitation, public health, and malaria control.[30] All the U.S. wartime program initiatives—Lend-Lease, the expansion of the role of the Export-Import Bank, and the Institute for Inter-American Affairs—brought increased cooperation and closer ties between the United States and Ecuador. However, the most important area of collaboration was in the establishment of U.S. military bases in Ecuador.

## U.S. Bases in Salinas and the Galápagos Islands

After Pearl Harbor the United States moved to set up air and naval bases in sixteen Latin American nations, the most important of which were in Panama, defending the canal, and in Brazil, where bases were necessary for flying aircraft from the United States to Africa and from there to Europe. Ecuador's principal contribution to the Allied war effort was its participation in the forward defense of the Panama Canal, providing U.S. air bases on the Salinas Peninsula (on the southwestern tip of Ecuador) and in the Galápagos Islands.

Throughout Ecuador's history its cash-starved governments had periodically given serious consideration to leasing or selling the Galápagos Islands. When Kemmerer came to Quito in 1926, Ecuadorian officials approached him to see whether he could help arrange the sale of the islands to the United States. In 1932 President-elect Neptalí Bonifaz considered transferring the Galápagos Islands to the United States in exchange for cancellation of Ecuador's foreign debt.

Later that year, H. S. Swarth, a curator at the Carnegie Institution of Washington, wrote the organization's president, John C. Merriam, recommending that the Galápagos be set aside as a natural wildlife preserve. The only thing preventing tourism to the Galápagos, Swarth said, was the lack of transportation. At the time only private yachts called at the Galápagos. Ecuador's representative in Washington, Colón Eloy Alfaro (the son of martyred Ecuadorian President Eloy Alfaro), shared Swarth's enthusiasm for making the Galápagos Islands into a nature preserve; both men correctly foresaw that the islands had vast future potential for ecotourism but only if something were done to keep the islands in their natural state. The great tortoises, the namesake of the islands, were at serious risk of extinction—locals killed them to make lamp oil, and sailors from passing ships gathered them up to replenish their food stores for lengthy voyages. In 1934 Colón Eloy Alfaro headed an Ecuadorian delegation that met with U.S. officials to discuss the idea of making the Galápagos Islands into a nature preserve. During the next three years he sent eighty-nine messages to his superiors about this project, his favorite topic, but his government took no action.

In July 1938 FDR visited the Galápagos and came away convinced that the islands had to be made into a scientific reserve. Acting on Roosevelt's initiative, in April 1940 the Smithsonian Institution and the U.S. State Department began exploring the possibility of setting up a U.S.-operated wildlife preservation station in the Galápagos. But beyond FDR's desire to protect the natural beauty of the Galápagos was his fear that the islands, as well as Chile's Easter Island and the Cocos of Costa Rica, might fall into enemy hands. The reality of Japanese aggression in the Pacific was changing the nature of the conversation.

Even in the 1930s Ecuador had suspected that Japan, working with Peru, had ideas about taking the Galápagos. During the 1930s Japan established closer relations with Peru: by 1935 Japan was sending naval officials to Peru, Japanese warships and aircraft carriers called at Callao, and about a hundred Peruvian officials and technocrats went to Japan on an official mission. When Japanese commercial agents made repeated trips to the central coast region of Ecuador, ostensibly to arrange coffee exports from the province of Manabí, some Ecuadorian officials suspected that they were really spies, scouting for invasion landing sites. As Colón Eloy Alfaro warned in January 1936, Ecuador had better start to worry about "the unfolding expansionist policies of Japan."[31] By the late 1930s Ecuadorian officials were gathering bits of evidence that suggested to them that Japan would assist Peru in invading Ecuador in exchange for Japanese control of the Galápagos.

As World War II loomed, the possibility of Japanese air bases in the Galápagos Islands—bases from which air strikes against the Panama Canal could be launched—raised increasing U.S. concern. In October 1939 Sumner Welles expressed to Ecuador the "urgent necessity" to secure the defense of the Galápagos.[32] In November 1939 Colón Eloy Alfaro met with top-ranking U.S. military officials to discuss the matter. But stories in the press complicated U.S.-Ecuadorian negotiations. On January 20, 1941, the Associated Press ran a story from *El telégrafo* of Guayaquil claiming a deal was in the works: if Ecuador permitted U.S. air bases in the Galápagos Islands, Washington would agree to arbitrate the boundary dispute between Ecuador and Peru.[33] President Arroyo del Río denied the report, although rumor had it that he was *El telégrafo*'s source. (It could have been a trial balloon to gauge Ecuadorian public opinion about the temporary transfer of the Galápagos.) The story aggravated Peruvian worries that Washington was going to start pressuring Peru about the boundary dispute. Ignoring the denials by U.S. Secretary of State Cordell Hull (1933–44), the Peruvian foreign ministry issued a press release stating its concerns in February 1941.[34]

In October the *New York Daily Mirror* published a story, later picked up by Guayaquil's *El telégrafo,* asserting that Nazi influence in Ecuador was holding up the acquisition of a U.S. base in the Galápagos Islands.[35] The article further suggested that there might be a secret German submarine base there too.

As U.S.-Japanese relations worsened through 1941, U.S. pressure for naval access to Ecuadorian waters and docking rights for U.S. warships in the Galápagos Islands and Guayaquil increased. A week after Pearl Harbor, Sumner Welles spoke with the Ecuadorian ambassador to the United States about arranging U.S. patrols of the Ecuadorian coast and the Galápagos. In response, Ecuador proposed the idea of establishing U.S. bases in Ecuador. Given Ecuadorian sensitivities, the arrangements for any transfer would have to be careful. The United States could not simply annex the Galápagos. Ecuadorian public opinion would never allow it, and in all events President Roosevelt had pledged under the Good Neighbor policy not to take any Latin American territory.

Meanwhile the Ecuadorian press was investigating whether the Peruvians and Japanese were about to seize the islands. *El globo* in Bahía de Caraquez ran a story on December 19, 1941, that discussed the increasing Japanese influence in Peru. The Ecuadorian press widely reported that Japanese officers and technical advisers were helping Peru. However, there is no evidence that the Japanese or Germans ever supplied military training to Peru in the years before World War II. (The French were actually the key trainers of Peru's military from 1896 to World War II.) On April 1, 1942, *El globo* ran another story about the possibility of Japanese attacks on the Galápagos Islands and coastal Ecuador as part of a larger effort to seize the Panama Canal.[36] In this atmosphere, with Ecuadorians increasingly fearful of a Peruvian-Japanese attack on the islands and the United States eager to acquire a base in the islands to provide for the forward defense of the Panama Canal, the two nations agreed in January 1942 to establish two U.S. military bases in Ecuador.

Construction began at once. Salinas, on the western tip of the arid Santa Elena Peninsula, was the site for a base designed for refueling aircraft. An existing landing strip was nothing but dirt and sand. U.S. personnel set to building an all-new facility, a paved runway, and an array of support facilities, including a desalination plant and a hospital. All told, the United States spent $3 million constructing the Salinas base. The United States stationed twenty-five hundred men there and set up two combat squadrons (about thirty-five aircraft in all) to patrol the Galápagos Islands, the western approaches to Central America, and the Panama Canal. At the Galápagos the United States established an air base on the previously uninhabited Seymour Island, spending $9 million to construct the runway, radar station, and all the support facilities for twenty-three hundred men. The base went into operation in May 1942.

Yet, as it turned out, none of the aircraft positioned in Ecuador ever saw the enemy. U.S. fears of a Japanese attack on the canal began to dissipate after the Battle of Midway in June 1942. It was increasingly apparent that neither German nor Japanese aircraft or naval vessels were going to attack the Panama Canal. In mid-1944 the United States began to scale back operations at the Ecuadorian air bases. The thoughts of both U.S. and Ecuadorian officials turned to the postwar disposition of the facilities, and a long, difficult process of negotiation ensued. The result suited neither side and generated considerable long-term mutual distrust.

In 1944 FDR renewed his call for making the Galápagos Islands into a nature park, one controlled by Ecuador but administered collectively by the twenty-one American republics. But Ecuador could never support such a proposal as it offered Ecuador absolutely no advantage. Why would Ecuador want to surrender its national territory, turn it over to be run by others, and get nothing in return? U.S. Secretary of State Edward Stettinius (1944–45) decided to open informal talks with Ecuador to explore the establishment of ninety-nine-year leases for U.S. use of the Galápagos and Salinas bases. However, Ecuadorian President Arroyo del Río was already unhappy with the idea of the Americans' staying on in Salinas and the Galápagos Islands after the war. Arroyo del Río informed U.S. Ambassador Bob Scotten that the United States had to prepare to leave the bases right away; waiting even one year would be too long. The Ecuadorian legislature, having read the proposed lease agreement, shared Arroyo del Río's view.

When Velasco Ibarra replaced Arroyo del Río as Ecuador's leader later that year (1944), he reopened consideration of the lease arrangement with the United States. Washington now proposed to hand over the Salinas facility in exchange for the right to maintain a U.S. base in the Galápagos. Velasco Ibarra was interested but added a new condition: the price for continued U.S. use of the Galápagos base after the war would be $100 million.

In July 1945 top-ranking Ecuadorian, State Department, and Export-Import Bank officials met in Washington. Ecuador was seeking to set up a $20 million line of credit with the Export-Import Bank for development projects. For collateral Ecuador sought to use the $100 million that Velasco Ibarra believed the United States was going to pay for the use of the Galápagos. The Ex-Im Bank board approved an initial $1 million loan for Ecuador to formulate a public works plan, with an agreement in principle for a line of credit totaling $20 million. However, the bank board retained ultimate authority; it would have to approve each project as planning went forward. But there was a problem: the United States had not actually agreed to pay $100 million for the base on Seymour Island. U.S. Secretary of State James F. Byrnes (1945–47) made clear the U.S. position in an internal memo dated August 1945: "Apart from the . . . [previously] mentioned million, no credit [to Ecuador] until Galápagos base treaty satisfactorily concluded."[37]

On August 17, 1945, Ecuador's ambassador to the United States, Galo Plaza Lasso, presented the U.S. State Department with a draft treaty for continued U.S. control of the Galápagos air base. The reaction was not positive. As John Campbell White, the U.S. ambassador to Peru, summed up the situation, the United States was "not interested in . . . the Galápagos as long as Ecuador held control and always provided that no other non-American power obtained occupational rights." He added that the navy considered it unsuitable for a coaling station.[38] Moreover, if the United States did hand the base over to Ecuador, it would be better that the facility not be in running order. This was essential, White believed, because "Ecuador is unable to defend it." If for some reason the United States chose to keep the base, White said, it should offer to pay only about $250,000 a year and certainly not a lump sum of $100 million. The notion that Ecuador could now borrow $20 million from the Ex-Im Bank, using as collateral the modest user fees it could probably get from the United States for continued use of the

Galápagos Islands base was, White felt, utterly ridiculous. "The Ecuadorans have very exaggerated ideas of the value to others of the Galápagos Islands," he concluded.[39]

With the end of the World War II the United States was losing interest in maintaining the Galápagos base, especially if the price was too steep. The War Department no longer could support plans to pay Ecuador $20 million for its use, no matter how much Ecuadorian Ambassador Galo Plaza Lasso insisted that it was Ecuador's minimum price. Somehow the sum of $20 million had become common knowledge in Ecuador; public opinion would accept nothing less. Meanwhile in January 1946 the State Department suggested that the Export-Import Bank should approve a $3 million loan to Ecuador for potable water works as a way of sweetening the most recent U.S. Galápagos base proposal. Although such a contingency violated the bank's strict regulations, Ecuador's loan approval depended on accepting U.S. wishes about the Galápagos Islands base arrangement. Spruille Braden, an assistant secretary of state, brought the proposal to Galo Plaza Lasso in Washington in February 1946, informing him that free U.S. use of the Galápagos base could mean generous repayment terms on an Export-Import Bank loan. That would be the best deal the United States could offer, Braden said.[40]

As these discussions continued, the United States turned the Salinas facility over to Ecuador on February 1, 1946, without conditions, removing U.S. vehicles and planes but leaving trained personnel to ease the transition. This act of generosity, it was hoped, would make Ecuador more flexible regarding the Galápagos base. But in a meeting on February 26 with the State Department, Ecuadorian Ambassador Plaza complained that there was an overall lack of appreciation in the United States for Ecuador's sacrifices during the war. Plaza noted that although the Ex-Im Bank had loaned Ecuador $5 million during the war for a program run by the Ecuadorian Development Corporation, the sum had been so unwisely expended that his country had practically nothing to show for the money it owed. As Henry Dearborn of the State Department's Division of North and West Coast Affairs recounted the meeting, Plaza said that "a good part of the loan was spent to promote the rubber and cinchona programs of the United States in obtaining raw materials for the war and to finance the construction of the Manta-Quevedo Highway, the costliness of which was scandalous."[41]

Privately, State Department officials agreed that the Ecuadorian Development Corporation projects had indeed been designed to benefit the United States as much as Ecuador and that the United States bore at least half the blame for the program's many failures. Plaza suggested that maybe in exchange for continued use of the Galápagos base the United States could loan Ecuador some money, with payments to start in four or five years or so. After Plaza left the room, however, the U.S. officials privately noted that the United States was now seeking bases all over the world, and if they paid Ecuador $20 million for this one, they would never be able to afford all the other bases they wanted.

In March 1946 Secretary of War Robert P. Patterson and James Forrestal, the navy secretary, wrote in concurrence with this opinion. In their letter to the secretary of state, Forrestal and Patterson argued that if Ecuador were permitted to kick the United States out of the Galápagos, other little nations might follow, with the potential loss of bases in Iceland, the Azores (Portuguese territory), and Greenland (Danish territory). The war and navy secretaries emphasized that the United States had borne all the costs of building the bases in Ecuador, and therefore, they reasoned, "as Ecuador is unable to maintain a military air base in the Galápagos it would seem that permitting the United States to utilize two small, relatively uninhibited [uninhabited?] islands would be a fitting contribution of Ecuador to hemispheric security."[42] The United States should be allowed to stay and use the bases free of charge, Forrestal and Patterson believed.

By April 1946 Ecuadorian officials had come to recognize that they were going to get nothing for the base: not $100 million, not a $20 million loan from the Export-Import Bank, nothing. Public sentiment in Ecuador was against giving the base to the United States, and especially for free, and so the Americans were asked to leave. Accordingly, the United States pulled out of the Galápagos on July 1, 1946, dynamiting, burning, or dumping into the Pacific Ocean whatever could not be pried up and hauled away. Jeeps, radio equipment, telephones, refrigerators, ovens, and other supplies and equipment were tossed into the sea. The United States left behind two hundred empty buildings and two runways. Nevertheless, Ambassador Scotten reported that the transfer ceremony "was carried out in [an] atmosphere [of] harmony and goodwill [on] both sides."[43] Top Ecuadorian officials attended the event, flown in on U.S. aircraft, and told Scotten that they wanted the United States to stay on and help maintain the facility.

Acting Secretary of State Dean Acheson informed Scotten that he should tell Ecuador not to expect any help with the Ex-Im Bank loan, noting that Congress's support for further expenditures on the base was doubtful.[44] With the use of air refueling the U.S. military no longer really needed an air base on Ecuador's Galápagos Islands anyway. Ecuador would make renewed offers in the future, but the United States was just not interested anymore. By 1947 the United States had Latin American bases only in the Panama Canal Zone and in Guantánamo, Cuba.

## Conclusions

Connections between the United States and Ecuador increased markedly from 1925 to 1945. This could be seen in many ways, large and small. The Yale debate team had come and participated—in Spanish— at a competition at the University of Guayaquil in 1930. By the 1940s more Ecuadorian audiences were watching U.S.-made films, even in the heretofore isolated highlands. Ads for English lessons appeared in small-town papers like *El globo* of Bahía de Caraquez. Even in the remote sierra city of Cuenca, newspapers featured ads for U.S.-made oil, tires, refrigerators, radios, stoves, lamps, paint, fire extinguishers, pills, underwear, Coca Cola, jam, "Campbelis" soup [sic], and antacids.[45] Advertisers were also now paying more attention to using images and text that better suited Latin American audiences. The ad for Goodyear tires, for example, pictured an Inca messenger and text in Spanish that read: "Run, run, and run."[46]

U.S. cultural, diplomatic, and economic influence could be great but not as overwhelming as some have maintained. In *The Ordeal of Hegemony,* Guy Poitras, historian of U.S.–Latin American affairs, writes: "When a great power like the United States is hegemonic, its share of the economic and military resources is so preponderant that it can control international and even domestic outcomes of a region to suit itself. . . . What the United States wants in Latin America, it usually gets."[47] But while this may be true in most instances, what the exchanges between the United States and Ecuador in 1925–45 demonstrate were the limits of U.S. power and that the United States did not always choose to use this power, especially in places or on issues it did not care much about.

It would be a mistake to read the Kemmerer mission to Ecuador as just another example of U.S. economic imperialism, the imposition of U.S. will on recalcitrant innocents. Ecuadorian President Ayora and the military junta invited Kemmerer to Ecuador because they knew what he would say. He could be counted on to recommend precisely the policies that he did. Kemmerer did not impose alien financial systems on an unwilling Ecuador. He recommended policies that leading Ecuadorians already wanted, policies that they were, in fact, already adopting. Ayora wanted to legitimize his plans to close down the coastal banks, and Kemmerer provided cover for this agenda, supplying the imprimatur of objective reform. Beyond this, Ayora and others in leadership understood that getting the Kemmerer stamp of approval was the only way to gain access to new lines of foreign credit. Ecuador was not being forced by Kemmerer to adopt these policies; it wanted to. Moreover, when Ecuador decided to drop these economic orthodoxies, it did. When the Great Depression hit, Ecuador threw most of the Kemmerer measures over the side.

The U.S. government did not always act to defend U.S. capitalists abroad in all cases at all times, especially if the company lacked influence or was just too small to worry about. Washington tried to get Ecuador to pay off the railway bondholders, investors whose claims for repayment Ecuador steadfastly ignored. However, the railroad bondholders were a small interest without political clout in Washington. Consequently, no one in a position of authority in the U.S. government felt sufficiently moved to do anything about the bondholders' plight.

Sometimes Ecuadorian dictators tried, not very artfully, to play one great power off another. For example, in February 1941 President Arroyo del Río intimated to U.S. Ambassador Boaz Long that some Ecuadorians supported the Nazis. However, Arroyo del Río offered, if he could hold a public ceremony that featured Ecuadorian pilots in new airplanes provided by the United States, and if the Americans were to throw in maybe a couple of ships, or even just one small one, so the Ecuadorian navy could cruise by, perhaps Ecuadorians would see the advantage of supporting the United States in the global conflict against fascism. Ambassador Long dutifully reported Arroyo del Río's proposal to the State Department, but this transparent ploy never had a chance of acceptance.[48]

During World War II Washington sought Ecuadorian bases as part of a forward defense of the Panama Canal. However, this was clearly not a case in which the United States bullied Ecuador into accepting its demands. In fact, Ecuador desperately wanted a U.S. military presence in the islands. Ecuador feared that Peru, in league with Japan, might try to seize the islands for use as a Japanese base, with the territory controlled by Peru. Ecuador knew it could not defend the islands itself, that it had to have U.S. help. Ecuador wanted the United States to use its power to defend the islands against a Peruvian or Japanese attack. The placement of U.S. troops and equipment in the Galápagos was a success for Ecuadorian foreign policy—Ecuador got exactly what it wanted.

As the war drew to a close, the United States initially sought to maintain control of the Galápagos base. The United States tried everything, from persuasion and bribery to threats. But in the end Ecuador did not like the deal offered and told the United States to pack up and get out, and so it did. Perhaps if U.S. officials had seen a greater national interest in maintaining the base, they would have tried to compel Ecuador to relent. But it was like this in most matters involving these two nations. The U.S. government just did not see sufficient reason to force the issue, and so Ecuador got its way.

**The Cold War in Ecuador:**
**The 1940s to the 1960s**

With the end of World War II and the worsening of relations between the United States and the Soviet Union, U.S. policy makers came to place the threat they perceived from international communism above all other foreign policy concerns. Over time this fixation became all consuming. During the 1950s the U.S. secretary of state, John Foster Dulles, held annual meetings in Washington, D.C., with all the Latin American ambassadors, and his theme was always the same: anticommunism. In October 1957 Dulles brought in the Latin American ambassadors and lectured them on the nature of the Soviet menace. Not once did he mention Latin America. Dulles called the Latin American ambassadors back in May 1958 for another of his talks about communism, again not offering a word about Latin America. In April 1959 the new secretary of state, Christian A. Herter, summoned the Latin American ambassadors for a meeting, and, following Dulles's example, Herter told the group about the Communist menace. He did not mention Latin America. In September 1959 Herter offered a repeat performance, discussing with the Latin American ambassadors the Soviet Union, Europe, NATO, Vietnam, and Laos but not Latin America. In May 1960 Herter spoke with the group about Berlin, Nikita Khrushchev, NATO, Charles de Gaulle, U-2s, and Red China. This time, however, Herter did say a word or two about Latin America but only after prompting by Ecuador's ambassador, José R. Chiriboga.[1]

Despite these hectoring sessions, few Latin American and Ecuadorian leaders genuinely shared the U.S. preoccupation with the Soviet Union. They did not see the Soviets as embarking on a plan of world conquest, and they certainly did not believe that the Soviets had much influence in the Latin American nations. But if U.S. officials seemed to think about only the Soviet Union, Ecuador had a different fixation. In the wake of Peru's 1941 invasion, Ecuadorian officials were deeply concerned about any signs of renewed Peruvian aggression. In nearly all foreign policy considerations Ecuadorian officials were thinking about their fear and hatred of Peru: combating all potential threats from Peru, getting even with Peru, or, best yet, figuring out some way to get their land back from Peru.

Yet although most Ecuadorian officials did not typically share U.S. perceptions of the threats posed by international communism, Ecuador's leaders nevertheless found great utility in taking an anti-Communist stance. They came to understand rather quickly how to play upon U.S. anxieties in order to induce Washington to provide economic, and especially military, aid. If Ecuador spoke to the United States of a Peruvian menace, it would get no attention, but if Ecuador could somehow maintain, however implausibly, that the weapons it sought were really going to be used for the common defense of the western hemisphere against the threat of international communism, the United States would provide planes, warships, and tanks, as well as boatloads of guns and munitions. Ecuadorian officials knew just what to say.

One key cold war belief of U.S. officials was that the Soviet Union and its puppet states were constantly probing the world, looking for weaknesses to exploit—that if the West let down its guard anywhere, communism would penetrate. For Ecuador, Americans' cold war beliefs meant that the United States would now pay more attention to it. The United States became more engaged with Ecuador—it cared more about what was going on in Ecuador; it cared more about what Ecuador was doing in inter-American and international forums—and, as a result, for the first time the United States began to consistently use its great power advantage against Ecuador. The United States began to push its way into Ecuadorian internal affairs, sometimes playing a significant role in shaping political outcomes, and to use its considerable resources to impose its will.

## The Banana Age

U.S. influence could be seen in a variety of ways, including economic. For Ecuador the decades after World War II brought significant economic growth, although the country suffered some serious financial reverses along the way.[2] Ecuador's gross domestic product (GDP) saw an average annual increase of 2.9 percent from 1950 to 1973, a rate faster than that of most Latin American nations and faster even than the GDP of the United States (2.3 percent from 1950 to 1973). Yet Ecuador's growth was uneven and slowed considerably by the mid-1950s. From 1944 to 1949 the Ecuadorian GDP grew at an annual rate of 5.2 percent and from 1950 to 1955 at 3 percent a year before dropping to 0.9 percent a year from 1955 to 1968.

U.S. products dominated Ecuador's imports, although the U.S. market share was declining year by year. In 1949 Ecuador bought 70 percent of its imports from the United States, receiving principally manufactured goods, drugs, chemicals, and oil. But by 1952 the U.S. share of Ecuador's imports had dropped to 65 percent. By 1964 it was 46 percent and in 1967, 40 percent. Nevertheless, Ecuadorians maintained a taste for certain things American. They certainly liked Hollywood movies. Photos of Anne Baxter, June Allyson, and other U.S. movie stars decorated the pages of Ecuadorian newspapers. Even the comics were typically translations of U.S. favorites such as *They'll Do It Every Time, Henry,* and *Blondie.*[3]

Ecuador's exports rose considerably in the postwar period, quadrupling from 1941 to 1948, with rice and cacao shipments making up two-thirds to three-quarters of all overseas sales. High prices for rice and cacao exports on international markets raised the value of Ecuador's exports from $23.6 million in 1945 to $43.6 million in 1948. After 1949, however, competition in rice production from the United States, Egypt, and Italy glutted world markets, and Ecuador, which was using outdated and inefficient farming methods and producing lower-quality rice, could not compete. Cacao exports showed a similar pattern. Ecuadorian cacao sales initially rose in the postwar years, but by 1949 prices had declined on international markets. Ecuador's total exports fell in value by more than half from 1948 to 1949.

Beginning in the 1950s, however, Ecuador emerged as the world's leading producer of bananas, the growing sales bringing a new age of prosperity to the nation.[4] The emergence of banana production in

Ecuador was swift. The country had not even exported bananas before 1934, and a decade later bananas still accounted for less than 1 percent of exports. But as U.S. consumer demand for bananas rose in the postwar period and production in Central America and the Caribbean declined, the way opened for Ecuador.

Beginning in the 1930s plant diseases such as Panama disease and Sigatoka became an increasing problem in Central America and the Caribbean, forcing plantation owners there to replant on new land every ten years. Devastating hurricanes in 1947 further reduced production in Mexico, British Honduras, Nicaragua, Cuba, the Dominican Republic, and Haiti. From 1945 to 1955 banana production in Central America and the Caribbean remained stagnant, while global demand, chiefly from the United States, rose 35 percent. Banana prices rose steadily in the 1940s and into the early 1950s.

Ecuadorians saw opportunity in this situation, and banana trees soon spread across the Ecuadorian coastal lowlands, especially around Machala in the Pacific Coast region south of Guayaquil. Lands left abandoned since the collapse of the cacao economy in 1922 were now planted with row upon row of bananas. In 1948 Ecuador had only thirty-seven thousand acres of bananas but ten times that many by 1954. Exports rose dramatically, with two-thirds of banana shipments headed for the United States. In 1945 Ecuador exported 18,000 tons of bananas; in 1955, 613,000 tons; in 1959, 886,000; and in 1964, 1.2 million tons of bananas. By 1951 bananas had become Ecuador's leading export, and by 1953 Ecuador was the world's top producer, in some years selling nearly a third of the world total. Ecuadorian banana exports rose in value from $2.8 million in 1948 to a peak of $90 million in 1960. Bananas made up more than half of all Ecuadorian exports from 1958 to 1964 and reached nearly two-thirds of all exports in 1959 and again in 1961. Ecuador became a banana monoculture.

Rising banana production stimulated other developments in Ecuador. Before the 1950s Ecuador had no real national highway system, but as banana farms spread beyond the rivers and into the coastal jungles, the government cut new roads, providing access and bringing more areas under production. The Ecuadorian government, using money borrowed from the United States for road construction, built 2,175 miles of high-way between 1944 and 1967, a modest beginning but still a 50 percent increase. Ecuador also used money borrowed from the U.S. government to add new port facilities to handle the rising trade in bananas and the flood of imports that arrived in return.

In contrast to Central America, where large U.S.-owned banana plantations predominated, in Ecuador the fruit was grown mostly on medium-sized and small farms. By 1964 Ecuador had about three thousand banana farms, most fairly modest in size, averaging about 158 acres. But if domestic growers dominated production, large foreign firms still played the central role in the marketing of bananas. By 1954, 80 percent of Ecuador's banana exports were handled by just five companies, with half the trade controlled by three firms, Standard Fruit and United Fruit from the United States, and the Noboa group from Ecuador. These companies laid claim to the lion's share of the profits, leaving all the production risks but little of the money to the small and medium-sized growers.

A good illustration of the complexity of the U.S. presence in Ecuador was the role of the United Fruit Company. Ecuador had only one large U.S. banana estate, the United Fruit plantation at Tenguel, and while it never produced more than 5 percent of Ecuador's bananas, it nonetheless came to have large symbolic significance. United Fruit first arrived in Ecuador in 1934 when it bought up the failed cacao estate at Tenguel on the southern coast. As Ecuador's banana sales grew, United Fruit constructed a massive complex at Tenguel, one that became a remarkable, if singular, example of enlightened corporate generosity. The company showered its workers with benefits, providing low-cost housing; pure drinking water; subsidized meat, rice, and milk, and even set up sports teams, paying for everything—the fields, the balls, and the uniforms. United Fruit also operated a first-rate hospital for workers at Tenguel. Workers received sick leave and paid vacations, their wages four times what farmworkers made elsewhere in Ecuador. United Fruit was generous for many reasons, but perhaps most of all because of its bad experiences with angry and organized workers in Central America.

But while the banana boom brought commercial success for Tenguel, export companies, some producers, and others in Ecuador, the nation as a whole failed to use its windfall to lay the foundation for long-term economic growth. Ecuador made little progress toward industrialization. Of course, Ecuador could not really have done much to advance in this direction. Like other small poor nations, Ecuador did not have an adequate domestic market. The middle class was too small, and urban markets were poorly served by the nation's infant highway system. Nevertheless, Ecuador tried some state-directed attempts at industrialization during the 1950s. Following the recommendations of the United Nations' Economic Commission for Latin America, Ecuador adopted the Import Substitution Industrialization model, a policy direction it followed ever more closely in the early 1960s. As a consequence, more light industry appeared, centered in Guayaquil and Quito. Yet compared with the rest of Latin America, the Ecuadorian impulse toward industrialization was feeble. For Latin America as a whole, industry's contribution to GDP expanded from 17 percent in 1940 to 25 percent in 1970, but in Ecuador it remained stagnant, at 16 percent of GDP in 1940, rising to only 17 percent in 1970. Like the earlier cacao age, the banana boom would come and go, generating riches for a time, favoring some but not most, and leaving the structure of the Ecuadorian economy essentially unchanged.

## Population and Poverty

Some social changes did come to Ecuador in the postwar years. Ecuador's population grew from 3.1 million in 1942 to 4.5 million in 1962 and to 6.5 million in 1974.[5] The population growth rate increased from 1.8 percent a year in the 1930s to 2.2 percent a year in the 1940s to 3 percent a year in the 1950s and to as much as 3.2 percent a year in the 1960s, one of the highest rates in the world at the time. The nation became more urban. The population of Guayaquil increased from 125,000 in 1925 to 266,000 in 1950 and to more than 510,000 in 1962. Quito's population increased as well, although not as much, reaching 355,000 in 1962.

The migration of people from the sierra to the coast, which had been reduced to a trickle when the cacao era ended, started up again during the banana boom. Impoverished peasants renewed their exodus from the sierra, fleeing conditions of landlessness and abuse. The 1950 census, Ecuador's first, revealed that three-quarters of the land in the sierra was held by large haciendas. Working conditions in the highlands were, as before, highly exploitative. Only 2 percent of the sierra workforce actually received wages. Instead, most *serrano* peasants labored as *huasipungos*, which meant that they would turn over a large part of their harvest to the *hacendado* in exchange for access to a small plot of land. Given these conditions in the sierra, more and more ordinary people saw little incentive to stay, while the relative shortage of labor on the coast meant that wages there could be two to three times higher. For the first time in Ecuador's history, its demographic balance tipped in favor the coast. In 1942 two-thirds of the population lived in the sierra and one third lived on the coast. By 1950, 58 percent of Ecuadorians lived in the sierra and 41 percent lived on the coast; in 1962, 51 percent lived in the sierra, 48 percent on the coast; and by 1974 the coast was home to 49 percent of the national population, with 48 percent remaining in the sierra.

Most Ecuadorians lived in poverty. In 1955 Ecuador's infant mortality rate (deaths of infants younger than a year per thousand live births) was 112.8, one of the highest levels in Latin America. In 1962 two-thirds of all homes in Ecuador had no potable water, indoor plumbing, or electricity. Most people received little education: in 1950 only about half of elementary school–age children attended school, and only 4.5 percent of high school–age young people actually went to school. Adult literacy rates were appallingly low: 56 percent in 1950, although improving to 68 percent in 1960.

Given Ecuador's failure to address its social concerns, Protestant missionaries arrived from the United States in increasing numbers, motivated, at least in part, by their desire to help the most needy. U.S. missionary efforts in Ecuador dated from 1931 when Clarence Jones and Reuben Larson of the World Radio Missionary Fellowship arrived in Quito. Together they founded the HCJB Radio station (Hoy Cristo Jesús Bendice, or Heralding Jesus Christ's Blessings), "The Voice of the Andes." From its modest, two-hundred-watt beginnings, HCJB grew to have an enormous million-watt transmitter capable of broadcasting its signal literally all the way around the globe.[6] In 1953 the Summer Institute of Linguistics, an affiliate of Wycliffe Bible Translators, also arrived in Ecuador. Focusing on the indigenous peoples of the Oriente, institute officials said they were going to construct a record of native languages in the Ecuadorian Amazon region before they were lost forever. However, this claim was disingenuous: the institute was on a proselytizing mission. Other religious groups, the Salesian order, the Franciscans, the North American Gospel Missionary Union, joined in the effort to spread their faith to the Indians of the Amazon. But the natives were suspicious, and missionaries felt compelled to use force to gather the reluctant converts within earshot of their message of God's love. Sometimes missionaries kidnaped native children in order to place them in church schools. The missionaries also cooperated with government authorities to relocate and consolidate Indian communities, reasoning that this would be the most effective way to provide schools, clinics, and, of course, religious instruction. But natives did not want to be uprooted from their ancient lands or turned away from their sacred cultural practices. Worse, gathering the natives together in larger communities (like the *congregaciones* of the colonial period) meant that infectious diseases spread rapidly among this epidemiologically naive population. Under the missionaries' care the native peoples of the Amazon withered. In terms of health conditions, infant mortality, life expectancy, literacy, and other social measures, the people of the Amazon remained the poorest of Ecuadorians. Despite the vast riches of the banana age, all across Ecuador—in the Amazon, in the mountain valleys of the sierra, and on the coast—poverty abounded and social inequality remained the rule.

## The Domestic Political Context

Ecuador's unequal and unfair social situation extended into the nation's politics. Most Ecuadorians did not enjoy suffrage rights, as literacy requirements still eliminated most potential voters. In 1948, 9 percent of the population voted. Two decades later only 18 percent did. By comparison, in much of Latin America during this period about 30 to 50 percent of the population voted.[7] The difference was that in Ecuador the popular classes were too weak to insist upon incorporation into the political process. Unionized urban workers and a modern middle class, the groups that historically led the drive for the right to vote in other lands, scarcely existed in Ecuador, and the thinness of industrialization stunted the growth of these key political actors. Moreover, Ecuador's regionalism made it doubly difficult to build national working-class solidarity; the few worker groups that formed tended to split into two, one for the coast, another for the sierra.

The elite of Ecuador generally had little but contempt for the *chusma*, the poor, the people of color, the great mass of ordinary women, men, and their families. However, economic change was slowly beginning to re-configure Ecuador's social structure, gradually forming the groups and classes that could apply the most pressure for democratization, opening fissures in elite domination, and prying open the political process.

Among the elite there existed not only class fractions, landowners versus merchants, but regional fractions. Thus fragmented, the Ecua-dorian elite did not construct a shared vision of domination, an elite "project." About all they could agree upon was their desperate effort to hold back the social and political pressures from below, using the military, the *perros de la oligarquía* (dogs of the oligarchy), to defend their interests and repress the masses. The most determined opponents of change among the elites, the sierra landholders, also enjoyed the great-est sway with the military. Even into the 1960s nine of ten military of-ficers came from Ecuador's highland regions, and as a consequence the military tended to favor the interests of the sierra, the conservative heartland of Ecuador. Ecuador's recurrent military coups, as John Fitch demonstrated in his brilliant 1977 study *The Military Coup d'Etat as a Political Process*, functioned to forestall "basic changes in [the] social and economic structure" and thereby reinforced the status quo.[8]

Within this context a key political development in the post–World War II period in Ecuador was the emergence of populism. However, populism in Ecuador was different from that found elsewhere in Latin America, "neither particularly incorporating nor particularly reform-ist," as David Schodt has noted.[9] Populism in Ecuador was also unique in that it split into two separate movements, one led by five-time president José María Velasco Ibarra and the other led by the Guayaquil-based political party the Concentración de Fuerzas Populares (Concentration of Popular Forces, or CFP). The rise of the CFP in Guayaquil after 1948 owed much to the charisma and resourcefulness of its leaders, first Carlos Guevara Moreno and then Assad Bucaram. Both men served terms as mayor of the port city, deftly channeling government favors to their loyal clientele to secure support.

Populist José María Velasco Ibarra spoke in his many campaigns for the presidency of punishing the oligarchy and fighting for the poor, but once in office he showed little interest in real reform. He started many public works projects but saw nearly none through to completion. He increased the size of the government bureaucracy but mainly to reward supporters with sinecures. In truth, Velasco Ibarra lacked any abiding political philosophy, more interested in gaining office than in actually governing. A political chameleon, Velasco Ibarra sought and obtained the backing of nearly all political groups in Ecuador at various points in his career, reinventing himself with each new electoral campaign.

His impact on democratization in Ecuador is ambiguous. In his election campaigns Velasco Ibarra reached out to the previously excluded and ignored, and though they were denied the right to vote, ordinary men and women nevertheless turned out in record numbers to hear Velasco Ibarra's fiery speeches. In this way he raised the democratic expectations of the popular classes, encouraging the drive for democratization. Yet once in power Velasco Ibarra demonstrated that he had little use for democracy, repeatedly shutting down the congress and ruling by decree. Moreover, he failed to support any significant measures to advance suffrage rights for illiterates in Ecuador.

Velasco Ibarra was barely tolerated by the elite and usually not for very long; when he went too far in his rhetorical attacks, the rich looked to the obliging military to remove him. The generals, for their part, would at times support Velasco Ibarra but only if he lavished funding upon them. When he failed to do so, they would depose him, especially if the elite asked them to. All told, Velasco Ibarra was ousted four times: in 1935, 1947, 1961, and 1972. Although he was sworn in as president five times, he completed his full term of office just once.

Such frequent extralegal changes of government seriously undercut the efforts of Ecuador's diplomatic corps. Ecuador was the most unstable nation in Latin America from 1930 to 1948, and diplomats lost their jobs each time the government changed hands, leaving Ecuador in a position of starting over with new people every year or so. However, the years that followed, 1948 to 1960, proved a time of relative political stability for Ecuador, something made possible by the sizable increases in government revenues from the banana boom. Export taxes swelled government coffers; national government revenue increased 11.3 percent a year from 1945 to 1955 before slowing to 4.4 percent a year from 1955 and 1960. Three consecutive leaders, Galo Plaza Lasso (1948–52), Velasco Ibarra again (1952–56), and Camilo Ponce Enríquez (1956–60), each came to power in reasonably honest elections, albeit in a still highly restricted democracy. Each president completed his full term in office, something no Ecuadorian leader had accomplished since José Luis Tamayo (1920–24).

Galo Plaza, a sierra landowner and son of former president Leonidas Plaza, was favorably disposed toward the United States. U.S.-educated, Galo Plaza had served as Ecuador's ambassador in Washington, D.C., from 1944 to 1946. He opened a period of friendlier relations between the two nations, visiting the United States at the invitation of President Harry Truman in June 1951.

Velasco Ibarra's third presidency was the term of office that he completed, due in large measure to the broad but disorderly public works program he launched. While banana exports had increased government income, the treasury still was not large enough to pay for Velasco Ibarra's public works program. Most projects never got far, abandoned shortly after the ground-breaking ceremonies and left forever unfinished, slowly growing over with weeds and forgotten. In 1956, as Velasco Ibarra finished his term, the banana boom was winding down, the government's money was all gone, and the nation was plunging toward bankruptcy. Overall, then, in the postwar period the Ecuadorian landscape was one of economic boom and bust, social inequality and poverty, political exclusion of the popular elements, and some tentative first steps toward democratization. Within this domestic context Ecuador would seek to construct its foreign policy.

## Ecuadorian Foreign Policy in the Postwar Years

After World War II, Ecuador sent representatives to all the principal international forums.[10] At these meetings Ecuador officials—with Peru's aggression very much in their minds—looked for every opportunity to win respect for international adherence to the rule of law, not the use of force, in the resolution of international relations. Ecuador also used the international forums to advance the call for economic fairness for underdeveloped nations. At the founding of the United Nations in June 1945 and the meeting in London that followed in February 1946, Ecuador's representatives spoke out on behalf of poor nations, putting forward a proposal to consider the economic and social plight of the people of Latin America, especially with respect to the prices that less-developed nations fetched for their products on the world market. At the meetings in Havana from November 1947 to May 1948, Ecuador continued to press the case for fair prices, emphasizing the declining terms of trade for nations that exported raw materials.

Regionally, Ecuador sought in the postwar period to reinvigorate friendly relations and cooperation among the nations that had once comprised Gran Colombia: Ecuador, Colombia, Venezuela, and Panama. The goal was to create a larger collective power base for fending off the demands of the United States. Ecuador brought these nations together, hosting the Gran Colombian Economic Conference in Quito from May to July 1948. However, the Carta de Quito that resulted from the meetings amounted to not much more than an agreement to lower tariffs.

For Ecuador a critical foreign issue was the U.S. role as one of four guarantors of the 1942 Río Protocol (along with Brazil, Chile, and Argentina) that had settled the boundary dispute with Peru. Ecuadorians believed that the United States had somehow forced Ecuador into signing the disastrous Río treaty. U.S. officials did not understand this complaint and thought that they had been helping Ecuador. By the mid-1940s the neutral multistate Boundary Commission had marked 95 percent of the border, and the United States offered to carry out aerial photography of the remaining forty-seven miles of Amazonian territory left to demarcate. The mapping of this remote region proved a dangerous task, costing the lives of fourteen Americans.

The final report of the Boundary Commission in February 1947 brought the Río treaty back to front pages in Ecuador. U.S. aerial photography had revealed a different course of the Cenepa River than had heretofore been thought, and it also identified a new mountain spur, the Cordillera del Cóndor. Technically, these findings meant that the 1942 treaty was geographically flawed. Ecuador pounced on this new information and renounced the whole treaty, seizing the opportunity to renew its longstanding demand for an outlet to the Amazon River. Ecuador insisted that Peru withdraw from the "disputed" territory.

In 1951 skirmishes broke out along the border, and in Guayaquil a mob attacked the Peruvian consulate. Troubles continued into 1953, leading to the expulsion of the Peruvian ambassador from Quito. In 1955 Ecuadorian leaders feared that Peru was readying an invasion, and Ecuador's ambassador to the United States, José Ricardo Chiriboga Villagómez, went before the Organization of American States (OAS) to deliver an urgent appeal for outside help. Chiriboga alleged that Peru had massed thirty-thousand troops along its border. The guarantor nations quickly dispatched military inspectors to examine the situation. They soon reported that they saw absolutely nothing that would support Ecuador's claims: no concentration of Peruvian forces on the border, and the Peruvian navy resting peacefully at port in Callao. Chiriboga, who had given his speech on the orders of the Ministry of Foreign Relations in Quito, felt utterly humiliated. His credibility, and that of his nation, had been seriously compromised.

Because Brazil was one of the four guarantor nations, the U.S. ambassador to Brazil, Ellis O. Briggs, came to be drawn into the controversy. In a long telegram to the State Department in 1957, Briggs took a nononsense approach. "Fact is," Ambassador Briggs began, "Ecuador considers [itself] swindled by [the] 1942 [Río] Protocol and is out to wreck it." Ecuador should be told, Briggs recommended, that the boundary was already marked and would stand as is. "Ecuador may . . . [be] unhappy, but so what?" Briggs asked.[11] The State Department's leadership felt much the same way. The United States could spare little attention for Quito's principal foreign policy concerns; it had an entirely different agenda.

## The Cold War Comes to Latin America and Ecuador

Anticommunism was not just an important foreign policy concern of the United States in the postwar years, it was an overriding concern, a fixation even, that colored its foreign policy everywhere. In Latin America the United States insisted that all nations sever ties with the Soviet Union. This demand was rather ironic, for previously, in the 1920s and 1930s, most Latin American nations had *not* recognized the Soviet Union, and, in fact, they had extended recognition only at the urging of the United States when the Soviets joined the Allied cause during World War II. During the war Latin America's Socialist and Communist parties grew in size and won prestige by virtue of their ties to the Soviet Union, viewed at the time as an honorable ally of the United States and others in the fight against fascism. But as the cold war commenced, the United States demanded not only that the Latin American states break with the Soviet Union but also that they close down their Communist and Socialist parties and eliminate left-wing labor unions.

Latin American and Ecuadorian leaders believed that during World War II they had been faithful allies of the United States, especially in supplying critical economic support for the Allied war effort. Now that the fighting was over, they believed it was time for them to be repaid for their loyalty and sacrifices. Instead, soon after World War II ended, the United States began to focus its attention on new cold war hot spots in Europe, extending $12.4 billion in grants beginning in 1948 under the Marshall Plan to help rebuild the continent. Latin American leaders could only look on with considerable bitterness as the United States provided generous assistance for the postwar reconstruction of even Japan and Germany, while the Latin Americans got next to nothing.

From 1948 to 1958 Latin America received only 2.4 percent of U.S. foreign economic assistance, less than Belgium and Luxembourg. As one State Department official noted in an internal memo, "Many Ecuadorans feel that . . . [U.S.] assistance has been niggardly, particularly in comparison with what are considered to be our munificent outlays in Europe."[12] To the Ecuadorian diplomat Dr. Julio Prado Vallejo, the United States poured money into other nations but ignored Latin America because it did not see a Communist threat there. Perhaps what Latin America needed to do was import some Communists, Prado Vallejo observed dryly.[13] Latin American leaders felt increasingly abused, believing that the United States was pushing them hard on matters it cared about while ignoring legitimate Latin American concerns.

In August 1947 delegates from Latin America and the United States met in Quitandinha, Brazil (near Río de Janeiro) for the Inter-American Conference for the Maintenance of Continental Peace and Security. The United States wanted to use the meeting to construct an anti-Communist collective security treaty with Latin America, cementing the U.S. sphere of influence and freeing it to focus energy on other regions that the United States viewed as of greater concern. Latin American delegates wanted to use the conference to negotiate a Marshall Plan for Latin America. Their view was that in exchange for giving the United States what it wanted—a collective anti-Communist commitment (which it got in the 1947 Río Pact, drawn up at the conference)—Latin America should receive U.S. aid. But U.S. officials found such thinking absolutely infuriating. Why should the United States have to *pay* Latin America for the privilege of defending it against international communism? Secretary of State George C. Marshall (1947–49) refused to even consider it, telling the Latin American delegates that all such matters would have to be taken up at an economic conference later. Ecuador, for its part, was willing to go along with U.S. insistence on arranging a hemispheric anti-Soviet military alliance but also wanted an intrahemispheric arrangement. That is, Ecuador pushed the idea of mutual defense not only against extrahemispheric attacks but also in the event of intrahemispheric acts of aggression, as, for example, Peru against Ecuador in 1941. This measure would forestall future Peruvian invasions, Ecuador reasoned, and perhaps even reopen discussion of the territorial implications of the previous one. Ecuador found little support for its proposal. Rebuffed, Ecuador dragged its feet in ratifying the Río Pact.

In 1948, at the founding meeting of the Organization of American States (the Ninth International Conference of American States in Bogotá, Colombia), Ecuador continued to push for more effective mechanisms to avoid warfare among the American states. Ecuador also again raised the issue of the declining terms of trade for Latin America, lobbying for greater fairness for nations that exported raw materials. The latter proposal was popular among the Latin American states, but Marshall told the delegates that they would not be getting special trade considerations, nor would they get any Marshall Plan aid. Look instead to private investors, he advised.

U.S. policy makers were not listening to Latin American critics. Indeed, if anything, the cold war fixation of the United States was intensifying. In 1950 George Kennan, the U.S. diplomat who promulgated the U.S. policy of Soviet "containment," traveled to Latin America to report on conditions for the State Department and upon his return articulated the hardening U.S. position. "The activities of the communists," Kennan warned, "represent our most serious problem in the area. They have progressed to a point where they must be regarded as an urgent major problem. . . . We must concede that harsh governmental measures of repression may be the only answer."[14] Previously, in the years right after World War II, the United States had pressured Argentina, Brazil, and Paraguay to move toward adopting democratic forms of governance. Now, with the onset of the cold war, those days were over. Democratic governments, U.S. policy makers believed, could not be counted upon to be sufficiently anti-Communist. Henceforth the United States would encourage the development of reliably anti-Communist governments, authoritarian or otherwise. In keeping with this practice, in 1954 President Dwight D. Eisenhower (1953–61) bestowed the U.S. Legion of Merit award on the brutal Latin American dictators Marcos Pérez Jiménez of Venezuela and Manuel Odría of Peru.

In 1954 at the OAS meeting in Caracas, U.S. Secretary of State John Foster Dulles (1953–59) sought a resolution directed against the Guatemalan leader Jacobo Arbenz, whom Dulles and other U.S. officials believed to be a Communist threat to U.S. security. In an effort to secure Ecuador's support, Arbenz dispatched former president José Arévalo to Quito to speak with Velasco Ibarra. But it was no use. U.S. pressure and threats were too great, and in the end Ecuador and nearly all of Latin America voted to support the United States. Only Guatemala voted in opposition, with Mexico and Argentina abstaining. After twisting arms to line up support for the U.S. position on Guatemala, Dulles left without even listening to Latin America's pleas for economic assistance. The Central Intelligence Agency's overthrow of President Arbenz came two months later, arousing deep suspicions in Latin America of a new U.S. policy of interventionism. As the historian Gordon Connell-Smith notes, the cold war had revived "the tradition of United States intervention in . . . [Latin American] internal and external affairs which had been broken only partially by the Good Neighbor policy."[15] Naturally, U.S. diplomats did not look at the matter this way; fighting Communists was different. The United States did not consider overthrowing the elected Guatemalan government in 1954 an act of intervention.

In 1956 Ecuador strongly condemned the Soviet invasion of Hungary, although Ecuador's position probably had less to do with its support of the United States in the cold war than with its opposition to powerful nations' invading small ones and getting away with it. Ecuador voted in the United Nations to denounce the British and French invasion of Egypt in 1956 but, again, not so much in support of the U.S. position on this issue as to stand up for the principle that big nations should not be allowed to attack little ones.

One area in which the United States was willing to help Latin America was military aid. Washington wanted to strengthen the Latin American militaries in order to build up the hemispheric defense against communism. Toward this end, in 1951 the U.S. Congress passed the Mutual Security Act, which extended military assistance to Latin America through bilateral pacts with individual states. The United States also sought to use this military aid as leverage to compel compliance with its foreign policy agenda. A case in point was Ecuador's refusal to sign the 1947 Río Pact. Ecuador was troubled by language in the accord stipulating that treaties between nations could be modified only by consent of both parties, and Ecuador wanted out of the 1942 Río Protocol with Peru. In 1949, however, as a $1.5 billion foreign aid bill for Latin America's militaries worked its way through the U.S. Congress, the State Department informed Ecuador that it would see none of that money unless it joined the Río Pact. Cornered, Ecuador signed the treaty in 1950.

But there were limits to how much leverage the arms shipments could give the United States over Ecuador's foreign policy. Ecuador found itself in an unusual position of power in 1950 when the Korean War broke out and Ecuador held a seat on the United Nations Security Council. Pleasing the United States, Ecuador voted to back Washington's position on Korea, although Ecuador's vote no doubt had less to do with currying favor with the United States than with Ecuador's fixation with Peru. Ecuador was always opposed to any nation that invaded another nation. But the United States wanted more from Ecuador than its Security Council vote: it wanted Ecuador to send troops to fight in Korea. Colombia sent a thousand troops (the only Latin American nation to do so) and, in the words of the Ecuadorian military attaché in Washington, was rewarded with military assistance and economic aid on a "grand scale." The United States demanded that Ecuador send eighteen hundred men, offering to pay for the "training, equipment, arming, and transport" of the battalion.[16] Ecuador refused this "blood quota" and instead shipped five hundred tons of rice to South Korea.

In the end Ecuador's signing of the Río Pact and its vote in the Security Council proved enough to win military aid from Washington. In January 1952 Ecuador became the first Latin American nation to ratify a new bilateral military accord with the United States. Most other Latin American nations quickly followed. In exchange for U.S. military aid, Ecuador and the other Latin American nations pledged to halt all trade with the Eastern bloc, help the United States in Korea and in future conflicts, and to use the weapons received only in the fight against international communism, not in wars against their neighbors. Under the bilateral military program, from 1951 to 1961 the United States transferred $66 million a year in arms to the Latin American states. The number of U.S. military personnel stationed in Latin America also increased to

eight hundred, not counting U.S. troops in Panama and military attachés. Latin American officers began to receive training in Panama and
at bases in the United States. The United States now monopolized the
foreign supply and training of the Latin American militaries.

Nowhere was the disconnect between U.S. and Ecuadorian foreign
policy priorities more clear than in the area of military assistance and
arms sales. As Ambassador Chiriboga noted, the United States saw the
military buildup it sponsored across Latin America as an effort to create
"an effective defensive counter force against the threat of Soviet aggression."[17] But for Ecuador the enemy was Peru, not the Soviet Union, and
Ecuador looked on with considerable alarm as the United States stepped
up its military aid to Peru, which appeared to get more of everything—
planes, ships, submarines, tanks, guns, ammo, troop training—than did
Ecuador. Peru obtained three destroyers; the United States refused to
sell Ecuador even destroyer escorts. The United States, Ecuador complained, was fueling an Ecuadorian-Peruvian arms race. U.S. military
assistance to Peru rose from $100,000 in 1952 to $9.1 million in 1956,
and, overall, Peru received $73.2 million in U.S. military support from
1952 to 1967, the third-highest total in Latin America, after Brazil and
Chile.[18] To Ecuador's complaints, U.S. officials replied that Peru was
getting more than Ecuador because it paid for much of the military
hardware it received with cash, while Ecuador always bought on credit
and then proved lax in paying. The Ecuadorian government typically
lacked the funds to buy even its designated allotment of U.S. planes
and weapons and could not afford to properly maintain the equipment
it did receive. Ecuador found little comfort in the State Department's
bland assurances that the United States would never permit Peru to
attack Ecuador.

In addition to U.S. military assistance to Latin America, both loans
and grants, came economic assistance, nearly all in the form of loans.[19]
But when it came to paying back borrowed money, Ecuador had a bad
reputation. The World War II Lend-Lease agreement had brought the
transfer of $6 million-worth of military equipment to Ecuador, although
after the war the United States asked for only $575,000 in repayment. Yet
despite this more than 90 percent reduction in the amount due, Ecuador

was still slow to pay the debt. Ecuadorian treasury officials repeatedly promised full and prompt payment but did not send any money. When in 1955 the United States renewed its request for repayment, Ecuadorian authorities said they had lost the paperwork. U.S. officials, who had forwarded the documents three times already, sent new copies. At length Ecuadorian officials suggested the they could perhaps pay off the debt during the next ten to fifteen years, making payments in Ecuadorian sucres, not in dollars. The U.S. Treasury Department rejected the proposal. Only in 1956 did Ecuador finally work out an agreement for retiring its World War II Lend-Lease debt to the United States, in dollars, over the next several years.

From 1945 to 1957 the United States extended $2.6 billion in all forms of economic and military grants and credit to Latin America, but only about 2 percent of the total, $48.5 million, went to Ecuador. The money came through a variety of initiatives. One was the Point Four Aid Program (in operation from 1949 to 1961), run through the Technical Cooperation Administration from 1949 to 1954 and the U.S. International Cooperation Administration from 1955 to 1961. "Point Four" came from Truman's 1949 inaugural speech in which he called for U.S. aid for the poorest nations of the world, especially in the areas of industrial and scientific advancement. The Point Four Program was Truman's answer to critics who felt the United States had provided Marshall Plan aid only to European nations and nothing to the rest of the world.

The leading source of U.S. economic aid for Ecuador was the Export-Import Bank. Spruille Braden, a State Department official, recommended in an internal 1946 memo that Ecuador receive special Export-Import Bank help, noting that "Ecuador had accepted a highly unpopular boundary settlement in 1942, and was persuaded to do this largely as a result of US promises to assist that country economically."[20] The loans provided by the Export-Import Bank funded a wide array of projects in Ecuador: highway construction, including a road from Manta to Quevedo serving the central coastal region; public water supplies for Quito, Latacunga, and elsewhere; rebuilding after the devastating 1949 earthquake in Ambato; street paving; housing construction; new port facilities for Guayaquil; airports for Quito and Guayaquil; an electrical plant for Quito (at nearby Cunucyacu) and electricity programs in seventeen other cities and towns; railroad construction; farming development, including initiatives for sheep raising and African palm production; fishing industry development; a program to encourage colonization of the Amazon; and an initiative to build a new hotel and several buildings in Quito so that Ecuador might host a meeting of the Organization of American States. Yet despite this considerable generosity, U.S. lending generated scant goodwill in Ecuador.

For one thing, loans meant a loss of freedom of action for Ecuador. President Galo Plaza (1948–52) invited an International Monetary Fund mission to Ecuador in 1949, and the IMF insisted that Ecuador adopt a series of strict monetary policies, as well as currency and credit tightening, in exchange for a line of credit. After it got its loan, Ecuador ignored these strictures, following instead its own council. Annoyed, IMF director Camille Gutt wrote that "the Fund could not do other than conclude that the monetary authorities of Ecuador had acted without the approval of the Fund" and in a manner "inconsistent with the obligations of Ecuador under the Articles of Agreement." All this, wrote Ecuadorian Ambassador Augusto Dillon, was like "a father saying 'I won't punish you this time but you had better behave in the future.'"[21]

The Ex-Im Bank could be overbearing, micromanaging the public works projects it sponsored in Ecuador. For example, to get approval for the Manta-Quevedo road project in the 1950s Ecuador had to agree to a finely detailed plan for how the money was to be spent, granting Ex-Im Bank the right to approve all building plans. When construction did not go forward in precisely the way the bank wanted, it threatened to pull the loan. Some loans brought even greater intrusions. In 1957, as the banana economy began to go slack, the Ponce government turned to the IMF for a $15 million loan for coastal road construction and other infrastructure work. In order to get the loan Ecuador had to agree to IMF mandates regarding Ecuadorian domestic credit and fiscal policies as well as to give multinational corporations greater freedom to operate in Ecuador. From 1963 to 1966 the government obtained much-needed loans only after it instituted a tough fiscal austerity program—tight credit policy, currency devaluation, higher gasoline prices, and a hike in electricity rates—and fired two hundred workers at the Quito power plant.

Of course, the IMF and U.S. aid officials held that Ecuador made such intrusive measures necessary. For example, in overseeing a loan to fund the extension of potable water lines in Quito in the 1950s, the Ex-Im Bank demanded that the municipal treasury submit monthly reports on potable water revenues. However, the bank took this action only after the Quito city government repeatedly failed to deposit its potable water revenues in the Banco Central de Ecuador, as Quito had expressly promised. On other occasions U.S. aid agencies charged that Ecuador was using loan funds in unauthorized ways. Sometimes this was a result of the highly decentralized nature of the Ecuadorian bureaucracy, for no one in the Ecuadorian government seemed to be accountable, no one understood the whole picture, and no one seemed to know what was going on. Often the Ecuadorian government did not have enough money to put up its promised share of the costs of the externally funded development projects, and as a result much of the loan money never got used. Exasperated by these and other problems, the Export-Import Bank gave up on trying to work with Ecuador. As Ex-Im Bank president Samuel C. Waugh explained, "Promises . . . on their part . . . have not been kept."[22] Another Ex-Im Bank officer added: "Every loan to Ecuador is a headache."[23]

So while some loans came to Ecuador, they were never as large as what other Latin American nations received, never big enough to match Ecuadorian needs, and seemed in the end only to generate misunderstandings and disputes. Export-Import Bank loans to Latin America from 1962 to 1987 totaled $10 billion, $64.6 million of which (0.6 percent) went to Ecuador. Ecuador received less than Paraguay, less than Jamaica, and a quarter of what Peru got.[24] Total U.S. government loans and grants to Ecuador in the same period amounted to $661 million, 2 percent of the Latin American total. Peru received twice what Ecuador got. Haiti and Guatemala received more than Ecuador. Moreover, the relatively smaller sums Ecuador did receive came with strings. Ecuador's ambassador to the United States, José R. Chiriboga Villagómez, defiantly vowed in a meeting with U.S. State Department officials that Ecuador "would not and could not permit . . . [others] to dictate the economic development policies of the country."[25] But Chiriboga was wrong about this. Ecuador was paying for external aid with increasing losses to its autonomy.

## The Decline of Bananas

Despite the intrusive conditions and strings attached, Ecuador desperately sought loans from the United States in the late 1950s and the early 1960s because Panama disease was threatening banana production. As the disease spread, the rate of growth of banana exports slowed markedly: from 1950 to 1955 banana exports had risen at a rate of 25 percent a year, but from 1955 to 1960 the growth rate was only 12 percent a year. At the same time Central American banana production began to recover. Prices slumped as the market became glutted. Coffee and cacao prices also began to fall off markedly, slowing Ecuador's overall economic advance.

For the United Fruit Company the arrival of Panama disease cut into profits to the point where it could no longer afford to be as openhanded as before. United Fruit began to lay off the Tenguel workers in the early 1960s. Before long the goodwill the company had created came completely undone. In 1962 former employees, disillusioned and angry, seized United Fruit property, only to be evicted by government troops.

Banana exports continued to be important to Ecuador in the 1960s (and are still important today) but were no longer as dominant in the economy. With prices dropping, Ecuador's banana industry changed. One reform was the introduction of a new type of disease-resistant banana, the Cavendish, which replaced the Gros Michels. The Cavendish could be grown on the same land repeatedly, yielding four times more per acre than the Gros Michels. However, Cavendish bananas were fragile, required expensive mechanized transport from the fields, extensive use of pesticides and fertilizers, and the placement of pipes and other equipment to assure a regular water supply. Banana farming became more capital intensive, and production shifted back to the great estates in Central America and away from Ecuador. By 1965 bananas accounted for only 38.5 percent of Ecuador's exports, although Ecuador hung on as the world's number one banana producer until 1983.

These negative economic developments had political implications. Conservative Camilo Ponce Enríquez (1956–60) was the last president of Ecuador's "democratic parenthesis," the period in which banana boom revenues had provided some measure of political stability. Ponce, never very popular, had taken the 1956 election with only 29 percent of the vote and a winning margin of but 3,043 votes. In 1959, as Ecuador's economic troubles deepened and unemployment rose, people poured out into the streets in mass protests. Police repression left about two hundred dead and wounded.

In the elections of 1960, as Peter Pyne has noted, the perennial candidate José María Velasco promised "a land of milk and honey in the immediate future."[26] Inspired by Velasco Ibarra's words and impatient for the good times to begin again, the aroused populous launched demonstrations in Quito in late August 1960, forcing Ponce to resign the presidency six hours before his term of office was legally due to expire. Velasco Ibarra jumped into action, immediately cashiering forty-eight top military officers and firing thousands from the government's bureaucracies, filling the vacancies with loyalists. But as the banana economy shut down and coffee prices continued to decline, Velasco Ibarra found he could do little to meet the popular expectations that he had done so much to raise. The reforms he had promised—land reform, tax cuts for the poor—were not going to happen, after all. Velasco Ibarra tried to change the conversation, focusing on enacting his foreign policy agenda, but at this he was equally ineffective.

## The Eleventh Pan-American Conference and Velasco Ibarra

Planning for one of Velasco Ibarra's foreign policy goals had begun even before he took office: securing for Ecuador the honor of hosting the Eleventh Pan-American Conference. In 1958 Ecuador had received a $2.5 million loan from Export-Import Bank to help cover the costs of the meetings. The conference, held by the OAS every five years, was set for Quito in 1959. Ecuador used its U.S. loan for an ambitious spate of construction: a new Quito airport, a legislative building, the remodeling of the Palace of Government and the Ministry of Foreign Affairs, international radio equipment, and, most impressive of all, the beautiful new Hotel Quito, the conference meeting site. When construction soon ran into delays, the OAS decided to postpone the meetings until 1960.

In helping Ecuador prepare for the conference, the U.S. State Department emphasized the need to take steps to prevent Communists from ruining the meetings. To this end the United States offered its assistance in flushing out Communist agents, silencing Communist propaganda, and alerting all Ecuadorians about the danger of potential Communist infiltration. The United States also supplied antiriot weapons to Ecuadorian security forces. Ecuadorian planners said they agreed with the United States about the nature of threats to the conference, although Ecuadorian officials added that they believed that the Peruvians were working with the international Communist conspiracy to plan disruptions. Of course, all this placed Ecuador in something of a double bind. On the one hand it had to assure Washington that it had the Communists under control or risk its chance to host the OAS meeting, but on the other hand it had to maintain that Communists were a serious threat in Ecuador in order to get the military aid money.

In December 1960 the *New York Times* reporter Tad Szulc, based in Venezuela, wrote a story that claimed that Cuba and Ecuador were entering into closer relations, that Castro wanted to make Ecuador an outpost for Communist revolution. Szulc claimed to have information that Castro was offering arms to Ecuador in the event of war with Peru. "The opinion is growing in Latin-America that the Ecuadoran situation is quickly becoming the most serious problem in the Western Hemisphere," Szulc wrote. "Ecuadoran intelligence reports, based on intercepted Communist party documents, indicated that the Communists planned major violence at the [Quito] conference in order to discredit the inter-American system. According to the documents, the Communists intended to use the border dispute with Peru to organize riots against the parley," Szulc wrote.[27] There was no truth to any of this.

Planning for the meetings ran into more trouble when President Velasco Ibarra announced his intention to use the conference as a forum to air his views on the Peru boundary question. With this, Peru said it was not coming. Washington was also angry about Velasco Ibarra's announcement; the United States had planned to use the conference to line up united opposition to Communist Cuba, not hear Ecuador complain about Peru. In the midst of all this news broke in April 1961 of the failed effort by U.S.-supported Cuban exiles to overthrow Castro with the Bay of Pigs invasion. This latest renewal of U.S. interventionism deeply troubled Latin American leaders. Opinion in Ecuador and across Latin America ran hard against the United States. As Philip Agee, a CIA agent in Ecuador, noted at the time, "They just hate U.S. intervention more than they hate communism."[28] Several Latin American nations called for canceling the OAS meeting in Quito. Ecuador accepted the postponement. It was not ready anyway; the buildings were still not finished, and civil unrest against the troubled Velasco Ibarra administration was spreading. Later, in 1964, the OAS suggested that Ecuador go ahead and hold the meetings, but now Costa Rica and Venezuela said they would not attend. Peru also announced, again, that it would not come if Ecuador planned to bring up the boundary question, and Bolivia said it would not attend unless it *could* bring up its boundary questions. Given all this, Ecuador decided it did not want to host the OAS meetings after all. Shortly thereafter the OAS abandoned the idea of five-year meetings altogether.

Velasco Ibarra tried other foreign policy ploys in a desperate effort to maintain popular backing. One sure-fire winner was denouncing Peru and the boundary settlement, and so on August 17, 1960, he declared the Río Protocol null and void. Dutifully, the Ecuadorian legislature voided the treaty. On December 8, 1960, the four guarantors, meeting at Peru's request, ruled that Ecuador could not unilaterally abrogate the treaty. This ruling prompted angry public responses in Ecuador—rocks hurled at the U.S. and Peruvian embassies in Quito and at the U.S.-Ecuadorian Clubs in Quito, Guayaquil, and Cuenca, as well as the torching of the

U.S. consul's car in Guayaquil. Meanwhile Velasco Ibarra hinted that if the United States would not come to Ecuador's assistance, then perhaps the Soviet Union would.

In dire need of money to shore up the sagging economy, in 1961 Velasco Ibarra agreed to raise taxes in return for a loan from the International Monetary Fund. Naturally, this action was enormously unpopular, and by August 1961 much of the nation had risen in opposition to the president. Characteristically, Velasco Ibarra responded with repression, jailing opposition lawmakers and using thugs to beat up opponents. In October 1961 members of the congress crawled under their desks as outraged citizens packed the gallery and threw rocks and rotten fruit, while other lawmakers traded gunfire.

Among the more active participants in the gunplay at the legislature was Velasco Ibarra's vice president, Carlos Julio Arosemena Monroy. As vice president Arosemena Monroy served as head of the congress, and he used his leadership position to build considerable support for himself within the deliberative body. Now he began to distance himself from the president, and as pressure against Velasco Ibarra increased in October and November 1961, Arosemena Monroy spoke out forcefully for the opposition. Strikes and street protests erupted almost every day, with thirty-five killed and one hundred injured.

Matters came to a head on November 6, 1961. President Velasco Ibarra had Arosemena Monroy arrested, claiming that the vice president was trying to seize power and make himself dictator. As the chaos spread, the armed forces dithered, unable to agree about what to do. Some in the army wanted Velasco Ibarra removed, others rather favored keeping him, but no consensus emerged. On November 7, 1961, the army leadership decided that the best thing would be for both Velasco Ibarra and Arosemena Monroy to go. The air force disagreed and on November 8, 1961, came to the support of Arosemena Monroy, threatening to start bombing runs against the army. The army caved. Velasco Ibarra was out, having lasted but fourteen months this time. The legislature elected Arosemena Monroy to the presidency, and Velasco Ibarra left for exile in Mexico, vowing to return.

## The Alliance for Progress

Against this troubled domestic scene Ecuadorians learned of U.S. President John F. Kennedy's dramatic initiative in foreign policy for Latin America, the Alliance for Progress. Kennedy's announcement came two months into his administration (1961–63), delivered in a special address to Congress. The program was consistent with the youthful president's overall approach and vision, one of powerful self-assurance, bold action, and boundless optimism. Latin America could be substantially reformed, Kennedy and his top advisors believed, provided it accepted U.S. guidance and aid. U.S. action, Kennedy and his staff asserted, could raise Latin America to the "take-off" point for self-sustaining economic development. The United States would show the Latin American republics the way, helping them set into place the right economic and social foundations upon which to build strong democracies. In this way, Kennedy and his advisers held, the United States could prevent the spread of communism in Latin America.[29]

Several forces had come together by the late 1950s and early 1960s to make Kennedy's Alliance for Progress possible. Certainly Nixon's disastrous May 1958 trip to Latin America had prompted reconsideration of U.S. hemispheric policy. In Lima angry students threw rocks at Nixon, and someone moved up from the crowd and got close enough to spit in the vice president's face. In Caracas a mob attacked Nixon's motorcade and rocked his car before he escaped. These events left many in Washington wondering why people in Latin America hated the United States so much. At the same time Brazilian President Juscelino Kubitschek's "Operation Pan-America" proposal for economic development, and the subsequent OAS Committee of 21's Act of Bogotá in 1960 (in which Ecuador took a leading role), prompted U.S. worries that Brazil could lead Latin America out of the U.S. orbit.

As always, there was conflict and contention in the construction and carrying out of U.S. foreign policy, and the competing array of impulses that gave rise to the Alliance for Progress included a push for democratization and a call for social and economic justice. But mostly the alliance was a response to Fidel Castro. Unless the United States acted to make reform possible in Latin America, more nations would move into the socialist camp, Kennedy feared. Above all, the Alliance for Progress was the U.S. effort to forestall "more Cubas."

To achieve these aims the alliance offered an extremely ambitious ten-year agenda, seeking to foster industrialization, reduce unemployment, end income maldistribution, carry out land reform, put more children through school, abolish illiteracy, and much more. Latin American leaders, meeting at Punta del Este, Uruguay, in 1961, were ecstatic. At last the United States was listening to Latin America and, better still, was opening its wallet. Washington pledged $20 billion for the alliance. Latin America had received just 3 percent of all U.S. aid under Truman and 9 percent under Eisenhower. Under Kennedy and Lyndon B. Johnson (1963–69) Latin America would take almost 18 percent of U.S. aid. Whereas U.S. economic aid to Latin America averaged $204 million a year under Eisenhower, it averaged $1.3 billion a year under Kennedy and Johnson.[30] Across Latin America ordinary people responded with great affection for Kennedy, cutting out his picture from magazines to hang on the walls of their homes. In the highland Ecuadorian city of Loja, city fathers renamed the main boulevard Avenida Kennedy. The image of the United States in Latin America reached its highest level, before or since.

But just two years after the celebrated launching of the Alliance for Progress, many in the United States and Latin America had already began to view the program as a failure. Little had turned out as they had hoped. For one thing there was a great deal of disquiet regarding how the monies were disbursed. All Latin American proposals for using alliance funds had to be vetted by a nine-man council of U.S. experts, the "nine wise men," and their often aloof ways engendered considerable rancor. As the alliance historians Jerome Levinson and Juan de Onís have noted, "The resulting situation . . . [was] the worst of both worlds. The people of the United States . . . [felt] that their generosity . . . [was] not . . . appreciated . . . , while Latin Americans generally resent[ed] the restrictions placed on use of the funds . . . , as well as the patronizing attitude [of the U.S. officials]."[31]

Total U.S. aid to Latin America during the 1960s reached $22.3 billion, by far the largest sum the United States had ever extended to the region. Yet for all this largess the money was still not enough to make much of a difference, amounting to only about $10 a person per year. Moreover, unlike the earlier Marshall Plan for Western Europe, nearly three-quarters of the alliance money came in loans that had to be repaid, not grants. And there were other problems. Perhaps as much as three-quarters of the alliance money allocated by the U.S. Congress never made it to Latin America, instead getting hung up somewhere along the way, hopelessly snarled in red tape. Funds that did get through were commonly earmarked for the purchase of U.S. goods only, and these often sold at noncompetitive prices. Moreover, too much of the alliance money went for payments on Latin America's foreign debt (that is, the money was deposited in U.S. banks). The Latin American elite generally viewed the alliance goals of land reform and progressive taxes with considerable hostility anyway, although they certainly liked the idea of tapping into alliance money for projects that benefited them, such as new ports and roads, but that they preferred not to pay for themselves. Perhaps worst of all, aid money often wound up in the hands of corrupt authoritarian leaders, most notoriously the brutally repressive military government that seized power in Brazil in 1964.

Of course, some alliance programs were beneficial. Of particular note in this regard was the Peace Corps. The six thousand Peace Corps volunteers who came to Ecuador (from the 1960s to the present) did much to assist the needy and to improve what Ecuadorians thought of Americans. Still, most of the social and developmental aspects of the alliance came to be completely overshadowed by the anti-Communist and military agenda of the program. Panicked at the notion that Communists in other Latin American nations would follow Castro's revolutionary lead, the United States focused ever more intently on building up the counterinsurgency capabilities of the Latin American military and police forces. The United States supplied light arms ideal for fighting guerrillas, counterinsurgency training for thousands of Latin American military and police personnel at the School of the Americas in Panama (known to critics as *la escuela de golpes*, the school of coups), and in 1962 opened the

Inter-American Defense College at Fort McNair, in Washington, D.C., for Latin American military officers. U.S. military aid to Latin America grew from $66 million a year from 1953 to 1961 to $172 million a year from 1961 to 1964.

As the historian Federico G. Gil sums up, "The United States' most consistent [Alliance] goal . . . was to preserve stability, to oppose communism, . . . and these goals . . . [were] not always compatible with reform."[32] In the end the Alliance for Progress mostly meant military aid to combat internal insurgencies. The net result of U.S. policy was the reinforcement of repressive, authoritarian regimes in Latin America. In this manner the Alliance for Progress contributed handsomely to the rise of military governments across Latin America, which saw six military coups in 1962–63 alone. In 1961–69 sixteen civilian governments in Latin America were removed and replaced by the military. Most coup leaders had trained in the United States or in the Panama Canal Zone. After Lyndon Johnson assumed the presidency, he focused his attention on Vietnam, sharply cutting alliance funding. When Richard M. Nixon (1969–73) took office, he dropped the alliance altogether.

## The Cuba Question

A leading foreign policy objective of the United States in these years was the isolation of Castro's Cuba in the hemisphere, but in Ecuador the confused domestic political situation made it enormously difficult for Washington to realize this goal. After the military removed Velasco Ibarra in November 1961 and Vice President Carlos Julio Arosemena Monroy, the fantastically wealthy son of Guayaquil notables, assumed office (1961–63), hopes were widespread that things would improve in Ecuador. Yet little changed. The wild legislative sessions continued, with more food fights, fisticuffs, and gunfire. When members of the congress turned their attention to lawmaking, they focused mainly on staged hearings designed to smear their opponents.

In an effort to demonstrate his political independence, President Arosemena Monroy reestablished relations with socialist Poland and

Czechoslovakia. He then departed for the Soviet Union and spoke of reestablishing relations. Naturally, the United States did not approve of any of this. Matters came to a head at the Eighth Consultative Meeting of Foreign Ministers held in Punta del Este, Uruguay, in January 1962 (Punta del Este II). U.S. Secretary of State Dean Rusk (1961–69) sought OAS approval of several anti-Castro measures, including suspension of Cuba from the OAS. The Ecuadorian delegation voted for all the measures condemning Castro's Cuba except the last one: Ecuador, along with Argentina, Brazil, and Chile, abstained in the vote to place a trade embargo on Cuba and suspend it from the OAS. Nevertheless, sixteen Latin American nations backed the U.S. position and the measure passed easily.

In time Arosemena Monroy broke relations with Cuba too. In Havana on December 11, 1961, a truck broke through the gates of the Ecuadorian embassy; the eight people aboard were seeking political asylum. The Cuban military opened fire, killing three and wounding four. After considering the situation, Arosemena Monroy changed policy direction and broke relations with Cuba on April 3, 1962.

If President Arosemena Monroy's policies could be somewhat unsteady, his personal conduct was even more so. Arosemena Monroy had a serious drinking problem, and every day it was becoming more and more obvious. Arosemena Monroy got drunk before important presidential duties, such as his meeting at the White House with President Kennedy. When Chilean President Jorge Allesandri Rodríguez came to visit Ecuador, Arosemena Monroy became so intoxicated that he could not stand up to deliver the greeting. In December 1962 the major Guayaquil newspaper, *El universo*, ran photos of a visibly inebriated Arosemena Monroy. His drinking may even have led to criminal conduct, perhaps including murder, at least according to Philip Agee, then a CIA operative in Ecuador. According to Agee, Arosemena Monroy went bar hopping in Guayaquil one night in March 1963, winding up at a lowbrow tavern, the Cuatro y Media, at some point after midnight. Blind drunk, Arosemena Monroy began bellowing taunts at a homosexual waiter, ordering him to put a lampshade on his head. Arosemena Monroy drew his pistol and fired at the lampshade but hit the man in the head, Agee reported.[33] When, on July 10, 1963, Arosemena Monroy arrived drunk and staggering at a state banquet, it was too much. The military had seen enough: Arosemena Monroy was a national embarrassment. The next day tanks surrounded the Presidential Palace. Soldiers loaded Arosemena Monroy onto a plane and saw him off to exile in Panama. Military government followed from 1963 to 1966.

## The CIA in Ecuador

One critical aspect of U.S. activities in Ecuador—something that quietly underlay all elements of the relationship between the nations—was the role of the CIA. Ordinarily it is all but impossible to gain knowledge about CIA covert operations, but for Ecuador there exists first-hand information. Philip Agee, posted in Quito as an assistant attaché in the U.S. embassy's political section from 1960 to 1963, was in fact a CIA agent. Agee quit "the company" in 1969 and wrote an exposé, *Inside the Company,* in which he made public the full extent of his knowledge of secret CIA activities in Ecuador.

Agee provided a wealth of details. The main goal of U.S. foreign policy in the early 1960s was to thwart Communist influence, and the CIA, Agee confirmed, labored hard to force Ecuador to break relations with Cuba. Velasco Ibarra's indifference to the purported threat of communism—a threat he seemed to regard as not real—aroused deep U.S. concern and action. When Velasco Ibarra took a neutral attitude toward Castro's Cuba, the United States began to work behind the scenes to engineer the president's removal from office.

The CIA went about its work in many ways. "High on the list of priorities" Agee reported, "[was] . . . the framing of Soviet officials in diplomatic or commercial missions in order to provoke their expulsion."[34] Part of Agee's job was also to discredit the Ecuadorian left and to induce the government to harass left-wing political parties and left-leaning unions. Another of Agee's duties was to tamper with the judicial system. Agee faked documents in order to rig trials and to get suspected Communists and other enemies thrown in prison. Agee's work also involved election fraud, including "the formation of 'goon squads' to intimidate the opposition" or "buying votes and vote counters."[35] In an effort to achieve the political outcomes it sought, the CIA funneled money to right-wing political parties and made use of "[e]conomic . . . [w]arfare . . . to aggravate economic conditions" to destabilize the already-rocky Velasco Ibarra administration.[36] The CIA also paid for "spontaneous" anti-Communist demonstrations or for the disruption of visits by Cuban or Eastern bloc diplomats.

Another key CIA undertaking was the recruitment of people to serve as agents and assist in covert operations. The CIA paid well. The CIA penetrated Ecuador's left-wing political organizations, with the planted agents providing a steady stream of details regarding the groups' activities. The CIA also established agents in the leading student groups. These student agents proved especially useful in disseminating CIA propaganda. Sometimes the CIA printed up "black" propaganda, for example, handbills ostensibly from left-wing organizations but really drawn up by the CIA and designed to show leftist groups in an unfavorable light. Likewise, the CIA paid students to spray-paint walls with extreme or salacious slogans that were then attributed to the left. The CIA paid for and helped run the student newspaper *Voz universitaria* (University Voice). The editor, Wilson Almeida, was on the CIA payroll.

Some agents recruited by the CIA were especially valuable, notably the journalist Gustavo Salgado, the author of a popular column in *El comercio*, the leading Quito newspaper. In exchange for cash payments Salgado published CIA propaganda and disinformation, especially forged documents designed to discredit those the CIA opposed. The campaign to influence the press in Ecuador was in keeping with Kennedy's larger goal to control at least one major daily and one major radio outlet in each Latin American nation.

Other CIA agents in Ecuador proved equally valuable. The CIA was able to read transcripts of the deliberations of Ecuador's military junta from 1963 to 1966, because the woman who took shorthand at the meetings was the girlfriend of a local CIA asset. The agent passed copies of the minutes on to the CIA, and Agee bragged that often the CIA got to read the minutes of the meetings even before junta members did. The

CIA had leading police and military officers on its payroll, as well as high-ranking politicians, up to and including the mayor of Guayaquil, Emilio Estrada Icaza; Ecuador's U.N. ambassador, Manuel Naranjo; Juan Sevilla, minister of the treasury; the minister of labor, José Baquero de la Calle; and even at one point the vice president of the nation, Reinaldo Verea Donoso. When Verea Donoso, a longtime CIA asset, became vice president after Velasco Ibarra was deposed in November 1961, the CIA raised his pay from $700 a month to $1,000. "If he gets to be President," Agee added, "we'll pay him even more."[37] In 1961 both the second and third in presidential succession were on the CIA payroll.

One project that took up a large amount of Agee's time involved reading mail from Cuba, the Soviet bloc, and China, most of it written by Ecuadorians traveling in these places. The CIA had an agent in the central Quito post office whose job was to take the international mail pouches arriving from the Eastern bloc and Cuba and pass the bags along to his brother, who delivered them to the CIA staff at the U.S. embassy. There Agee and others would steam open the mail, read it, photocopy anything they found of interest, and then reseal the envelopes and return everything to the post office for delivery. Usually, they opened and read thirty to forty letters a day. From this work the CIA generated a list of who it wanted to keep an eye on.

Not everything Agee tried worked out well. When Velasco Ibarra decided to allow Czechoslovakian diplomats back into Ecuador, Agee and the CIA had to hurry to plant a clandestine listening device in their new embassy building. The construction site was protected by guard dogs that would have to be drugged, and so Agee decided to test a potential sedative on his own dog. Agee got the dosage wrong, sending his pet into an irreversible coma. Bugging the Cuban embassy also went wrong. The planted listening device somehow got dialed into a local radio station, recording hours and hours of popular Ecuadorian music.

Thanks to Agee, we know what the CIA was doing in Ecuador from 1960 to 1963. After this time our window on CIA activities closes, although obviously this does not mean that CIA activities stopped. Unfortunately, we have no information on Soviet or Cuban clandestine activities in Ecuador, although both nations clearly had a vastly smaller presence in Ecuador than did the United States.

CIA activities in Ecuador, in conjunction with other U.S. actions, had several serious implications. One long-term U.S. goal was to undermine left-wing unionism in Ecuador. Washington made economic aid conditional on shutting down left-wing labor unions. The U.S. government paid to fly Ecuadorian labor leaders to the United States and offered instruction in the virtues of anti-Communist unions. The CIA actions added to these efforts to eliminate independent unions and replace them with tame, right-wing unions funded by the CIA. As the labor historian Jon Kofas notes, "Washington expended considerable financial, technical, and personnel assistance to undermine" the left-wing organized labor movement in Ecuador.[38] Therefore, it is fair to conclude that the historical weakness of labor unions in modern Ecuador is at least in part a result of U.S. actions.

Another implication of CIA activities in Ecuador was the loss of civil liberties. The CIA maintained a list of people it thought were Communists or potential Communists, assembling names from information obtained from paid informants, mail it opened, and from airline passenger lists of those traveling to Soviet bloc nations. When the military came to power in 1963, it closed down all left-wing political parties and unions, imposed censorship, set a curfew at 9 p.m., canceled elections, and banned all strikes. Then, using the CIA's "subversives" list, the military rounded up and jailed 125 people, politicians, labor leaders, newspaper reporters, intellectuals, writers, and others. University professors whose names showed up on the list were fired. In this manner, then, the United States contributed actively to the undermining of civil liberties in Ecuador.

Most serious was that the CIA worked assiduously to create an atmosphere of political instability in Ecuador. Because President Velasco Ibarra (1960–61) and subsequently Arosemena Monroy (1961–63) refused, at least for a time, to break relations with Cuba, the CIA worked hard every day to bring these governments down, paying for staged protests, loudly broadcasting distortions and lies, and seeking to exacerbate tensions and create a mood of crisis and social breakdown. Ecuador suffered from chronic political instability, but, the evidence shows, this was in no small measure a direct result of U.S. actions. As Agee wrote, "We aren't running the country but we are certainly helping to shape events in the direction and form we want." [39]

## Conclusions

Ecuador's principal foreign policy concern in the postwar period was Peru, not the Soviet Union. Peru had attacked Ecuador, and Ecuador's number one foreign policy goal was to make sure that it would never happen again. Ecuador wanted U.S. arms and wanted the United States to use its influence to control Peru. For Ecuador this Peru fixation was all consuming, its stance on the leading international issues of the day formulated with the Peru issue in mind. Ecuador favored the notion of international disarmament, backing, for example, the 1958 Soviet proposal for the United States to join in cutting military spending, because Ecuador could never hope to keep up with Peru in an arms race. Ecuador disapproved of nations' adding to their territory through war because Ecuador had lost territory to Peru in the 1941 war. Ecuador consistently stood against large nations' invading small ones because of Ecuador's own experiences. Ecuador always spoke out in favor of the peaceful settlement of problems with other nations because of its history with Peru.

But even though few Ecuadorian leaders shared the anti-Soviet fixation of the United States, they saw advantage in appearing to. Ecuador learned its lines in the cold war script well. In 1953 Ecuador's ambassador to the United States, José R. Chiriboga Villagómez, reported that "the U.S. would assist those governments that made a wall against communism." [40] It was plain what Ecuador would need to say if it wanted to get military aid. Ecuador had to maintain it was facing a Communist threat. U.S. officials were usually quick to accept such claims, although the perfect argument for Ecuador—that the Peruvians were Communists—would have looked too obviously like overreaching. Sometimes

U.S. officials spotted the hand of the Communist menace in Ecuador even when no one else could see it, but going along with the United States on this had no down side for Ecuadorian leaders. In fact, not only could it bring more aid, it also provided a handy reason for repressing political opponents.

Of course, the anticommunism of some Ecuadorians was genuine enough, especially among the military officers who had received a heavy dose of anti-Communist indoctrination at the School of the Americas in the U.S. Canal Zone in Panama or at bases in the United States. But for most Ecuadorian leaders, anticommunism was something less than authentic, its origins residing in obsequiousness. Chiriboga, in a meeting with State Department officials in May 1957, claimed that communism was on the rise in Ecuador and that President Ponce had his hands full trying to contain the threat. Guevara Moreno and the CFP had ties to the Communists, Chiriboga warned. Worse, Czechoslovakian Communists were stirring up trouble in Ecuador, he reported. Perhaps too transparently, Chiriboga told U.S. officials that President Ponce would be willing to expel the Czechs in exchange for $16 million in aid. On another occasion Chiriboga reported to the Ministry of Foreign Relations in Quito that the United States considered Ecuador to be one of the places where the Soviet Union might seek a trade opening in Latin America. Chiriboga recommended fanning these fears. In fact, Chiriboga went even further, suggesting that Ecuador open full diplomatic relations with the Soviet Union, reasoning that this action would lead the United States to offer more loans and military aid.[41] Sometimes artfully, sometimes not, Ecuador sought to use the Americans' cold war fears to further its own aims.

As one Ecuadorian official, Dr. Julio Prado Vallejo, put it, U.S. policy makers suffered from a "psicosis comunista."[42] The policies that grew out of the United States' cold war fixation, and its lack of genuine understanding of Latin America, had many negative consequences. Military aid was particularly harmful. The warships that the United States provided to Latin America offered no military protection against communism; the ships were hopelessly out of date and would have been no match against modern Soviet vessels. More to the point, the Soviet Union was not planning to attack Latin America. The Latin American nations purchased the vessels solely to threaten their neighbors. Moreover, these ships came at a hefty price that Latin American nations could ill afford to pay. Warships, planes, tanks, rifles, ammunition—the United States lavished military aid on Peru, Ecuador's archenemy. Ecuador tried to keep up, seeking to block U.S. arms sales to its rival while buying more and more weapons itself. U.S. policy led to an Ecuador-Peru arms race.

In the cold war years Ecuador grew more dependent on the United States, making it Ecuador's sole supplier of weapons and military supplies—even the lubricants used by the Ecuadorian armed forces had to be purchased through the Pentagon. Ecuador relied on the United States for loans and aid. But Ecuador's increasingly close ties to the United States had implications for its sovereignty. U.S. officials micromanaged Ecuadorian public works projects, the most extreme example of which was the Manta road project funded by the Ex-Im Bank. Ecuador could not just build a road where it wanted or how it wanted; it had to yield to the choices made by its U.S. supervisors. The claim by U.S. officials that Ecuador lacked the necessary engineering expertise was both condescending and untrue. Nevertheless, dependence on U.S. loans meant that nearly all decisions about what public works would be built in Ecuador were made by a handful of officials in Washington, D.C. These men did the picking and choosing; it was pointless for Ecuador to appeal their decisions. All verdicts were final. This was, as Ecuador's ambassador to the United States, José Chiriboga Villagómez, rightly put it, an "economic dictatorship."[43] The United States used the leverage provided by its military aid and foreign loans to attempt to force Ecuador to comply with its wishes. The United States held back desperately needed loans from the 1960–61 Velasco Ibarra administration to compel Ecuador to adopt a more clearly hostile stance toward Cuba. As Velasco Ibarra tracked rightward in his rhetoric, he lost critical left-wing support for his administration. The protests and nationwide strikes that followed brought down his government.

U.S. policy had other implications. During the cold war Ecuador's most extreme right-wing elements found that they had a powerful ally in the United States. Ecuadorian leaders learned that any act of political repression, no matter how savage, could be easily explained away by labeling the victims "Communists." The United States induced Ecuadorian leaders to interpret every social protest, every land invasion, every march for social justice as part of a broader Communist plan for world domination. U.S. actions precipitated an Ecuadorian red scare.

The United States actively supported the military dictatorship that came to power in 1963. In that year alone the United States provided more than one million dollars' worth of guns and ammunition to the military government and stepped up counterinsurgency training in Panama for Ecuadorian police and military. In an especially telling exchange, in September 1963 the Ecuadorian ambassador to the United States, José A. Correa, met in Washington, D.C., with the Secretary of State Rusk.[44] In their conversation Rusk was particularly keen to ask Correa about Cuban Communists, quizzing the ambassador about possible infiltration into Ecuador. In response Correa reported with some pride on the wide array of repressive measures taken by the new military junta, adding without a hint of embarrassment that Ecuador should be seen by the United States as a friendly nation with a *democratic* orientation. The U.S. secretary of state offered no criticism of the military coup or the regime's repression, instead promising U.S. support for the dictatorship.

In this postwar period the United States for the first time began to effectively use its great power to impose its will on Ecuador. The United States now noticed Ecuador, and Ecuador suffered from the attention. The United States accomplished its goals in Ecuador: the banning of progressive political parties; the persecution of left-wing unions; the firing, jailing, beating, exile, and murder of independent-minded intellectuals, professors, and newspaper reporters; and the undermining of governments it did not like. Through its actions United States contributed significantly to political instability and undermined the goal of building democracy in Ecuador.

# 6  Tuna, Oil, and Trouble: The 1960s to the 1980s

The decades of 1960s through the 1980s brought serious difficulties to relations between Ecuador and the United States. Two major controversies developed, and economic issues stood at the center of both. A continuing conflict developed regarding Ecuador's claims to a two-hundred-mile territorial sea boundary. Ecuador wanted to reserve for itself the amazingly rich fishing zones off its coastline, waters fed by the Humboldt Current, which abounds in tuna and other sea life. When, in defiance of Ecuadorian law, U.S.-owned fishing boats began to push in anyway, Ecuador seized the vessels and assessed heavy fines. The U.S. government retaliated with cuts in aid. The acrimonious and long-running dispute that ensued was the low point in U.S.-Ecuadorian relations.

Economic issues were also at the core of the dispute that arose in connection with the U.S. role in the development of Ecuador's oil resources. U.S. companies discovered the oil and initially took the lead in drilling and export operations, supplying critical assistance to Ecuador in the commercial development of its oil resources. But in time the U.S. companies concluded that they could not work in Ecuador; the highly restricted conditions imposed by the Ecuadorian government made this impossible, and they pulled out of Ecuador. The subsequent legal fights between Ecuadorian interest groups and U.S. oil companies continue to cloud relations between the nations even today.

## Population and Poverty in Ecuador

From the 1960s to the 1980s Ecuador's story demographically and socially was one of explosive population growth and widespread and persistent poverty. The population of Ecuador grew at its swiftest rate ever in the 1960s and 1970s, rising 3.27 percent a year from 1962 to 1974, dropping to the still rapid growth rate of 2.52 percent a year from 1974 to 1982. The national population, 4.6 million in 1962, reached 7.1 million in 1979.[1] Ecuador became more urban, and by 1975 Quito's population had reached 592,000 and Guayaquil's hit 1.1 million.

Rapid population growth and urbanization placed greater burdens on the already-strained social conditions in Ecuador. Inequality was at the core of the problem, and in 1975 one-fourth of the population held nearly three-quarters of the wealth. This maldistribution of wealth bred many social ills. Infant mortality rates in Ecuador were appallingly high, remaining in the 60s in the 1970s and 1980s, one of the worst rates in all Latin America.[2] Education was another problem area. In the 1980s almost half the children who started elementary school failed to finish, with most completing only a year or two. The problem was cost; most families could not afford to pay for the uniforms, textbooks, and other school supplies that were required. As a result illiteracy was widespread. In rural zones at least 40 percent of the population was completely illiterate, and many more, though counted as literate, could do little more than sign their own name. As throughout its history Ecuador remained a land of vast social inequality and deep poverty.

## Political Failings

Ecuador's governments remained unequal to the challenge of addressing these social concerns, and continued political instability followed. After the military leadership ousted the erratic Carlos Julio Arosemena Monroy in 1963, the expectation was that the generals would follow their customary practice and quickly hand back the reins of government to trustworthy civilians. But this time the generals wanted to try their hand at reforming the nation—they had a plan—and remained in control for three years (1963–66). The program they undertook was a mishmash of contradictions: denunciation of communism but a state-directed industrialization program; vigorous repression of labor and the left but an attempt at land reform. Lamentably, none of junta's reform efforts amounted to much, least of all its vaunted 1964 land reform.

The military wanted land reform to be its signature accomplishment, one that would supply a justification for seizing power. Talk of change was in the air; the Alliance for Progress and the rhetoric of Velasco Ibarra had placed land reform on the agenda. But in 1966—*after* the military's land reform—0.4 percent of the population (or thirteen hundred estate owners) still held 45.1 percent of the farmland, while 73.1 percent held but 7.2 percent of the land.[3] Because of this and other failures, popular approval of the military junta, never high to begin with, soon spiraled downward. The situation worsened in March 1966 when the military brutally attacked protesters at Quito's Central University; the students were the sons and daughters of the elite and the middle class. As public outrage swelled, the military, having now alienated nearly all sectors of Ecuadorian society, elected to return to its barracks.

With the end of military government in 1966, an interim government briefly governed Ecuador, followed by the election of the Guayaquil businessman Otto Arosemena Gómez (1966–68) (cousin of former president Carlos Julio Arosemena Monroy). Arosemena Gómez's administration came to be distinguished most by the president's outspoken stances on key foreign policy issues. At the inter-American meeting of Latin American presidents held at Punta del Este, Uruguay, in 1967, he rose to his feet and bitterly denounced the failings of the Alliance for Progress, sharply criticizing the United States for not extending more foreign aid to the poor nations of Latin America. At the close of the meetings Otto Arosemena Gómez alone refused to sign the conference's final declaration. He continued his attack on the United States later that year, charging that alliance aid came only in the form of U.S. goods purchased at inflated prices. Openly dismayed, the U.S. ambassador to Ecuador, Wymberley Coerr, told the press that Arosemena Gómez's discourse was destructive.[4]

## The "Tuna Wars"

President Arosemena Gómez led Ecuador into another controversy with the United States, a bitter confrontation about Ecuador's territorial sea limits.[5] The problem had festered for a long time. In 1952 Ecuador joined Chile and Peru in asserting a two-hundred-mile limit, the Declaration of Santiago. Washington rejected this claim—like nearly all nations, the United States recognized only a twelve-mile limit. The matter took on greater significance and urgency in the mid-1950s when modern, large-scale fishing operations sailing out of California began to work the Pacific waters off Ecuador, especially from January to April when the tuna migrated in and the fishing was good. U.S.-based vessels were cruising in and hauling off boatload after boatload of valuable cargo, their holds packed with tuna. At the inter-American meetings in Caracas in 1954 Ecuador pushed its position further, also claiming the right to all natural resources found on the ocean floor within its two-hundred-mile zone. Peru and Chile supported Ecuador's proposal, and the conference approved it, despite the determined objections of the United States. Emboldened, in March 1955 Ecuador seized two U.S. fishing boats, the *Santa Ana* and the *Antarctic Maid,* surprising their crews while they were working the waters off Santa Clara Island in the Gulf of Guayaquil. One U.S. sailor, William Pack, was injured during the capture of the vessels. In response the United States recalled Ambassador Sheldon T. Mills for consultation. But more ship seizures followed. Ecuador assessed heavy fines on the captured ships and insisted that all vessels entering its two-hundred-mile limit pay a fee for fishing rights.

The United States would not allow fishing vessels owned by its citizens to pay the fees Ecuador was demanding, for such payments would constitute a de facto recognition of the two-hundred-mile limit. Beyond this, U.S. officials needed to assert the restrictive twelve-mile limit because of cold war considerations. A twelve-mile limit would allow U.S. warships to continue to defend Formosa against attack from mainland China, and it would allow U.S. submarines to maintain patrols off the coastlines of the Soviet Union. A two-hundred-mile limit would not. Understanding this, Ecuador had to find some compromise solution. It could never hope to prevail if the United States resolved to make a fight over the issue. But one thing Ecuador could absolutely *not* do was suggest some lower territorial limit, like seventy miles, or fifty or twenty-four, for this would make the assertion of a two-hundred-mile limit look all the more capricious.

Above all, Ecuador wanted to protect its emerging fishing industry. From 1957 to 1961 Ecuador's offshore fish haul increased from 26,000 to 60,000 metric tons. In 1957 Ecuador exported 33,000 cases of canned tuna; by 1961 it shipped 266,000. So periodic seizures of U.S. shipping vessels continued. Washington tried to pressure President Carlos Julio Arosemena Monroy, blocking a loan for highway construction unless he renounced the two-hundred-mile limit, but Arosemena Monroy refused. In response, Washington cut Ecuador's access to credit.

In May 1963 the Ecuadorian navy seized two more U.S. tuna boats off Salinas. This time, however, nineteen other U.S.-owned fishing boats working in the area moved in and surrounded the captured vessels, forming a blockade. The U.S. government intervened and Ecuador backed down, releasing the two boats. At this point the United States approached Ecuador's military government with a deal, offering to drop the demand that Ecuador renounce the Santiago Agreement, provided that Quito simply stop enforcing the two-hundred-mile limit. Ecuadorian Ambassador Neftalí Ponce Miranda recommended acceptance, noting that Ecuador lacked the naval power to enforce the two-hundred-mile limit anyway. "The existence of this zone is merely theoretical," he conceded.[6] Ecuador would lose nothing by agreeing to this modus vivendi, Ponce-Miranda advised. Moreover, because it was to be a secret agreement, Ecuador would not even have to explain to it Chile and Peru. So in 1963, under pressure from the United States, the new military junta signed the secret accord, promising not to enforce the two-hundred-mile limit. In return Ecuador received several U.S. loans. Relations between the nations appeared to be on the mend.

This changed abruptly in 1966 when Arosemena Gómez took office. Having already angered Washington with his outspoken denunciation of the Alliance for Progress, President Arosemena Gómez now provoked even deeper wrath by suddenly renouncing the verbal agreement previously entered into by the military government. Ecuador resumed its ship seizures. As the controversy heated up in 1967, President Arosemena Gómez declared Ambassador Coerr persona non grata and expelled him from the country.[7] The U.S. Congress responded with the

Pelly Amendment to the Foreign Military Sales Act of 1968: henceforth the U.S. government would pay the fines imposed by Ecuador on private U.S. vessels and then deduct the sums from the amount of aid that Ecuador would otherwise have received.

Nevertheless, subsequent Ecuadorian governments, first civilian and then military, continued the policy of sporadic enforcement of the two-hundred-mile limit. Seizures peaked in 1971 when Ecuador took custody of fifty-one U.S. tuna boats and levied more than $2.4 million in fines. The United States retaliated with a one-year suspension of military sales to Ecuador. Ecuador expelled the U.S. military mission from Quito. Through the 1970s Ecuador collected about $6 million from the owners of the more than one hundred tuna boats it captured, as the pace of seizures ebbed and flowed. After slowing in the late 1970s, seizures picked up again in 1981 when Ecuador nabbed ten more U.S. tuna-fishing vessels and levied fines totaling $10 million.

The nations finally moved toward resolution of the long-running conflict in the 1980s. The 1982 U.N. Convention on the Law of the Seas opened the way, establishing a twelve-mile territorial limit as well as a 188-mile exclusive economic zone for all nations, giving each dominion over all resources in those waters. By 1988 President Ronald Reagan (1981–89) had declared U.S. acceptance of the key parts of the accord, thereby ending the "tuna wars."[8] But other areas of contention between Ecuador and the United States did not find resolution.

## Oil and the Military Government

One central area of controversy in Ecuadorian-U.S. relations, and one with a long and continuing history, was the role of U.S. firms in the Ecuadorian oil industry. Ecuadorians long had believed that vast deposits of oil surely lay somewhere beneath the green carpet of the Amazon tropical rainforest. In 1919 Ecuador drew up legislation to make sure that when Ecuador did strike it rich, the oil would not be "monopolized by U.S. oil companies" or "empresas yankes [sic]."[9] In the 1930s Texas oilmen, notably Gilard Kargl, president of Kargl Aerial Surveys of San Antonio, led the hunt for oil in Ecuador, but they found nothing.

Ecuadorian President Galo Plaza lost faith, declaring in 1949 that the idea of Amazonian oil was just a myth.[10]

In 1967 Texaco-Gulf struck oil at Lago Agrio in the Ecuadorian Amazon near the Colombian border; drillers had tapped into what quickly proved to be a vast underground sea of petroleum. By 1972 oil was rushing through a newly constructed 313-mile pipeline, built at a cost of $130 million, traveling up and over the Andes mountains and connecting the Amazon oil fields to a terminal at San Lorenzo on Ecuador's north coast. A more practical solution, using neighboring Colombia's existing oil pipeline, was never considered. Ecuador wanted control of its oil.

It appeared that the task of prudently husbanding Ecuador's petroleum windfall would fall to the wildly unpredictable populist José María Velasco Ibarra, who had returned to power in 1968. Velasco Ibarra's fifth and final presidency proved as troubled as his earlier turns in office. His campaign aroused popular expectations, but once in office Velasco Ibarra embarked on an austerity program, governing from the right. By late 1969 schoolteachers and government employees were on strike, and by April 1970 students were marching in daily street protests in the capital. Citing the need for social peace, in June 1970 Velasco Ibarra seized dictatorial authority, closing down the legislature and the universities, but unrest continued, with growing protests against poverty and government corruption. Government employees had gone unpaid for months while Velasco Ibarra's cronies stole money from the public till with shameless abandon. (About 180 officials were later charged with theft of government funds.)

Viewing the unfolding chaos, military leaders concluded that only they could restore order to the nation. Velasco Ibarra was clearly unacceptable, and his likely replacement in the next election, the Guayaquil populist Assad Bucaram, looked even worse, someone most officers regarded as a crude and deeply dishonest opportunist. In February 1972 the military decided to act, a move actively encouraged by the nation's elites. Velasco Ibarra was sent into exile in Argentina (he would return to Quito to die in 1979) and Assad Bucaram denied the presidency. The military would handle Ecuador's oil.

Heading the coup was Gen. Guillermo Rodríguez Lara (1972–76), a member of the military leadership although not the highest-ranking officer. The coup should not, however, be read as a blow against democracy, because the Velasco Ibarra government was, after all, a dictatorship. Instead, the coup amounted to the replacement of an unpopular and ineffective civilian dictatorship with a somewhat unpopular and only partially ineffective military one. The military government was also a good deal different from its counterparts then in control in Brazil and across the Southern Cone. There the generals initiated "dirty wars" of atrocities and terror, campaigns designed to "cleanse" their nations by removing the left from the political spectrum once and for all. But in Ecuador the military did not need to demobilize and discipline the popular elements because they had never been incorporated in the political process in the first place. Ecuador's military did not define its mission as one of torture and repression. As Anita Isaacs has noted, the Ecuadorian "armed forces . . . inherited a longstanding . . . commitment to social reform." [11] They believed that *they* had saved the nation from "bank rule" in 1925 and from that time forward carried a deep and abiding commitment to progressive social change. The military saw itself as the nation's one incorruptible institution. General Rodríguez Lara sought to follow this tradition by putting in place reforms that would help ordinary people, a program he labeled "revolutionary nationalism." [12]

Because Rodríguez Lara had attended the U.S. School of the Americas in Panama and received further instruction at Fort Leavenworth, Kansas, he might have been expected to forge strong ties with the United States. However, Ecuador's relationship with the United States actually diminished as the generals looked to the *Peruvian* military for inspiration and leadership—a curious development, indeed, given the longstanding enmity between Ecuador and Peru. But in Peru the generals, led by Juan Velasco Alvarado (1968–75), had recently launched their own experiment in military-led social reform and state control of the nation's oil and other natural resources. The Ecuadorian junta looked to Velasco's government for inspiration and example. Ecuadorian military leaders traveled frequently to Lima to seek advice.

The Ecuadorian military expected the newfound oil reserves to fund its ambitious social agenda. Production soared, rising from 27 million barrels in 1972 to 73 million in 1978. Ecuador's exports rose from $195 million in 1971 to $1.4 billion in 1977, a more than sevenfold increase, with oil making up about half the export total. Even better, Ecuador's emergence as an oil exporter coincided with a spike in world prices from $2.37 a barrel in 1972 to $35.26 in 1980 on the heels of the Iranian Revolution. The wealth created by oil exports brought a near tripling of Ecuador's total gross domestic product from 1971 to 1977.[13] From 1968 to 1971, before the discovery of oil, the GDP had grown at an annual rate of 5.03 percent, but from 1973 to 1977, with the swift growth in oil exports, the Ecuadorian GDP grew at an annual rate 8.7 percent. Total national economic output increased from $4.3 billion in 1970 to $10 billion in 1979. Per capita GDP increased from $260 in 1970 to $1,668 in 1981, as Ecuador rose from being one of the poorest nations in Latin America by this measure to the middle of the pack, or about equal with Colombia and Peru.

The oil was owned by Ecuador, the revenues from sales flowing directly to the state. For the first time in the nation's history, government in Quito enjoyed an independent source of money, and with this came political autonomy. The national government in Quito was no longer dependent on revenues collected at the customhouse in Guayaquil. Political power in Ecuador shifted away from the coast. The share of national government revenue from oil sales increased from about one-third in 1973 to nearly two-thirds by 1975. Total government income increased dramatically, quadrupling from 1971 to 1977. Public spending rose at the astonishing rate of 12 percent each year from 1972 to 1982, increasing from one-fifth of GDP to a third of GDP.

Although Ecuador owned the oil, foreign capital played a central role in production and export. This was the first time in Ecuador's history that foreign money was essential to the development of its key export. U.S.-based Texaco-Gulf carried out the most expensive operations, undertaking nearly all the exploration and drilling for oil. Rodríguez Lara consistently sought Ecuadorian control of the oil industry and took a critical step toward this objective when he named Gustavo Jarrín Ampudía, a former navy captain, to head the Corporación Estatal Petrolera Ecuatoriana (CEPE, the Ecuadorian State Oil Corporation) in 1972. Jarrín, who served as head of CEPE from 1972 to 1974, revised the terms under which foreign, principally U.S., companies could operate in Ecuador, putting in place new, retroactive oil taxes; increasing state royalties on exports; and renegotiating all foreign concessions—by 1973 more than 13.8 million acres of oil land had been handed back to Ecuador. Jarrín pushed to build state-owned refineries (the first came on line in 1976), acquire state-owned oil tankers, and capture 51 percent Ecuadorian control of the powerful Texaco-Gulf consortium. Under Jarrín's leadership Ecuador joined the Organization of Petroleum Exporting Countries (OPEC) in 1973, and in 1974 he served as OPEC president when the organization met in Quito.

Rodríguez Lara wanted the Ecuadorian people to benefit directly from the oil windfall, but the policies he adopted did not and could not accomplish this. He failed to use the oil revenues wisely. Property taxes and other key imposts on the elites actually fell during the oil boom, as, in effect, the military government substituted oil revenues for taxes on the rich. These policies led to increasing income concentration. The military regime also sharply increased defense expenditures, an especially wasteful choice, given that relations with Peru were very much improved at the time.

Under the military government the state's role in the economy reached its zenith. The military sought to "sow the oil," using petroleum revenues to foster long-term economic growth. The government took over whole or partial ownership of a wide array of economic activities: oil certainly; telephone service; electricity and gas utilities; airlines; the fishing industry; leading sectors of agriculture, including sugar, dairy, fertilizers, and seed production; tourism; textiles; munitions; hotels; travel agencies; banks; and the fledgling steel industry. The state also used oil revenues to build infrastructure, but the key beneficiaries were the wealthy entrepreneurs with the best connections to the government, and the junta even made loans available at negative interest rates to the business elite. As of result of these policies Ecuador experienced some small growth in industrialization, and by 1980 industry contributed one-fifth of the nation's GDP. Still, this was not as much as in the rest of Latin America, where industry contributed a quarter of GDP.

Ecuador's program of state-led development cannot be judged a success. The military had acquired mostly cash-hemorrhaging enterprises, the generals seemingly specializing in buying up private concerns that were about to go under. Not surprisingly, government spending raced ahead of even the swiftly rising oil revenues. (In fact, the government spent *projected* oil money even before the pipeline was finished.) With outlays outpacing revenues by about 20 percent, the military turned to foreign borrowing to cover even day-to-day government operating expenses.

Meanwhile, the military's social reform efforts floundered. Emblematic in this regard was the troubled 1973 land reform. Rodríguez Lara proposed a worthwhile measure, but the landowning elite managed to gut the proposal and kill the reform impulse, using, as David Corkill and David Cubitt put it, "a combination of political pressure, economic sabotage and violent thuggery which included the murder of peasant union leaders."[14] Rodríguez Lara's resulting 1973 land reform proved even more feeble than the 1964 effort (that of the military regime that ran Ecuador in 1963–66). In its principal failings the 1973 law surely resembled that of 1964: making available mostly marginal land that nobody wanted; taking land only from those lacking political connections; and failing to provide government support for the few who actually got land. As before, the state made no provision for assistance with seed, fertilizer, water, or credit. By the late 1970s most of those who had received land had already sold it back to the large landowners. By the 1980s 80 percent of the landowners in Ecuador controlled only 15 percent of the arable land, while the richest 5 percent of landowners held 55 percent of the croplands. After two land reforms the land tenure situation remained much as it had been before; Ecuador continued to have one of the most unfair land distributions in all Latin America. In Ecuador, land reform left most people landless.

Rodríguez Lara had sought to follow the path of progressive reform set by the military government of Velasco in Peru, but Rodríguez Lara was no Velasco. Rodríguez Lara's attempted reforms—land for the landless, benefits for workers—failed because Rodríguez Lara never really tried to establish popular support for this progressive agenda. Rodríguez Lara could just not bring himself to trust ordinary people. He feared popular organizations.

In 1972 the elites had begged the military to remove Velasco Ibarra from office and prevent Assad Bucaram from becoming president. But the elites found the military government disappointing as well. The elites were hard to please. Nothing Rodríguez Lara did for business seemed enough, not the tax breaks he doled out, not the easy credit, nothing. Instead, the elites objected to the state's increasing role in the economy: under Rodríguez Lara the public sector's contribution to the Ecuadorian economy had grown from 16 percent in 1972 to 23 percent in 1976, reaching its highest level ever. Moreover, Rodríguez Lara's efforts at social reform—for all their failings—had frightened the elites. And although workers and peasants were not effectively organized, Ecuador's rich merchants, large landowners, and nascent industrialists—the forces of capital—*were* organized. Together, they united in opposition to Rodríguez Lara. And because he had done so little to secure popular support for his social reform policies, when the organized elite interests attacked these programs, almost no one defended them.

The elites were most concerned about being shut out of policy making. As the political scientists Catherine Conaghan and James Malloy note: "The military did not set up formal channels through which business interest groups could participate in key decisions concerning the economy. These frustrations led the domestic bourgeoisie to search for a political alternative to military authoritarianism and for an economic model that embodied their . . . vision of capitalism."[15] The elites wanted more reliable access to government decision makers.

The elites began calling for a "return" to democracy, although what they clearly had in mind was a return to the highly restricted form of democracy that Ecuador had before the coup. Elites were betting that their money would give them influence in political decision making under a civilian authority; they had a good deal of experience at dominating and controlling these governments and were willing to take their chances again. The elites reasoned that they really had little to fear from

allowing some democracy; the popular elements were so poorly organized that they posed little threat. Whatever the exact details were of
the economic policy that might emerge, the elites knew that its main
dimensions would be something they liked, for they knew that they
would play the major role in creating it. So elite interests began calling,
somewhat disingenuously, for a return to greater political freedom, an
appeal designed to draw other groups to their cause. What the elites
were after was a political opening wide enough that they could push
in, but one not so wide as to allow unmanageable popular elements to
gain entrance. But once the door of popular political participation was
ajar, the masses would shove it open the rest of the way.

## The Texaco-Gulf Production Boycott
## and the Fall of Rodríguez Lara

Popular elements joined in opposing the military government for
several reasons, not least of which was the slumping economy. What
triggered the downturn was a drop in production. Drilling and pumping were largely in the hands of foreign firms, especially Texaco-Gulf,
and under Gustavo Jarrín CEPE's regulations had become quite tough,
with laws now so restrictive that U.S. and other foreign oil companies
refused to drill for or extract oil. Seeking to deal with the crisis, Rodríguez Lara fired Jarrín in 1974, but Texaco-Gulf was not assuaged.
In 1976 the company gave up and pulled out altogether, saying that
restrictions made it impossible to earn a reasonable profit.

Because of the problems with Texaco-Gulf, Ecuador's oil exports fell
by half in 1975, which caused government revenue to fall by half. To
deal with the budgetary shortfall, the Rodríguez Lara government adopted a wide array of austerity measures that hit the popular classes
the hardest. As anger with Rodríguez Lara spread, the elites spearheaded the protest movement, broadcasting widely their message of
opposition. Because Ecuador's was not a Southern Cone–style military
regime—there was no crackdown on public expression; free press and
free speech continued largely unabated—the elites were able to amply

ventilate their views in the newspapers and on radio and television, providing a steady din of anti–Rodríguez Lara broadsides. This effort worked, and the poor joined the elite in opposition to Rodríguez Lara, staging a massive general strike in November 1975. At the same time those elites with liquid assets began to transfer their money out of Ecuador, deepening the economic crisis.

As protests mounted, the military became divided, with the younger officers backing Rodríguez Lara, while the older, conservative, higher-ranking officers wanted him out. In August 1975 Gen. Raúl González Alvear instigated a coup—the "funeral parlor revolt" (the operation was planned in a funeral parlor)—against Rodríguez Lara. General González led his troops into central Quito and launched an all-out armed assault on the Presidential Palace. González and his men managed to seize the building but in the process killed about one hundred people, mostly civilians who happened to be shopping when the soldiers began firing automatic weapons in the crowded downtown. Tipped off in advance, Rodríguez Lara was not in Quito at the time, having fled to Riobamba, miles away. González had missed his quarry. Moreover, by taking the Presidential Palace at such a high cost in lives, González had squandered any possible support for his coup, either in the military, among leading elite groups, or with the public. González gave up and slid off into exile.

But now it was becoming clearer that much of the military itself had tired of Rodríguez Lara. High-handed and idiosyncratic, Rodríguez Lara had alienated too many of his fellow officers. The second coup attempt, led by Rear Adm. Alfredo Poveda Burbano in January 1976, proved successful. Once in power, Poveda Burbano and the military leadership (1976–79) promised a quick return to civilian government. The military government turned its attention to replacing reformers with hard liners, disciplining labor, breaking strikes, and quashing demonstrations. Its most notable effort in this regard was the crushing of the sugar workers' strike at El Aztra in October 1977 that resulted in one hundred deaths. The military government pulled land reform off life support in 1977, with all pending land tenure cases decided in favor of the large landowners.

Despite the change in military leadership, the economic situation continued to deteriorate. Oil prices commenced a long downhill slide, and new oil finds became less frequent. Even though oil production rebounded by 1979, equaling 1973 levels, Ecuador's oil exports fell off, as artificially low domestic oil prices encouraged consumption. In 1972 nearly all of Ecuador's oil was exported; by 1979 only half was. As the economy unraveled, the military prepared to return to its barracks but not before going on a lavish last-minute spending spree with borrowed money. Ecuador's foreign debt rose twenty times over, from $209 million in 1970 to $4.2 billion by 1980. Debt servicing as a percentage of exports rose from 5 percent in 1977 to 23 percent by 1981, with two-thirds of the debt owed to U.S. banks. The military was leaving, the oil boom was coming to an end, and the nation was deeply in debt.

## The Transition toward Democracy

Into the 1970s Ecuadorian politics, as Anita Isaacs has noted, was "dominated by the traditional oligarchy . . . remarkably skilled at stymying the efforts at reform . . . that other Latin-American countries had pursued during the postwar era."[16] Yet Ecuador's exclusionary oligarchic system of political dominance was beginning to break down. Nascent industrialization, spurred by government policies, helped to create new groups—some industrialists, a budding middle class—that made problematic the continuation of unchallenged rule by the old elites. Gradually, as pressure built for political inclusion, voting rights had to be extended to more people in Ecuador. The 1978 Constitution granted suffrage rights to illiterates, and they voted for the first time in the 1979 presidential election. In 1979, 21 percent of the population voted; in 1984, 31 percent. The number of votes cast in presidential elections rose from 850,000 in 1968 to 1.6 million in 1979, 2.6 million in 1984, and 4 million in 1988.[17]

Across Latin America military governments retreated in the late 1970s and 1980s; for in 1979 Ecuador was the first to move away from rule by the generals to civilian government. Yet the transition toward democracy in Ecuador was not a smooth process. When the military saw that former Guayaquil mayor Assad Bucaram ("Don Buca") of the Concentración de Fuerzas Populares (CFP) was likely to win the 1979 election, the generals attempted to halt the voting and reinstate its dictatorship. Bucaram was unacceptable. After all, the military had seized power in 1972 to prevent him from coming to power.

The generals sent several democratization movement leaders into internal exile in the Amazon, and Washington made plain its disapproval. President Jimmy Carter (1977–81) dispatched his wife, Rosalynn, in 1977 to lend her voice to the call for a return to civilian government and the construction of democracy. This action came as President Carter was seeking to take U.S. foreign policy in a new direction, emphasizing human rights. Carter cut aid to Latin American nations judged guilty of human rights violations: Argentina, Bolivia, Chile, Guatemala, Haiti, Nicaragua, and Uruguay. While the Ecuadorian generals had been nowhere near as brutal as their Southern Cone counterparts, they had to be careful about overtly throttling the budding democracy movement in Ecuador, given Carter's foreign policy stance on human rights.

The Ecuadorian military found something of a compromise solution. Democracy could go forward, but Bucaram would not. The military government announced that Assad Bucaram was not eligible to run for president because his parents were not Ecuadorian citizens when he was born. This was true, for although Assad Bucaram was born in Ecuador his parents had been born in Lebanon. However, the 1978 Constitution stipulated only that the president be Ecuadorian born, and Bucaram was. Nevertheless, the military's decision was final: Bucaram was out.

The CFP ran a stand-in, Jaime Roldós Aguilera, a Guayaquil attorney and political unknown. What recommended Roldós was that he was Bucaram's nephew-in-law. Roldós's unofficial campaign slogan became "Roldós to the presidency, Bucaram to power." Roldós and his vice presidential running mate, Osvaldo Hurtado Larrea, a sociology professor from Catholic University in Quito and a socialist, won the election handily, taking 68 percent of the vote and defeating the conservative candidate, Sixto Durán Ballen. Bucaram also won an election, assuming the presidency of the congress. Most people, especially Bucaram, figured he would be the real power in Ecuador, Roldós a mere figurehead. Roldós did not agree.

## Conclusions

For Ecuador the discovery of oil had promised to change everything. But in some ways old patterns reasserted themselves. As with the cacao and banana eras, the rise of oil exports was a return to the familiar boom-bust cycle. Riches poured in, popular expectations soared, and some profited handsomely. But then, as before, prices collapsed, fortunes disappeared, and hopes deflated.

But in other respects something new was happening in Ecuador. The oil economy had quickened the pace of change in the Ecuadorian social structure, a process that had been accelerating during the century. This development, along with the relentless push of population growth and urbanization, was stimulating the creation of significant new groups and classes: a stronger industrial and commercial elite, a growing middle class, and the great mass of urban poor. These groups were getting too large and powerful to ignore. The old elite could no longer hold back the unstoppable pressure for political inclusion: mass democracy came to Ecuador. The United States under Jimmy Carter aided this process, and democracy went forward in Ecuador due at least in small measure to U.S. support. Especially for ordinary people in Ecuador, the achievement of democracy was a victory of historic proportions. Yet victories can be fleeting. In recent years democracy has come under serious threat in Ecuador, and U.S. economic power has come to play a decisive role in this most troubling development.

# 7 Democratization and Neoliberalism: The 1980s to the Present

The cold war ended with the collapse of the Soviet Union in 1991, and U.S. foreign policy became preoccupied with other issues. One leading U.S. concern in Latin America was the production and export of illegal drugs. However, the United States focused its attention on the nations that supply and process cocaine, Colombia, Peru, and Bolivia, not on Ecuador, which took part only in the money-laundering part of the trade. Another key U.S. concern in Latin America was undocumented immigration, but U.S. efforts concentrated on Mexico, the leading source of immigrants. As in the past, U.S. foreign policy concerns did not center on Ecuador.

But this did not mean that Ecuador did not experience U.S. power, for it surely did. However, when Ecuador had been subjected to U.S. power in the past, the instrument of application was usually the U.S. government. During the cold war the U.S. government sold or denied the sale of arms, the U.S. government supplied or cut off economic aid, and the U.S. government sent the CIA to shape political outcomes. What changed in the closing decades of the twentieth century was that U.S. power and influence became more economic than political. Now U.S. economic power, not its political power, came to most affect Ecuador.

Like most Latin American nations, Ecuador fell deeply into debt in the 1970s and early 1980s. In those years U.S. banks, flush with money, looked to Latin America as a good place to invest. Interest rates fell, and bank loan officers made arrangements for loans amazingly easy, so across Latin America government after government borrowed heavily. In 1982, however, the overextended Mexican economy collapsed, and suddenly the days of easy money were over for Latin America. With the disaster of the Mexican debt crisis, new loans to Latin America dried up and interest rates climbed sharply. For Latin America and Ecuador this meant serious financial problems. The money they had borrowed was all gone—sometimes spent wisely, more often squandered or stolen, but gone—leaving only bottomless debt. The interest due on the foreign debt had to be paid; default would lead only to certain and complete economic ruin. Not paying was not a realistic option. The trouble was (and is) that Ecuador and other Latin American nations did not have the money to service their debts, leaving them with no choice but to borrow more money to pay the interest due.

But before Ecuador and other Latin American nations could get new loans from U.S. commercial banks to pay the interest due on their debts, they had to carry out the economic reforms that the international banking community believed were necessary to make these countries sound credit risks. What U.S. and international lenders wanted was fiscal austerity and the adoption of free-market economic policies. Enforcement of these loan conditions was handled, indirectly, by the International Monetary Fund. All Latin American states were expected to enter into an accord with the IMF before getting new loans from U.S. commercial banks, and getting an agreement with the IMF required adoption of "structural adjustment policies," that is, fiscal austerity and free-market economic policies. With the latter in place the IMF would then extend a small loan to the nation, signaling the IMF's stamp of approval. This would, in turn, make lending available from the large commercial banks, usually headquartered in the United States.

IMF conditions were strict. The IMF required Latin American nations to adopt tough austerity measures, slashing spending to free up resources to pay the interest on the foreign debt. Moreover, borrower nations were required to set in place a comprehensive array of economic policies designed to reform their overall financial systems. These measures (termed *neoliberalism* in Latin America) were like the Kemmerer missions' recommendations of years before: they reflected the economic orthodoxies of the day. Neoliberalism involved the adoption of free-market economic policies of the sort generally championed by President Ronald Reagan (in word if not always in deed). For Latin America this meant privatizing state-owned firms, cutting government spending, raising taxes, elimi-

nating government subsidies and price controls, lowering tariffs, opening the market to foreign investors, and paying the interest due on the
debt—in a word, less government interference in the economy, a "new"
version of the classical liberalism of John Stuart Mill, David Ricardo,
and Adam Smith, ergo neoliberalism. These economic measures, championed by nearly all the leading financial and political authorities in the
United States, came to be known as the "Washington Consensus."

Ecuador and other Latin American nations had no choice but to enter
into these agreements with the IMF. Given the necessity of continuing to
make service payments on their foreign debt, they had no other option.
The implications of this imperative were extraordinary. For Ecuador it
meant that all major economic decisions and many minor ones were
made in Washington, D.C., where they would be handled by economic
experts at the IMF and World Bank, disciples all of the new economic religion of neoliberalism. The key decisions for any government are economic ones: taxing, spending, the rules for commerce. Removing these
decisions to the United States meant a serious loss of freedom of action
for Ecuador. In short, it meant dependency.

Although the IMF would force Ecuador to adopt neoliberal economic
policies, in truth it did not always have to. Many recent Ecuadorian
presidents have shown an authentic enthusiasm for neoliberalism, just
as during the cold war Ecuadorian leaders were sometimes dedicated
and true believing anti-Communists. As Jeanne Hey notes, Ecuadorian
and U.S. leaders often shared the same outlook and goals because they
had "similar upbringing, education, [and] culture."[1] In this sense neoliberalism in Ecuador was overdetermined. If a nation is forced to do
something, has no choice but to do it, and, as it turns out, also wants to
do it, *it will do this thing.* This chapter focuses on the ways in which the
debt and U.S. economic influence have in the recent past served to determine the direction of key Ecuadorian political and economic decisions.

## The Commercial and Social Context

The last decades of the twentieth century saw the emergence of
new exports for Ecuador but the continuation of old patterns of trade.

Commerce with the United States continued as before: the United States provided about a third of Ecuador's imports and bought a third to two-thirds of its exports. But within this trade some new Ecuadorian exports appeared. Along Ecuador's southern coast a shrimp exporting business developed in the 1970s and continues to grow today. In the sierra the cut flower industry, especially roses, emerged as Ecuador's fastest-growing new export. But Ecuador's leading exports remained traditional ones: bananas and oil. The banana industry continued its recovery, and by 2000 Ecuador had regained its place as the world's top banana producer. And despite some sharp drops in price at times, oil remained Ecuador's leading money maker, even if Ecuador has never supplied more than 0.5 percent of the world's oil.[2]

Tourism was another bright spot in the economy, as the Galápagos Islands emerged as a mecca for U.S. and Western European biology students and favored tourist destination, attracting about sixty-six thousand visitors every year. Expatriate remissions provided another important source of income for the Ecuadorian economy. Today as many as 2.5 million Ecuadorians make their homes in the United States, even though the emigrants typically have to pay $10,000 to $12,000 to smugglers to guide their clandestine and undocumented entry into the United States. The money they send home, roughly $1.4 to $1.6 billion a year, is Ecuador's second-largest source of foreign income.

For the most part Ecuador continued its twentieth-century demographic and social trends. Its population growth rate slowed but only modestly, dropping from 2.2 percent a year from 1982 to 1990 to about 2 percent in 2005. The nation's population continued to increase, from 10.8 million in 1991 to 12.4 million in 2000. Urbanization maintained its steady advance, with Guayaquil's population increasing from 1.9 million in 1995 to more than 2.5 million in 2002. Quito's population reached 1.6 million in 2002.[3]

Sprawling slum districts, filled with the homes of the many un- and underemployed, dotted the edges of both cities. Workers in the formal sector of the urban economy were in the clear minority; most people had to scratch out a living as best they could in the informal sector. But conditions in the rural zones were even worse. In the 1990s, 83 percent of the land was held by the wealthiest 20 percent of landholders, whereas the poorest 40 percent owned but 3 percent of the land. In Ecuador as a whole the richest 10 percent of the population took home 54.7 percent of the national income in 1997, while the poorest one-fifth of Ecuadorians were earning less than ever: in 1988 the poorest 20 percent took home 2.55 percent of national income but only 1.68 percent in 1993. Per-capita income did not grow in real terms from the 1980s forward.[4]

This great social inequality was at the core of Ecuador's widespread poverty and appalling health conditions. Clean drinking water remained scarce and expensive for most people. Across Ecuador only about half of the homes were hooked up to sanitary waste systems. Getting enough food, and especially animal protein, was a daily struggle for most families. Even today about two of every three Ecuadorian children do not get enough to eat. Ecuador was not a land devoid of resources. Oil, the leading export, had brought Ecuador about $32 billion between 1972 and 2005. Yet for all this wealth it was hard to see how ordinary people were better off. The nature, structure, and pattern of growth of the economy did not bring solutions to Ecuador's social dilemmas, nor did the programs and polices of Ecuador's political leaders.

## Roldós, Hurtado, and the United States

When Jaime Roldós Aguilera took office in August 1979, he was only thirty-eight years old (the youngest leader in the hemisphere), and his vice president, Osvaldo Hurtado Larrea, was thirty-nine. The tasks facing Ecuador's nascent democracy and young leaders were daunting. Ecuador confronted rapid inflation (15 percent in 1981; 63 percent in 1983), the declining value of the sucre (32 sucres to the U.S. dollar in 1981; 100 sucres to the dollar by 1983), lower oil prices, vast and growing trade deficits, increased gasoline consumption (rising 10 to 15 percent each year), decreasing oil exports, and the real danger that Ecuador might again become a net oil importer. In 1982 the economy grew at an anemic 1 percent (the per-capita GDP *fell* 4 percent that year); in 1983 the economy contracted by 3 percent; and in 1984 the economy was stagnant, with growth less than 1 percent. But by far the biggest economic concern was Ecuador's breathtaking public debt, a burden that was swiftly becoming unmanageable. In 1981 Ecuador's foreign debt totaled $5.868 billion; in 1982, $6.633 billion; and by 1983 it had reached $7.381 billion. The debt equaled roughly twice the amount of annual exports. Debt service payments totaled 30 percent of export earnings. Nearly all Latin American nations had acquired sizable debts, but Ecuador's situation was extreme. In 1975 Ecuador's debt had been 12.4 percent of its GDP, whereas in Latin America as a whole it was 18.8 percent of GDP. But by 1980 Ecuador's debt had reached a stunning 52.2 percent of GDP, while in Latin America as a whole it was 34.1 percent.[5]

The government had to try something, and Roldós thought austerity was the best remedy. One thing certainly would have to change: price controls made gas prices in Ecuador among the least expensive in the world. Roldós addressed the situation by tripling gas prices. But the Ecuadorian congress, led by Assad Bucaram, wanted economic policy to take a different direction and passed a spate of laws calling for generous wage hikes, a shorter workweek, and the like. Roldós replied with vetoes. The public answered with general strikes, the first coming in May 1981. As members of the legislature traded insults and on one occasion gunfire (two wounded, none dead), the conflict immobilized government. Roldós's agenda was sidelined; he concentrated his energies on killing bills that Bucaram had pushed through the congress. What emerged was essentially a battle of wills, but the callow Roldós did not know what to do with his determined and crafty uncle-in-law, Bucaram.

Then, on May 24, 1981, President Roldós, his minister of defense, and the president's staff were all killed in an airplane crash in the Andes. As provided by the Constitution, Vice President Osvaldo Hurtado of Riobamba became president of Ecuador (1981–84). But like Roldós, Hurtado was overwhelmed with trying to deal with Ecuador's financial predicament. Oil sales and government revenues were plummeting; the nation's economy was in a tailspin. In a television address to the nation Hurtado summed up the situation: "It is necessary to come to the conclusion that the petroleum is *finished* and as a consequence, we must forget the lavish spending that characterized the 1970s."[6] Hurtado saw no choice but to violate Ecuador's agreement with OPEC, selling 50 percent more oil than its allotted sales quotient. In August 1982 Hurtado allowed U.S. investors easier access to Ecuadorian markets, hoping to attract new money to drill for oil. Although he once had been critical of the U.S. oil companies that were operating in Ecuador, he had changed his mind. He realized he would get no new oil exploration without their help.

But for Hurtado and Ecuador everything was going wrong. In 1982–83 an el niño arrived, flooding the coastal regions and reducing the nation's agricultural output by almost a third. Ecuador's banking structure teetered on the edge of collapse. In an attempt to bring government spending in line with lower revenues, Hurtado deepened Roldós's austerity measures, triggering massive strikes and protests in September and October 1982. Hurtado declared a nationwide state of emergency, but the troubles continued. In 1983 food prices increased 80 percent, and the sucre lost half its value against the U.S. dollar.

Meanwhile, the stalemate with the congress continued. Legislators wanted to spend more on social programs, while Hurtado was trying to rein in spending. And he had other political enemies, especially big business. In some ways the depth of business's enmity toward Hurtado is hard to understand. True, he tried to balance the budget by actually enforcing the tax code and charged about seven hundred businesses with cheating on their taxes. But in other ways Hurtado was good to the business community, *very* good. He delivered into the hands of business a spectacular windfall in 1983 when he allowed them to use depreciated sucres to repay debts owed in dollars (the "sucretization" of the debt). This policy saved the wealthiest Ecuadorians from considerable losses at the expense of greatly increasing the nation's public debt. Yet these actions did not win Hurtado the favor of Ecuador's business interests. They just could not bring themselves to trust this leftist university professor. Elites called loudly for Hurtado's removal from office, actively seeking to recruit members of the military to do the deed.

## The IMF, Neoliberalism, and Hurtado

What Roldós and now Hurtado were attempting to deal with in Ecuador was part of a larger problem, the Latin American debt crisis of the

1980s.[7] The origins of Latin America's deteriorating economic situation were complex and reached far beyond the region. In 1973–74 and in 1979–81 OPEC had cut oil exports, resulting in much higher prices for gasoline and, in turn, vast profits for oil-exporting nations. These nations, seeking the safest place for their new earnings, deposited their money in U.S. banks. For the U.S. banks that took in these "petrodollars," these sums would count in their ledgers as debits unless the money could be loaned out to generate interest payments. And so the rush was on to find someone to borrow all this money (and pay interest). To the banks Latin America seemed like the next rising star, a real "go-go" area, and a good place to dump the money. Moreover, Latin American nations would pay higher interest rates than would industrialized borrowers.

Latin America's foreign debt rose from $30 billion in 1970 to $240 billion in 1980. The money was not hard to borrow and so easy to spend—how could anyone say no? The money disappeared fast, poured into massive and often questionable projects, doled out to cover day-to-day government operating expenses, or just stolen, spirited away to offshore accounts. Then the day of reckoning suddenly arrived, far sooner than anyone could have guessed. U.S. President Ronald Reagan and Paul Volker, president of the Federal Reserve Bank, ratcheted up interest rates in order to drive the U.S. inflation rate down. Latin America had been banking on low interest rates and high inflation, both of which favor borrowers. Now interest rates rose from 10 percent in 1978 to 18 percent in 1981. At the same time the prices for Latin America's exports of raw materials, including oil, fell dramatically. Latin America now had to borrow more and more money just to pay the interest due on its huge foreign debt. Latin America's total foreign debt rose from $99 billion in 1975 to $384 billion in 1985 and $431 billion by 1990.

To secure new loans from private U.S. banks President Hurtado needed to first obtain the IMF's stamp of approval, and to get this Ecuador was required to adopt severe austerity measures. Hurtado entered into an accord in October 1982, with the IMF mandating hikes in bus fares, higher prices for basic necessities, and the doubling of gasoline prices. To some it was surprising that Hurtado would take such a course of action, given his well-known views favoring income redistribution

and his purported hostility to business interests. But Hurtado had converted to neoliberalism.

Like Hurtado, business and political leaders in Ecuador and across
Latin America were increasingly captivated by the new economic religion of neoliberalism, that U.S.-born body of thought that saw everyone's salvation in free markets. The neoliberal agenda, as Conaghan
and Malloy have commented, "included an initial package of economic-
stabilization measures (currency devaluations, removal of price controls, reduction or removal of consumer subsides, . . . ) with long-term
policies to retract the role of the state from the marketplace (trade liberalization, liberalization of laws governing foreign investment, [and]
removal of protective labor laws)."[8] Economic elites and political leaders in Ecuador and Latin America were attracted to neoliberalism for
many reasons: their deep fear of the ever-expanding reach of government in state-led economies, the long-term floundering of their nations'
economies, the failure of all previous economic programs to do much
good, and the self-assured and appealingly clean philosophic purity of
neoliberalism. The trumpeting of Chile's success in using free-market
policies to improve its economic situation (success rather more apparent than real, at least to the underclass) set off a stampede to adopt
neoliberal policies across Latin America. This change, from the state-
directed Import Substitution Industrialization policies to wide-open
free-market neoliberalism, marked, as the political scientists Jeanne
Hey and Thomas Klak have put it, a truly "massive reorientation" in
economic policy in Latin America.[9]

In 1983 President Hurtado called for a meeting of debtor nations, the
Latin American Economic Conference (Conferencía Económica Latino-
americana). The United States and other industrialized nations were
not invited. But Hurtado, wary of angering the United States, promised
U.S. officials that the purpose of the meeting was not to form a debtors'
cartel. Quite the contrary, Hurtado said, this was a meeting to find ways
of *paying* the debt. Hurtado traveled to the United States to reassure
creditors, and one month before the conference Ecuador sent a delegation to Washington, D.C., to discuss its debt. Negotiators reached a bilateral deal on debt repayment just before the Quito debtors' conference.

Twenty-seven nations attended the two days of meetings in January 1984. Present were the secretary general of the Organization of American States (OAS), Alejandro Orfila, and the secretary general of the U.N., Javier Pérez de Cuellar. The tone of the meetings was clear: the conferees blamed the United States for Latin America's debt crisis. But the meeting produced nothing tangible. There would be no collective action; debtor nations continued to negotiate bilaterally with the banks. The final document that emerged from the meeting, the "Declaration of Quito," offered nothing but empty words. It was another illustration, as Hey put it, that "Latin American debt initiatives . . . rarely move . . . beyond rhetoric to meaningful proposals that creditors would sincerely consider."[10] After the meeting Hurtado sent Galo Plaza, the former president who was a long-time admirer of the United States, to Washington to discuss the Ecuadorian debt situation. President Reagan refused to meet with him.

On another front Hurtado showed some independence in foreign policy by denouncing U.S. actions against the socialist government in Nicaragua. This position was in keeping with the earlier stance taken by President Roldós, who had recognized the new regime in Managua. Both Roldós and now Hurtado rejected Reagan's view that Soviet or Cuban influence was behind the rise of left-wing movements in Nicaragua and Central America. Hurtado freely criticized the U.S. support for the *contras*, the guerrillas seeking to overthrow the Nicaraguan government.

Hurtado's defiant attitude brought no reprisals from the United States, and Washington made no effort to bully Ecuador into supporting its position. While Hurtado did discontinue the Roldós policy of providing financial support for the Sandinistas, it would be a mistake to read this as the result of Reagan administration pressure on Ecuador. The truth is that as much as Hurtado disliked the *contras*, he also had little use for the Sandinistas. Hurtado did not approve of revolutionaries and refused to help fund the Sandinistas for that reason. As Hey notes, "There is no evidence that the Reagan administration linked Hurtado's policy towards Nicaragua to US economic or diplomatic relations with Ecuador."[11] Ecuador was just too small for its opinion on this to matter much to Washington.

Hurtado came to the end of his term beleaguered by critics on all sides. Despite his embrace of neoliberal economic policies, the business community, especially those in the chambers of commerce in Guayaquil and Quito, harbored a deep hatred of the president. The elites in Ecuador lobbied the military ceaselessly to overthrow the Hurtado government. Hurtado had no real support from any important sectors; his economic measures killed his popular support but were not enough to win the backing of business. As Hurtado commented: "There isn't a cocktail party or a social event where there are members of the armed forces in which some civilians don't try to initiate a conspiracy to overthrow the constitutional regime."[12] Despite such promptings, the Ecuadorian military decided not to act, perhaps influenced by strong signals from the United States that it would oppose any coup attempt against Hurtado. In the end Hurtado was content just to finish out his term, taking at least a step toward the consolidation of democracy in Ecuador.

## Febres Cordero, Neoliberalism, and the United States

President León Febres Cordero (1984–88) followed Hurtado in office and attempted a new approach to the same problems. Campaigning under the slogan of *"Pan, Techo, y Empleo"* (Food, Housing, and Jobs), Febres Cordero, a self-made millionaire and chief officer of the Noboa Group, the richest company in Ecuador, offered himself as an ordinary guy, a man of the people, indeed, the Marlboro cowboy: he arrived at political gatherings on horseback, and his campaign posters featured him waving a white hat from atop a horse. Febres Cordero won the presidential runoff election in May 1984, defeating center-left candidate Rodrigo Borja, 52 percent to 48 percent.

Ecuador's economic situation worsened in the Febres Cordero years: the mid-1980s drop in world oil prices led to the greatest economic decline in Ecuador since the Great Depression. Oil prices had peaked in 1980 at $35 a barrel before fading to $11 in 1986, when petroleum made up 60 to 70 percent of Ecuador's export earnings.[13] Oil exports earned $1.8 billion in 1985 but fell to $900 million in 1986 and dropped to $700 million in 1987. The Ecuadorian economy stopped growing; in 1987 the GDP actually *contracted* by 9.5 percent. For the 1980s as a whole Ecuador's economy contracted at an annual rate of 0.7 percent, while that of Latin America as a whole contracted at 0.6 percent annually. For industry, which had begun to expand a bit under the Rodríguez Lara government's earlier Import Substitution Industrialization policies, growth halted too. Meanwhile, the foreign debt, owed mostly to U.S. banks, kept ballooning: in 1984, $7.596 billion; by 1987, $10.284 billion. Ecuador's debt reached an astonishing 59.3 percent of GDP in 1985; for all of Latin America it was 47.3 percent. Servicing these foreign obligations claimed nearly a third of Ecuador's export earnings.

Just one month into his administration President Febres Cordero, a free-market enthusiast, pressed for expanding the neoliberal agenda. Acting on the advice of the coterie of Ecuadorian-born but U.S.-trained economists who packed his cabinet, Febres Cordero further reduced price controls on gasoline and electricity, slashed government subsidies, decontrolled currency exchange, lowered tariffs, loosened the regulation of foreign investment, kept wage hikes below the rate of inflation (which was growing), and raised interest rates. The IMF swiftly rewarded Febres Cordero with a new loan in March 1985 and another one in 1986.

However, problems with the legislature continued under Febres Cordero, who could depend on the backing of only sixteen of its seventy-one members. The Febres Cordero neoliberal agenda was far too ambitious to attract anything near a majority in that body of individuals. Instead, the legislature was determined to obstruct Febres Cordero's attempts to govern. Aggressively asserting its right of interpellation, the congress hauled in Febres Cordero's cabinet members and subjected them to endless hearings, harsh questioning, and bitter accusations. The legislature moved to impeach Finance Minister Alberto Dahik, charging him with corruption, and so savaged him during its months-long interrogations that Dahik suffered a nervous breakdown.

The Ecuadorian congress was gaining renewed notoriety as a rather unruly deliberative body. There was always trouble, with lawmakers getting into fistfights and pulling guns. Febres Cordero responded by dispatching troops to toss in smoke bombs. But the legislature was unbowed and defiantly removed all sixteen members of the Supreme Court, replacing them with judges the legislators liked better. Febres Cordero called in tanks and troops to block the seating of the new judges. For a time Ecuador had two supreme courts, one named by the congress, another by the president.

Because of his problems with the congress, Febres Cordero found a legal loophole that allowed him to rule by decree. Under the Constitution any presidential emergency decree had the force of law if not acted upon by the legislature within two weeks. But the congress, in a state of perpetual discord, was incapable of agreeing on much of anything, least of all within two weeks, and so Febres Cordero's "emergency" decrees became law. Febres Cordero enacted the planks of his neoliberal program by decree. Democracy was in trouble in Ecuador.

Febres Cordero's foreign policy was very pro–United States, a position he came by naturally. As a young man Febres Cordero had lived in the United States when he trained as an engineer in New Jersey. Febres Cordero really liked the United States and found a soul mate in Ronald Reagan. They had frequent contact: Febres Cordero made three trips to Washington, D.C.; U.S. Secretary of State George Shultz visited Ecuador in 1985; and Reagan came to Quito in 1986. Economic ties between the nations strengthened. In 1985 Ecuador sent 57.1 percent of its exports to the United States and bought 35.1 percent of its imports from there. Under Reagan the United States provided Ecuador with an average of $55.5 million in combined military and economic aid each year from 1984 to 1987.[14]

Febres Cordero's foreign policy showed a definite pro-U.S. tilt. He backed the U.S. position against the formation of a Latin American debtors' cartel. He defied OPEC and sold more oil than allocated, something that brought U.S. approval. At the OAS Febres Cordero supported the U.S. position on Chile, helping to block a resolution condemning the dictatorship of Augusto Pinochet (1973–90). Febres Cordero entered into an accord with the United States to cooperate in operations against illegal drugs, agreeing to crack down on any production, processing, and shipments. The Reagan administration had a friend in President Febres

Cordero and rewarded Ecuador with both increased aid and with help in obtaining a generous debt renegotiation package.

In a departure from previous Ecuadorian policy Febres Cordero proved broadly supportive of U.S. actions in Central America. However, in October 1985 he suddenly and unexpectedly decided to join the Contadora Support Group, a group critical of U.S. policy in Central America. Then, curiously, Febres Cordero lashed out at Nicaragua, alleging that the Sandinistas had helped infiltrate Ecuador with leftist guerrillas. (No evidence to support this charge has ever emerged.) In reply, Nicaraguan President Daniel Ortega (1984–90) criticized Febres Cordero, saying that he was obsequious to U.S. interests and pointing out that Febres Cordero was not governing in a very democratic manner. At this Febres Cordero broke formal diplomatic relations with Nicaragua, making Ecuador the only nation in Latin America to do so.

While some have viewed the severing of Ecuadorian-Nicaraguan relations as an example of U.S. influence on Ecuadorian foreign policy, that was probably not the case. Febres Cordero's decision to break relations with Sandinista Nicaragua was, in fact, not a carefully taken one. He did not consult with his foreign policy advisers before making the move, and the action was not part of any larger or coherent policy. Ecuador never put into place any sort of economic penalties or embargo against Nicaragua. At the same time the Reagan administration never made any open effort to get Ecuador to break relations with Sandinista Nicaragua.[15]

A better explanation of what happened lies in Febres Cordero's character. Ortega's remarks sent Febres Cordero into a rage. Toward the end of a long evening of heavy drinking and stewing in his anger, he determined to hit back. In his inebriated condition Febres Cordero simply forgot that he had only recently joined the Contadora Support Group. (In 1988 incoming President Rodrigo Borja conducted a sober reassessment of the situation and reestablished relations with Nicaragua.)

Febres Cordero saw himself as a tough-minded man of action; he liked it when people called him ¡el león! (the lion). Ecuadorians referred to his authoritarian style of governing as a rambocracia. But his self-image did not always square with his actions. On March 7, 1986, Air Force Gen.

Frank Vargas Pazzos rebelled, seizing the air base at Manta (in central coastal Ecuador). Charging that top-ranking defense officials were corrupt, Vargas demanded that they be removed. Febres Cordero agreed, but after Vargas surrendered, the president backed out of the deal, and Vargas and his supporters were taken into custody at a Quito air base. There, amazingly, Vargas somehow managed to seize control of the facility and issue a call for a general uprising against the Febres Cordero government. Troops loyal to the government retook the air base on March 14, 1986, at the cost of five lives.

The congress, led by emboldened opponents of the president, granted amnesty to Vargas. Febres Cordero set his jaw and refused to release the general. In response, on January 16, 1987, troops loyal to Vargas kidnaped Febres Cordero, killing two presidential guards in the process. Holding the president at gunpoint at the Taura air base near Guayaquil, the rebels threatened to kill him on the spot unless he freed Vargas. *¡El león!* complied immediately.

Then, on March 5 and 6, 1987, a series of ten earthquakes shook the Ecuadorian sierra, killing at least a thousand people and wiping out thirty miles of Ecuador's oil pipeline. U.S. Vice President George H. W. Bush visited Ecuador shortly after the earthquakes, pledging U.S. assistance and support. Febres Cordero asked for U.S. troops too, but the Ecuadorian legislature blocked this proposal, objecting to the presence of U.S. soldiers on Ecuadorian territory. While workers labored to repair the pipeline, Ecuador lost nearly six months of oil sales. Oil exports fell 40 percent and government revenues dropped 60 percent in 1987. Ecuador had to halt all debt servicing for a time. Febres Cordero ultimately adopted a plan of holding debt-servicing payments to the level of dollars earned from exports. The IMF was quite displeased with this arrangement and cut off support. With the economy in shambles Febres Cordero backed away from his commitment to neoliberalism.

Reeling from the earthquakes, economic slide, drop in oil prices, the finance minister's impeachment, the battle over the Supreme Court, a lost plebiscite to remake the Constitution to yield more power to the executive, and his kidnaping, Febres Cordero seemed to have lost enthusiasm for his job. At the end of his term he went on a budget-busting spending spree, showering projects on Guayaquil, his home constituency, before handing over the reins of power.

## Neoliberalism from Borja to Bucaram

Following Febres Cordero in office were presidents Rodrigo Borja (1988–92), whose politics can be described as center-left, and Sixto Durán Ballen (1992–96), a rightist. These two administrations differed markedly in their stated views on neoliberalism (Durán Ballen pro, Borja con), yet both worked hard to advance free-market economic policies in Ecuador. The straightjacket of foreign debt and IMF mandates left them no choice.

This was a period of flat oil prices and an economy that was performing poorly. The GDP fell by 0.3 percent in 1989 and grew only slowly after that, up 1.5 percent in 1990, 2.2 percent in 1991, improving to 2.6 percent in 1995, before slumping back down to 1.9 percent in 1996. The contribution of oil export revenue to the national budget declined significantly, falling from 50.1 percent of all revenues in 1990 to 34.5 percent in 1994. Meanwhile Ecuador's national debt reached $11 billion in 1989 and by 1993 topped $14 billion. Measured as a percentage of GDP, the debt was a heavier burden in Ecuador than elsewhere in Latin America: in 1990 Ecuador's debt equaled 63.5 percent of GDP, whereas in all of Latin America it amounted to 41.4 percent of GDP.[16]

Ordinary people suffered from further erosion of the threadbare social safety net. Despite the advance of neoliberal policies, which slashed social programs, the state still provided some help for the poor in the form of subsidies for cooking fuel, electricity, and bus fares; gasoline still sold at half the cost it took to produce it; and the number of public employees remained large, having swelled during the oil boom from 100,000 in 1974 to 500,000 by end of the 1980s. But each new accord with the IMF brought more hikes in fuel prices, increases in telephone and electricity rates, and the easing of restrictions on foreign imports and the rules governing foreign investment in Ecuador. Government's role in the Ecuadorian economy was being steadily reduced. Public spending as a percentage of the Ecuadorian GDP fell from 31.4 percent in 1987 to 24 percent in 1994. From 1988 to 1995 Ecuador privatized eleven public enterprises (worth about US$169 million). This latest round of neoliberal measures hit hardest at the poor. Real wages had already fallen by nearly a third between 1980 and 1985, and from 1986 to 1990 they dropped another 8 percent each year. The IMF's structural adjustment program, which Ecuador adopted in 1992, led to a 50 percent decrease in the standard of living for Ecuadorian families.[17]

### Abdalá Bucaram and the Crisis of Ecuadorian Democracy

Former Guayaquil mayor Abdalá Bucaram (brother-in-law of President Jaime Roldós and the nephew of Assad Bucaram) won the 1996 presidential election, defeating Jaime Nebot, a Febres Cordero protégé. Abdalá Bucaram would open a new chapter in Ecuadorian politics, a time when widespread popular disaffection with the "Washington Consensus" led ultimately to several serious blows to Ecuadorian democratization. During his campaign for the presidency Abdalá Bucaram made a strong appeal to the Ecuadorian underclass. He was like them, he said, a person of color, someone despised by the elites.[18] At his every campaign stop Abdalá Bucaram heaped ridicule on the wealthy. Nicknamed *el loco* (the crazy person), Abdalá Bucaram made campaign appearances that were noteworthy for their offbeat style. He would arrive by helicopter and have himself lowered onto the stage dressed as Batman. Accompanied by go-go dancers in hot pants, he would break into song, offering his own renditions of popular salsa tunes. (He recorded a CD, *El loco que ama*, The Crazy One Who Loves.) As he warmed to the task, Abdalá Bucaram would strip to the waist. As he addressed the crowd, he would boast of his sexual virility, claiming that he possessed superior testicles that produced high-quality semen, in contrast, he offered, to those of his effeminate opponents. Usually joining him at campaign appearances was his running mate, Rosalía

Arteaga, a conservative, politically inexperienced thirty-nine-year-old *serrana*. When the demure Arteaga arrived on stage, Bucaram liked to reach around and hoist up her skirts so the crowd could get a look at the legs of the vice presidential candidate. Still, Abdalá Bucaram's campaign was not all spectacle. In his speeches he sharply rejected neoliberalism, and he signed agreements with labor unions denouncing the austerity measures and free-market policies. Abdalá Bucaram promised to provide government subsidies for basic food necessities, block further privatization, and promote social programs.[19]

In December 1996, four months after taking office, President Abdalá Bucaram and his leading economic adviser, Domingo Cavallo, launched a neoliberal austerity program. It radically reduced government subsidies and price controls, and by January 1997 the cost of basic goods and services had risen dramatically, with the heaviest blows landing on the nearly two-thirds of the nation that lived in poverty. Prices rose dramatically, from trolley fares (up 60 percent since Abdalá Bucaram's arrival in office), gasoline (up 245 percent), electricity (up 300 percent), and telephones (up 1,000 percent). Bucaram raised taxes and then began privatizing the two hundred remaining state-owned firms. To those who had trusted Bucaram and voted him into office, these actions looked very much like betrayal. Angry protests followed, and the president's approval rating plummeted to 5 percent by early 1997.

Abdalá Bucaram had other problems. He was corrupt. Of course, the same could be said of other Ecuadorian politicians, but Bucaram's stealing (totaling about $22 million in just seven months in office) well exceeded what Ecuadorians expected their politicians to take. More grievously, Abdalá Bucaram was stingy, refusing to share the right to steal from the Ecuadorian people with anyone who was not a close friend or family member. In his former job as mayor of Guayaquil, Abdalá Bucaram had been charged with embezzlement and drug trafficking and had been jailed for a time. Now Abdalá Bucaram and his cronies became bolder, establishing an extortion scheme at the Guayaquil customhouse, demanding huge bribes before releasing any imported goods. From this operation alone Abdalá Bucaram pocketed about $25,000 a day. He was also assessing a 10 to 15 percent kickback from any firm doing business with the government. The U.S. ambassador, Leslie Alexander, publicly criticized Abdalá Bucaram: "Ecuador is gaining a reputation for pervasive corruption."[20]

Ecuador's elites had never liked Abdalá Bucaram; despite his wealth he was never really one of them. That he in turn clearly held them in great contempt did not help matters. The elites did not trust him, figuring, probably correctly, that he was planning to use the privatizations to channel state-owned resources to his family and friends. The elites were also terrified that Abdalá Bucaram's outrageous personal conduct, his corruption, and his nepotism were going to scare off foreign money and bring the whole economy down. Abdalá Bucaram's actions, they concluded, were making a laughingstock of their nation. (For instance, Abdalá Bucaram's frequent lunch guest was Ecuadorian-born Lorena Bobbitt, who gained celebrity after cutting off her husband's penis and tossing it out a car window into a vacant lot.)

Massive anti-Bucaram marches, protests in opposition to his neoliberal economic policies, his conduct, and his corruption, became daily events. A nationwide general strike began on February 5, 1997, with two million people spilling out into the streets to demand Abdalá Bucaram's resignation. Protesters set up roadblocks on the Pan-American Highway, the only road linking the nation, and Ecuadorian economic life came to a standstill. Three former presidents, Febres Cordero, Hurtado, and Borja, called on Abdalá Bucaram to resign. Should he refuse to go, they said, the congress should impeach and remove him. The military also had concerns about Abdalá Bucaram. The generals believed that he had besmirched the reputation of the armed forces by militarizing customs collections in Guayaquil, thereby involving the military in his corruption scheme. Abdalá Bucaram also was using military personnel to pass out donated Christmas toys, but because he was stealing from this charity too, the reputation of the military was being harmed by association.

Sensing the trouble he was in, on February 6, 1997, Bucaram announced a reduction in the electricity and gas taxes and said he was thinking of suspending all the neoliberal austerity measures. But it was too little and too late. Opposition forces in the legislature had decided to oust the president. Abdalá Bucaram lacked any measurable popular support, and millions were in the streets, demanding his removal from office. He had to go. But for the congress the problem was that impeaching and removing Abdalá Bucaram would require a two-thirds majority, and the leaders did not have the votes, not even close. One option, opening up a congressional investigation into Abdalá Bucaram's corruption, was rejected. It would take too long and in the end still might not produce enough votes to remove the president. Even more serious, at least from the congress's viewpoint, was that such a probe ran the real risk of sparking a broader investigation into political corruption, something that legislators knew they would have to avoid at all cost.

So, on the evening of February 6, 1997, the congress decided, by a simple majority, to remove Abdalá Bucaram on the ground of "mental incapacity." This action violated the Constitution. The civil code of Ecuador required that a judge order a psychiatric examination before an elected official could be removed from office because of mental unfitness; it also spelled out an appeals process. But the legislature was in a hurry and so elected not to follow the mandated procedure. Indeed, the bill removing Abdalá Bucaram from office, passed by only a three-vote majority, actually said nothing about the president's mental unfitness. No psychiatric evidence of any type was presented, for there could be none: Abdalá Bucaram may have been corrupt, he may have been an extraordinarily crass and vulgar man, but he was not insane. The congress named legislative chief Fabián Alarcón as interim president, something it also had no authority to do.

On February 7, 1997, Fabián Alarcón, Vice President Rosalía Arteaga, and Abdalá Bucaram all claimed the presidency of Ecuador. Abdalá Bucaram argued that the whole thing was a set-up, that lawmakers had sold their votes to the highest bidder, getting as much half a million dollars each to vote to remove him from office (a charge that had the ring of truth). Abdalá Bucaram tried offering the military a 25 percent pay hike in exchange for its armed support, but the generals were not interested. Seeing that it was over, Abdalá Bucaram left Quito on the evening of February 7, heading into exile in Panama. The United

States was happy enough to see him gone, but Ambassador Alexander said that the United States would not be able to recognize Alarcón as president. Vice President Arteaga should assume the presidency, the ambassador said.

But the Ecuadorian legislature did not care, for it was unwilling to place Arteaga in the presidency. Angry, Arteaga declared, "They usurped my power because I was a woman."[21] This claim, too, had the ring of truth. By February 11 the congress had it all arranged: Alarcón would take over as president, Arteaga would continue as vice president, and Abdalá Bucaram was out. The legislature had its victory. But by handling this matter in such a clearly unconstitutional manner, Ecuador's leaders had done serious harm to the project of building an authentic democracy, an action that may have been much more harmful to the nation than anything Abdalá Bucaram might have done. The U.S. ambassador refused to attend Alarcón's swearing-in, calling the whole thing a farce.[22]

In the months that followed, voters approved a plebiscite that called for the convening of a constitutional convention. Delegates soon wrote a new constitution, Ecuador's eighteenth. Alarcón served as Ecuador's interim president until new elections in 1998. (Shortly after Alarcón left office, he was jailed for illegal self-enrichment.) The winner was the former Quito mayor Jamil Mahuad, who defeated the right-wing candidate Álvaro Noboa. Yet within eighteen months President Mahuad (1998–2000) had also been ousted, as Ecuador's young democracy suffered another devastating hammer blow.

## Mahuad, Neoliberalism, and the Second Crisis for Ecuadorian Democracy

Mahuad's problems were many, although not all of his own making. It was not his fault that the economy collapsed, although he was, of course, blamed for this. In 1998 the economy grew only 0.99 percent, in part because of another el niño. In 1999 the GDP dropped even further, contracting by 8 percent. Nearly half of government revenue now went just to pay the interest on Ecuador's foreign debt.

But Mahuad's actions in dealing with the economic mess were what focused most of the popular anger against him. In accordance with the IMF strictures, Mahuad cut subsidies for cooking fuel and electricity. Meanwhile per-capital income levels dropped to 1980s levels, and income became increasingly concentrated. (Ecuador today has the third most unequal distribution of income of any nation in Latin America, after Brazil and Paraguay.) The economic slide under Mahuad triggered a severe banking crisis; more than a third of the banks in Ecuador collapsed. To halt a run on the banks, Mahuad froze all accounts in 1999; depositors could not access their money for a year. When accounts were finally reopened, rampaging inflation (the sucre dropped in value about 200 percent in 1999) had dramatically reduced the value of deposits. Most people's lifetime savings vanished. Mahuad also funded a $6 billion bank bailout. For Ecuador this was a great deal of money, about a quarter of GDP. Yet despite this, the bailout money was soon all gone, as leading bankers fled the country with their bank's assets, including funds from the bailout. To many people the bank bailout looked like a giant giveaway to rich bankers. When news broke of a secret and illegal $3.1 million donation to Mahuad's 1998 election campaign by Banco del Progreso owner Fernando Aspiazu, citizens were enraged. The bank bailout looked like standard-issue political corruption, and Mahuad could provide no accounting for the money. Meanwhile, to cover the cost of the bank bailout debacle, Mahuad cut social programs for the poor by half in 1999.

Objections also arose in regard to Mahuad's foreign policy. In 1999 he signed a deal providing the United States with a ten-year lease of an air base in Manta. This facility was to replace U.S. bases in Panama (lost with the handover of the canal and canal zone at the end of that year) that were central to ongoing U.S. efforts to interdict illegal drug shipments. Under the agreement that Mahuad signed, Ecuador received no rent for use of the base, although the United States promised to spend about $67 million on improvements at the airfield and linked facilities. Nationalist critics charged that Mahuad had gotten a lousy deal, and they fiercely objected to the presence of U.S. military personnel on Ecuadorian soil.

Serious, if unfair, complaints also emerged in regard to Mahuad's handling of the border dispute with Peru. The Amazon border area had been the scene of armed clashes in 1978, 1981, 1991, and again in 1995 (the fighting in January 1981, the bloodiest, left two hundred dead). The conflict centered on the Cenepa region, a seventy-eight-mile band of territory claimed by Ecuador but held by Peru. In 1998, in what can only be described as a singular act of statesmanship, President Jamil Mahuad signed an accord with Peruvian leader Alberto Fujimori (1990–2000), ending the conflict and settling the border question. Peru generously agreed to set up an international peace park in the disputed region (territory actually granted to Peru in the 1942 treaty that Ecuador signed) and gave Ecuador permanent access to the town of Tiwintza in the region. But in some segments of Ecuadorian society sentiment ran hard against the accord, especially among die-hard nationalists in the military. They could never accept what they saw as Mahuad's act of betrayal, a land giveaway to the enemy, an insult to national honor, an affront to the memory of the brave Ecuadorian soldiers who gave their lives defending the motherland. To other observers, however, especially Americans, the settling of this age-old conflict was a great achievement, an act of wisdom and courage for which both Mahuad and Fujimori deserved considerable credit, especially because there was so little else that might be construed as worthy of praise in the actions of either leader.

## The Emergence of Indian Militancy

On January 21, 2000, junior military officers joined with Ecuadorian Indians to overthrow President Jamil Mahuad. The emergence of Indians as a key political sector in Ecuador was an astonishing new political circumstance, one that can be understood only by taking a brief look at its origins. Step by step, Indian groups' shared experiences of mistreatment and abuse led them to come together and forge a highly effective collective organization to fight for the redress of their grievances.[23]

In the 1960s the Ecuadorian government had decided it would be a good idea to relocate land-hungry *serrano* peasants in the Amazon and in 1964 established the Instituto Ecuatoriano de Reforma Agraria y Colonización (Ecuadorian Agrarian Reform and Colonization Institute), an undertaking supported with money from the Alliance for Progress. With the failure of land reform efforts in 1964 and 1973, about 145,000 squatters moved into the Amazon region in the 1970s and 1980s. A subsequent rush of migration into the Amazon coincided with the oil boom. The population of the Amazon rose from 1.5 percent of the national total in 1950 to 3.9 percent by 1990.

The migrants slashed into the jungle, clearing and burning to make room for farms. Adding to the destruction were Texaco and Corporación Estatal Petrolera Ecuatoriana (CEPE). Oil production can be sloppy business, and, all told, Texaco and CEPE spilled about seventeen million barrels of oil into the fragile ecosystem. (By way of comparison, the *Exxon Valdez* disaster in Alaska in 1989 dumped about eleven million barrels into the environment.) Texaco also followed a policy (agreed to by the Ecuadorian government) of not pumping oil by-products back into the ground after removing the oil, although reinjection was standard practice in the United States. Instead, Texaco dumped the oil by-products into nearby pits, and some leeched into adjacent streams and groundwater. Trucks also sprayed the waste material on dirt roadways. The official explanation of this practice was that the oil by-products were being used to help keep dust down, although such argument made little sense, because more than one hundred inches of rain fall in the Amazon each year. With the first downpour the oil waste and by-products flowed off in all directions. (In 1993 Indian groups tried to sue Texaco-Gulf for $1.5 billion in U.S. courts, but the matter was rejected on jurisdictional grounds. In 2005 the case was being heard in an Ecuadorian court.)

Indian groups had long sought to fight back against these intrusions and many abuses. In 1956 the Huaorani used their spears to kill five Christian missionaries, and in the late 1960s and early 1970s, when the Summer Institute of Linguistics worked with the Ecuadorian government and the oil companies to push the Indians off their land, local Indians killed a dozen oil workers and migrants. In 1987 a Catholic bishop and a nun were murdered in the region, pinned to the jungle floor with twenty-one Huaorani spears.

But the Indians' actions were more than sporadic acts of violence, as the natives of both the Amazon and the sierra came together to form groups and take collective political action. Cooperation between Indian organizations had taken place as early as 1944, and even more had been accomplished during the periods of attempted land reform. In 1986, however, the first truly national Indian organization formed, the Confederación de Nacionalidades Indígenas del Ecuador (Confederation of Indigenous People of Ecuador, or CONAIE). In June 1990 CONAIE organized a mass *levantamiento* (uprising) calling for recognition of Indians' rights and demanding social programs from government. In what became CONAIE's signature protest tactic, Indians set up roadblocks on the Pan-American Highway, cutting down trees and setting tires on fire to block the way. Roadblocks forced the government's hand: it could not allow the obstruction of the nation's main road, the only highway that tied the country together. The government might have tried to smash through the roadblocks, but this would mean violence, bring down mountains of bad press, and probably would not have worked anyway, for there were too many roadblocks to clear and it was too easy to set up new ones. So the government chose to negotiate with the Indians. The indigenous people, finding success with this tactic, used this chokehold on the nation's internal transport and commerce again and again, as CONAIE emerged as the strongest Indian organization in all Latin America. In 1997 CONAIE blocked the main highway and joined the protests that helped bring down the government of Abdalá Bucaram. In January 2000 CONAIE played the leading role in the ouster of President Jamil Mahuad.

## Conclusions

President Jamil Mahuad's approval rating fell from 66 percent in August 1998 to 2 percent in January 2000. Everyone, it seemed, wanted him out of office. In a hasty, last-ditch effort to save his rapidly collapsing presidency, Mahuad "dollarized" the Ecuadorian economy, adopting the U.S. dollar as Ecuador's national currency. If this measure made economic sense to some (it did, in time, end inflation—91 percent in 2000; 9.36 percent in 2002), Mahuad's decision to dump the sucre for the dollar was nevertheless a humiliating blow to Ecuador's national pride. Because of its debt and the role of the IMF, Ecuador had long ago surrendered control of its fiscal policy. Now, with dollarization, Ecuador gave up control of monetary policy as well.

About ten thousand Indians streamed into the capital in January 2000, staging mass protests in opposition to Mahuad. Then, on January 21, the young officers guarding the congress stepped aside and allowed the Indians to occupy the building. The junior officers, outraged by Mahuad's apparent corruption, had decided to join the opposition movement. Together they formed the three-man Junta of National Salvation to govern Ecuador, led by Col. Lucio Gutiérrez; Antonio Vargas, head of CONAIE; and Carlos Solórzano, former chief of the supreme court. Within hours, however, the coup had been hijacked by senior military officers who handed the presidency to Mahuad's vice president, Gustavo Noboa Bejarano.

As the crisis unfolded, the United States insisted that Ecuador return to democratic norms. Washington expressed its opposition to the Junta of National Salvation, applying steady public and private pressure. The State Department issued warnings that should the coup stand, Ecuador's economic and diplomatic isolation would be like Cuba's. Following Washington's lead, the OAS came out against the coup on the day it seized power. U.S. Ambassador Gwen C. Clare privately threatened the junta with diplomatic isolation, vowing to cut off aid and to discourage foreign investment unless Ecuador followed its constitution. Clare spoke three times to Gen. Carlos Mendoza on January 21 before he launched the successful countercoup.

Installed by the generals, Gustavo Noboa (2000–2003) completed Mahuad's term of office. (After leaving office, Noboa faced charges in a bond swindle and fled into exile in the Dominican Republic.) In the subsequent 2003 elections one of the leaders of the coup against Mahuad, Lucio Gutiérrez, won the presidency, bolstered by the enthusiastic support of CONAIE's political party, Pachakutik. As a candidate Gutiérrez angrily decried neoliberalism, but almost immediately upon assuming office he entered into a fresh agreement with the IMF. Gutiérrez then launched a new round of austerity measures, raising gasoline prices and bus fares, and freezing wages. Cabinet members from Pachakutik quit in disgust. CONAIE began planning protests. In Ecuador democracy evidently means the right to pick between candidates who endorse neoliberalism and will happily carry out free-market measures, and candidates like Gutiérrez who speak out against neoliberalism but once in office adopt these policies anyway.

Mahuad was the second democratically elected president of Ecuador to be ousted in the space of three years. Between the restoration of civilian rule in 1979 and today Ecuador has endured fifty-four states of emergency. Given recent events, one can only conclude that Ecuador has not succeeded in creating viable democratic political institutions and has not observed democratic procedures when changing governments. In Ecuador, it is fair to conclude, democracy is not succeeding.

Part of the problem is the structure of Ecuadorian politics. Where political parties are strong, they play a critical role as opinion articulators, forcing discipline on party members, mainstreaming views, knocking off rough edges, tempering radicalism, encouraging compromise, and shoving everyone toward the center. But in Ecuador political parties typically stand for nothing; their chief function is the distribution of patronage to loyalists. All political parties are weak, nonideological vehicles created for the purpose of advancing the aspirations of contending political hopefuls. Because fourteen to seventeen political parties usually compete in elections, and typically ten or so gain seats in the congress, the strongest party in the legislature usually holds no more than about 20 percent of the seats. Given the desperate economic context in which all available policy options look bad, legislators have found that the safest course is simply to denounce any and all proposals put forward. Whatever anyone might offer will hurt someone and probably would not work anyway. Until recent changes in the law, the favorite pastime of legislators in Ecuador seemed to be interpellating members of the president cabinet, hauling them in and hectoring them by the hour for failing to come up with solutions that would solve all of Ecuador's problems. In Ecuador all presidents fail and leave in disgrace. As Jamil Mahuad put it, "It is a historical constant in Ecuador that a president arrives, has to make tough decisions, and falls out of popular favor."[24]

When ordinary Ecuadorians imagine a government that might at least try to act on their behalf, many think back to the military government of Rodríguez Lara. The people in Ecuador tend to have "favourable perceptions of military rule," as Anita Isaacs has noted, a "nostalgia for military rule."[25] Most ordinary people in Ecuador believe that the political system responds only to those with money, that it is not for them or about them. Most Ecuadorians have little confidence in democracy and have voiced a clear preference for strong-man rule. Polls show that only about a quarter of Ecuadorians believe democracy can solve their problems, and less than half of those polled think that democracy is the best form of government.

# Epilogue

In mid-July 2006, on the eve of what proved to be yet another rancorous presidential campaign, Álvaro Noboa, twice a candidate for Ecuador's highest office, contemplated withdrawing from the race, explaining that there was little likelihood that any president could complete a four-year term.

This was a sobering reminder of the political uncertainties and dangers in seeking power in Ecuador, whose people celebrated a quarter century of civilian rule in 2004 but in the decade since 1997 witnessed nine men enter and exit the presidential office. Little wonder, then, that many Ecuadorians—some out of nostalgia for the stability of previous military governments, others out of indifference but most from a disturbingly widespread loss of belief in traditional democracy—prefer strong-man rule. In its professions the United States has historically opposed such a political choice, in Ecuador and elsewhere in Latin America, but U.S. actions and policies have sometimes undermined or certainly weakened Ecuador's political institutions.

This book has sought to trace the arc of Ecuadorian-U.S. relations from their earliest beginnings to the present. Contact between the nations, slow to develop at first, increased in the second half of the nineteenth century, but the emerging relationship was in most respects unsatisfactory to both. The early twentieth century brought more exchanges between the nations, yet although this was an era of rising U.S. power, the United States often experienced great frustration in attempting to achieve its foreign policy objectives in Ecuador. At the mid-twentieth century Ecuador and the United States found they could work together in cooperative undertakings from which each might benefit. However, most ventures ended badly, generating lingering tensions and undermining the construction of lasting goodwill between the nations.

The nature of the relationship between Ecuador and the United States underwent a decisive change in the cold war era. Whereas Ecuador had

217

formerly demonstrated an uncanny ability to deflect U.S. power, for the first time the U.S. government consistently used its considerable power advantage against Ecuador, directly intruding in its domestic affairs and shaping events more to U.S. liking. Finally, in the closing decades of the twentieth century and into the twenty-first, the relationship between the nations was again reconfigured. But while the essence of U.S. power changed, its implications did not. The end of the cold war also ended the U.S. anti-Communist crusade, and as a result pressure by the U.S. government on Ecuador subsided greatly. However, in recent years Ecuador has been forced to confront the reality of the application of U.S. economic power.

Contrary to the endless U.S. pronouncements about the post–cold war world, democracy and free-market economies are not goals in perfect harmony. All Ecuadorian leaders, willingly or otherwise, must enact neoliberal programs. They have no choice. This is the price demanded by the IMF if Ecuador is to receive new loans to pay the interest due on its vast national debt and thereby stave off default and economic catastrophe. As Hey puts it, "The International Monetary Fund . . . and the World Bank [have] assumed the role of Latin America's economic police."[1] The most important decisions any government can make are those regarding taxes and spending, and because Ecuador no long controls decisions about these critical matters, its political system cannot be regarded as a democracy. Ecuador's key decisions are now made by a handful of IMF economic "experts," neoliberal true believers, in Washington, D.C.

Today there are signs—some more concrete than others—that despite its volatile politics and economic vulnerability, Ecuador may be challenging the U.S. grip. In 2006 widespread public pressure, largely from the nation's indigenous political organizations, prompted the government to enact the Hydrocarbons Law, which requires foreign oil companies to pay a 50 percent tax on crude oil profits and respect human rights and environmental concerns. Other South American governments— Bolivia, Brazil, Colombia, Guyana, Peru, Surinam, and Venezuela— have adopted similar laws in accordance with the Andean Treaty of Cooperation. In response the United States broke off free-trade discussions, which some Ecuadorian political leaders believe are vital to the nation's future. Efforts by President Luis Alfredo Palacio González (2005–2006) to restart the talks precipitated outcries and protests from indigenous political organizations and led Ecuador to cancel its contract with Occidental Petroleum, which since 2000 had come under fire because of its operations in the country. In the minds of U.S. leaders trying to counter the growing influence in the Andean region of President Hugo Chavez of Venezuela, these and other developments made Ecuador less the "useful" and more the defiant country.

Though strained, the Ecuadorian-U.S. connection has remained, and it is not likely to be severed by the continuing economic and political conflicts between the two governments. In time, and that day may well be fast approaching, the U.S. government may acknowledge that its security and interests in Ecuador would better be served by recognizing that a less dependent Ecuador offers a firmer foundation for a more democratic Ecuador, a condition that will benefit both nations. Certainly, those who chart U.S. policy must address undeniable and disturbing features of modern Ecuador—a volatile political system, enormous environmental damages wrought by development, long-standing suspicion between the country's fractured social and cultural groups, and the crime associated with Ecuador's rapid emergence as a transit country for cocaine trafficking and money laundering.

And both U.S. and Ecuadorian leaders must place greater value on other links as well, notably the at least 200,000 Ecuadorians who live and work in the United States and whose remittances to their homeland constitute a significant and ever-growing part of the nation's foreign exchange. But perhaps the least-valued contribution of the United States is its profession of an enduring creed—self-determination—that is etched in its citizens' collective conscience since the American Revolution and that it has often unknowingly broadcast to the world. Ecuadorians have absorbed that message, however much they decry U.S. actions and policies. That should be the lasting imprint of Americanization in Ecuador if "useful strangers" are ever to become valued friends.

# Notes

The notes to this volume are used to identify the sources of quotations, data, and sections drawn closely from specific texts. Data sources are presented in composite note format.

The many materials consulted in the preparation of this book are listed and discussed in the bibliography essay at the end of this volume, arranged by period and topical category.

Note: All monetary sums in the text are expressed in dollars current for the period stated, unless otherwise indicated.

## Abbreviations

DC      *Diplomatic Correspondence of the United States: Inter-American Affairs, 1831–1860*, edited by William Ray Manning, vol. 1 (New York: Oxford University Press, 1925); vol. 2 (New York: Oxford University Press, 1925); vol. 6 (Washington, D.C.: Carnegie Endowment for International Peace, 1935); and vol. 10 (Washington, D.C.: Carnegie Endowment for International Peace, 1935).

FRUS      *Foreign Relations of the United States*

MRE-CR      Ecuador, Ministerio de Relaciónes Exteriores, *Communicaciónes recibidas de la legación del Ecuador en Estados Unidos, 1888–1893*

## Introduction

1. This section on geography is drawn especially from Preston E. James, *Latin America* (Indianapolis: Bobbs-Merrill, 1976), 428–49; Linda Alexander Rodríguez, *The Search for Public Policy: Regional Politics and Government Finances in Ecuador, 1830–1940* (Berkeley: University of California Press, 1985), 5–13; George M. Lauderbaugh, "The United States and Ecuador: Conflict and Convergence, 1830–1946" (Ph.D. diss., University of Alabama, 1997), 18–20.

2. This section on farm products produced at different elevations is drawn from Rodríguez, *Search for Public Policy,* 5–13.

## Chapter 1

1. William Eleroy Curtis, *The Capitals of Spanish America* (New York: Praeger, 1969), 309.
2. Ibid., 332.
3. Treatment of diplomatic representation in this chapter is drawn from DC, vol. 6; Jorge W. Villacrés Moscoso, *Historia diplomática de la república del Ecuador,* tecer tomo (Guayaquil: Lit. e Imprenta de la Universidad de Guayaquil, 1982); and George M. Lauderbaugh, "The United States and Ecuador: Conflict and Convergence, 1830–1946" (Ph.D. diss., University of Alabama, 1997), 17.
4. John C. Calhoun, secretary of state, to Delazon Smith, special agent of the United States to Ecuador, January 7, 1845, in DC, 6:224.
5. James Buchanan, secretary of state, to Vanburgh Livingston, U.S. chargé d'affaires at Quito, May 13, 1848, in DC, 6:224.
6. Curtis, *Capitals of Spanish America,* 304.
7. Ibid., 317.
8. As the leading Ecuadorian history scholars Rafael Quintero and Erika Silva have noted, in Ecuador, as in most nations, a national mythology has grown up around the process of independence. However, the heroic version of the story offered to Ecuadorian children in schoolbooks does not correspond very closely with actual events (Rafael Quintero Lopez and Erika Silva Ch., *Ecuador: una nación en ciernes* [Quito: Abya-Yala, 1991], 1:25).
9. Roger Davis, "Ecuador under Gran Colombia, 1820–1830: Regionalism, Localism, and Legitimacy in the Emergence of an Andean Republic" (Ph.D. diss., University of Arizona, 1983), 48.
10. Ibid., 60.
11. Ibid.
12. Ibid., 71.
13. Ibid., 80–81. The separate regional pathways to independence in Ecuador cast a long shadow that is visible even today. The people of Guayaquil continue to emphasize their city's unique and separate experience in gaining independence. In Guayaquil people celebrate independence on October 9,

the day Guayaquil became an independent city-state. The rest of the nation observes August 10 as independence day, a less important holiday in Guayaquil.

14. Arthur P. Whitaker, *The United States and the Independence of Latin America 1800–1830* (New York: W. W. Norton, 1964), 117. Whitaker writes that in the period before Latin America's independence, "both the people at large and even the authorities at Washington were woefully ignorant in regard to Latin America" (v), but after independence, U.S. interest in Spanish America rose. The era 1810 to 1830 was a time of U.S. discovery of Latin America.

15. Richard Rush, interim secretary of state, to Caesar A. Rodney and John Graham, special commissioners of the United States to South America, July 18, 1817, in DC, 1:42–43.

16. John Quincy Adams, secretary of state, to Richard C. Anderson, U.S. minister to Colombia, May 27, 1823, in DC, 1:194.

17. This policy statement did not come to be called the Monroe Doctrine until the mid-nineteenth century.

18. *El patriota de Guayaquil* (Guayaquil), July 29, 1826, 14–16.

19. José R. Revenga, secretary of state for foreign affairs of Colombia, to Richard C. Anderson Jr., U.S. minister to Colombia, March 17, 1826, in DC, 2:1294–96.

20. Beaufort T. Watts, chargé d'affaires of the United States at Bogota, to Henry Clay, secretary of state, June 27, 1827, in DC, 2:1319.

21. *El patriota de Guayaquil* (Guayaquil), July 29, 1826, 14–16.

22. *El colombiano* (Guayaquil), September 17, 1832, 570.

23. On U.S.-Ecuadorian commerce in the nineteenth century, see especially Joedd Price, "Ecuadorean Opinion of the United States in the Nineteenth Century: An Attitudinal Study" (Ph.D. diss., University of North Carolina, 1968); and Quintero and Silva, *Ecuador,* 64–65, 168.

24. Alexander McLean, U.S. consul, to the U.S. Department of State, January 24, 1880, Despatches [*sic*] from U.S. Consuls in Guayaquil, 1826–1906.

25. Demographic data from Quintero and Silva, *Ecuador,* 53–54, 77, 139, 145, 169; and Alberto Acosta, *Breve historia económica del Ecuador* (Quito: Corporación Editora Nacional, 1995), 31.

26. Delazon Smith, special agent of the United States to Ecuador, to Calhoun, Quito, August 10, 1845, in DC, 6:253.

27. Rumsey Wing, U.S. minister to Ecuador, to U.S. Department of State, August 11, 1870, Despatches [*sic*] from U.S. Ministers to Ecuador, 1848–1906.

28. Smith to Calhoun, 255.

29. See, especially, Mark J. Van Aken, *King of the Night: Juan José Flores and Ecuador, 1824–1864* (Berkeley: University of California Press, 1989).

30. Thomas P. Moore, U.S. minister to Colombia, to Martin Van Buren, secretary of state, November 28, 1830, DC, 2:1365.

31. Our understanding of this and several other leading episodes in Ecuadorian–United States relations during this period has been greatly enriched by the pathbreaking scholarship of the historian George Lauderbaugh, and new evidence that he has uncovered forms the basis of much of what follows here (Lauderbaugh, "United States and Ecuador").

32. Lauderbaugh, "United States and Ecuador," 48.

33. Ibid.

34. Smith to Calhoun, 251.

35. Ibid.

36. Ibid., 254.

37. Ibid., 251.

38. Buchanan to Stanhope Prevost, March 24, 1847, in DC, 10:238.

39. Buchanan to Livingston, in DC, 6:224–25.

40. Manuel Gómez de la Torre, minister of foreign affairs of Ecuador, to Livingston, August 31, 1848, in DC, 6:264.

41. John Trumbull Van Alen, U.S. chargé d'affaires at Quito, to John M. Clayton, secretary of state, February 1, 1850, in DC, 6:264–68.

42. Courtland Cushing, U.S. chargé d'affaires in Ecuador, to Daniel Webster, secretary of state, March 13, 1852, in DC, 6:271–74.

43. Cushing to José Villamil, minister of foreign affairs of Ecuador, February 28, 1852, in DC, 6:271.

44. Cushing to Webster, March 13, 1852, in DC, 6:271–74.

45. Cushing to Webster, April 13, 1852, in DC, 6:279–81.

46. Cushing to Webster, March 13, 1852, and May 1, 1852, in DC, 6:271–74, 281–82.

47. Cushing to Webster, June 1, 1852, in DC, 6:286–87.

48. Villamil to Cushing, June 7, 1852, in DC, 6:284–85.

49. Cushing to Webster, July 1, 1852, in DC, 6:286–87.

50. Cushing to Webster, August 1, 1852, in DC, 6:288.

51. Gen. José María Urvina, president of Ecuador, to Cushing, October 21, 1853, in DC, 6:314.

52. Aaron H. Palmer, consul general of Ecuador to the United States, to Charles M. Conrad, acting secretary of state, October 8, 1852, in DC, 6:296–97; Villamil to William L. Marcy, secretary of state, November 1, 1853, in DC, 6:316–17.
53. Marcy to Villamil, November 2, 1853, in DC, 6:231.
54. White to Marcos Espinel, minister of foreign affairs of Ecuador, July 29, 1854, in DC, 6:329–31.

## Chapter 2

1. José Villamil, minister of foreign affairs of Ecuador, to Courtland Cushing, U.S. chargé d'affaires in Ecuador, April 6, 1852, in DC, 6:275–78.
2. On the shift in Ecuadorian outlook toward the United States, see especially Joedd Price, "Ecuadorean Opinion of the United States in the Nineteenth Century: An Attitudinal Study" (Ph.D. diss., University of North Carolina, 1968).
3. Cushing to Edward Everett, secretary of state, March 1, 1853, in DC, 6:301–2.
4. Marcy to Philo White, chargé d'affaires, August 14, 1854, DC, 6:233.
5. White to Marcy, September 20, 1854, in DC, 6:335, emphasis added.
6. The issue continued to come up. In 1857 President Francisco Robles considered mortgaging or selling the Galápagos Islands to the United States in exchange for a loan. Rumors arose in 1869 and 1883 about such a sale. In 1890 Harvard professor Louis Agassiz sought permission to go to Galápagos Islands to study fish, but his request provoked suspicion that the United States was again after the islands.
7. Price, "Ecuadorean Opinion," 209.
8. George M. Lauderbaugh, "The United States and Ecuador: Conflict and Convergence, 1830–1946" (Ph.D. diss., University of Alabama, 1997), 87.
9. Ibid., 89.
10. Lawrence A. Clayton, *Peru and the United States: The Condor and the Eagle* (Athens: University of Georgia Press, 1999), 45–46.
11. Manuel Bustamente, Ecuadorian minister of foreign affairs, to William H. Seward, secretary of state, April 25, 1866, in FRUS, *1866*, 2:465–66.
12. L. V. Prevost, consul, to secretary of state, May 13, 1866, in FRUS, *1866*, 2:466.
13. Secretary of state to secretary of legation, June 5, 1866, in FRUS, *1866*, 2:470.
14. Prevost, consul, to secretary of state, July 5, 1866, in FRUS, *1866*, 2:473.

15. Manuel Bustamente, Ecuadorian minister of exterior relations, to Frederick Hassaurek, U.S. legation in Guayaquil, October 25, 1865, in FRUS, *1866*, 2:451.

16. Hassaurek, to Seward, November 12, 1865, in FRUS, *1866*, 2:448.

17. Hassaurek to Bustamente, November 1, 1865, in FRUS, *1866*, 2:452.

18. Rumsey Wing, U.S. minister, to secretary of state, December 23, 1871, in FRUS, *1872*, pt. 1, vol. 1:171.

19. Translated from quotation in Óscar Efrén Reyes, *Breve historia general del Ecuador*, tomos 2–3 (Quito: Imprenta del Colegio Tecnico Don Bosco, n.d.), 169.

20. Alexander McLean, consul, to Department of State, January 24, 1880, Despatches [*sic*] from U.S. Consuls in Guayaquil, 1826–1906.

21. *La nación* (Guayaquil), December 17, 1885.

22. William Eleroy Curtis, *The Capitals of Spanish America* (New York: Praeger, 1969), 304.

23. Shanon M. Eder, consul, to Department of State, March 15, 1879, Despatches [*sic*] from U.S. Consuls in Guayaquil, 1826–1906.

24. Martin Reinberg, acting consul, to Department of State, March 10, 1887, Despatches [*sic*] from U.S. Consuls in Guayaquil, 1826–1906; Wing to Hamilton Fish, secretary of state, December 28, 1873, in FRUS, *1874*, 393.

25. Plácido Caamaño to the Ministry of Foreign Relations, October 1889, Ecuador, MRE-CR.

26. Delazon Smith to John C. Calhoun, secretary of state, August 10, 1845, in DC, 6:255–56.

27. Quoted in Lauderbaugh, "United States and Ecuador," 83.

28. Smith to Calhoun, secretary of state, August 10, 1845, in DC, 6:254.

29. Ibid., 254–55.

30. Curtis, *Capitals of Spanish America*, 306.

31. Ibid., 333.

32. Ibid., 335.

33. Ibid., 300.

34. Ibid., 304.

35. Ibid.

36. Price, "Ecuadorean Opinion," 6.

37. Thomas Biddle, U.S. Legation in Guayaquil, to secretary of state, April 20, 1875, in FRUS, *1875*, 1:442.

38. Peter H. Smith, *Talons of the Eagle: Dynamics of U.S.–Latin American Relations* (New York: Oxford University Press, 1996), 27.

## Chapter 3

1. Data on commerce, the economy, and demographics are drawn from Ronn Pineo, *Social and Economic Reform in Ecuador: Life and Work in Guayaquil, 1870–1925* (Gainesville: University Press of Florida, 1996); Lois Weinman, "Ecuador and Cacao: Domestic Responses to the Boom-Collapse Monoexport Cycle" (Ph.D. diss. University of California, Los Angeles, 1970); and Rafael Lopez Quintero and Erika Silva Ch., *Ecuador: una nación en ciernes* (Quito: Abya-Yala, 1991), 1:163, 273, 278.

2. See, for examples, *El grito del pueblo* (Guayaquil), January 1900; *El tiempo* (Quito), April 1904; *El meridiano* (Quito), June 1904; and *El telégrafo* (Guayaquil), 1923 passim.

3. *El tiempo* (Quito), April 6, 1904, 4.

4. *El telégrafo* (Guayaquil), 1923 passim.

5. See, for examples, *El grito del pueblo* (Guayaquil), January 1900; and *El telégrafo* (Guayaquil), January 1923.

6. A. Kim Clark, *The Redemptive Work: Railway and Nation in Ecuador, 1895–1930* (Wilmington, Del.: Scholarly Resources, 1998), 91–92. Sections on demography are drawn from Pineo, *Social and Economic Reform in Ecuador;* Quintero and Silva, *Ecuador,* 249, 268; Linda Alexander Rodríguez, *The Search for Public Policy: Regional Politics and Government Finances in Ecuador, 1830–1940* (Berkeley: University of California Press, 1985), 202–5.

7. Clark, *Redemptive Work,* 75.

8. Quintero and Silva, *Ecuador,* 268.

9. For competing views see Rodríguez, *Search for Public Policy;* David W. Schodt, *Ecuador: An Andean Enigma* (Boulder, Colo.: Westview, 1987); Osvaldo Hurtado, *Political Power in Ecuador,* trans. Nick D. Mills Jr. (Boulder, Colo.: Westview, 1985); Fredrick B. Pike, *The United States and the Andean Republics: Peru, Bolivia, and Ecuador* (Cambridge, Mass.: Harvard University Press, 1977); Agustín Cueva, *The Process of Political Domination in Ecuador,* trans. Danielle Salti (New Brunswick, N.J.: Transaction, 1982); Quintero and Silva, *Ecuador;* and Weinman, "Ecuador and Cacao."

10. "El protestantismo en sud-america," *El heraldo de la hostia divina* I (Cuenca), 1898, 110, quoted in Joedd Price, "Ecuadorean Opinion of the United States in the Nineteenth Century: An Attitudinal Study" (Ph.D. diss., University of North Carolina, 1968), 66.

11. Note to U.S. legation, March 11, 1899, in FRUS, *1899,* 259.

12. Ibid., 254.

13. Ibid., 260.

14. Huntington Wilson, acting secretary of state, to Williams C. Fox, U.S. minister to Ecuador, June 19, 1909, in FRUS, *1909*, 245–46.

15. U.S. legation in Guayaquil, March 22, 1912, U.S. Department of State, General Records of the Department of State Relating to Political Affairs in Ecuador, 1910–29.

16. Quoted in J. Lloyd Mecham, *A Survey of United States–Latin American Relations* (Boston: Houghton Mifflin, 1965), 64.

17. For a discussion of Alfaro's ideas see Alan Weaver Hazelton, *Eloy Alfaro: Apostle of Pan Americanism* ([Los Angeles:] International Faculty of the Andhra Research University of India, 1943).

18. Quoted in Lester D. Langley, *America and the Americas: The United States in the Western Hemisphere* (Athens: University of Georgia Press, 1989), 108.

19. Ibid., 115.

20. Quoted in Peter H. Smith, *Talons of the Eagle: Dynamics of U.S.–Latin American Relations* (New York: Oxford University Press, 1996), 53.

21. Ibid., 52.

22. Mecham, *United States–Latin American Relations*, 100.

23. Sections on the Ecuadorian railway are drawn principally from Eva Maria Loewenfeld, "The Guayaquil and Quito Railway," M.A. thesis, University of Chicago, 1944; Clark, *Redemptive Work*; Emily S. Rosenberg, "Dollar Diplomacy under Wilson: An Ecuadorean Case," *Inter-American Economic Affairs* 25, no. 2 (Autumn 1971): 47–54; and George M. Lauderbaugh, "The United States and Ecuador: Conflict and Convergence, 1830–1946" (Ph.D. diss., University of Alabama, 1997). See also "The Guayaquil and Quito Railway of Ecuador," *Railway Age* 8 (August 1902): 134–38; and W. S. Barclay, "The Geography of South American Railways," *Geographical Journal* 49, no. 4 (April 1917): 259–61.

24. Clark, *Redemptive Work*, 106.

25. Perry M. DeLeon, U.S. consul in Guayaquil, December 3, 1898, quoted in Loewenfeld, "Guayaquil and Quito Railway," 6.

26. *Monthly Bulletin of the International Bureau of the American Republics* 15, no. 2 (August 1903), 447, quoted in Loewenfeld, "Guayaquil and Quito Railway," 5.

27. DeLeon, December 3, 1898,

28. Mensaje del Presidente de la República al Congreso Nacional, August 10, 1905, in Alejandro Noboa, ed., *Recopiliación de mensajes dirigidos por los presidentes y vicepresidentes de la república, jefes supremos y gobiernos provisorios a*

*las convenciones y congresos nacionales* (Guayaquil: Imprenta de El Tiempo, 1908), 5:302, quoted in Loewenfeld, "Guayaquil and Quito Railway," 6–7.

29. Alberto Acosta, *Breve historia económica del Ecuador* (Quito: Corporación Editora Nacional, 1995), 55.

30. Clark, *Redemptive Work,* 83–84.

31. Ibid., 192.

32. Memorandum by President Leonidas Plaza Gutiérrez to Charles Hartman, U.S. minister, August 9, 1915, in FRUS, *1915,* 358–59.

33. Rutherfurd Bingham, chargé d'affaires in Quito, to secretary of state, May 4, 1912, in FRUS, *1912,* 415.

34. Huntington Wilson, assistant secretary of state, to the U.S. representative in Ecuador, April 17, 1912, in FRUS, *1912,* 412; and Wilson to Bingham, May 11, 1912, in FRUS, *1912,* 417.

35. Throughout its history Ecuador's legislative branch has changed in composition many times. Sometimes there were two chambers, other times one.

36. President Plaza's address to the Ecuadorian congress, August 10, 1914, quoted in FRUS, *1914,* 266.

37. R. H. Elizalde, Ecuadorian minister of foreign affairs, to Hartman, October 19, 1915, in FRUS, *1915,* 356.

38. Modesto A. Peñaherrera, Ecuadorian minister of the interior, to Manuel R. Balarezo, fiscal attorney for the Ecuadorian minister of the interior, May 13, 1915, in FRUS, *1915,* 350.

39. Robert Lansing, secretary of state, to Hartman, February 13, 1917, in FRUS, *1917,* 738.

40. Elizalde, Ecuadorian minister to the United States, memorandum on conference with secretary of state, June 4, 1918, in FRUS, *1918,* 409.

41. "Memorandum Regarding June 4, 1918 Meeting," in FRUS, *1918,* 410.

42. Frank Lyon Polk, an undersecretary of state, to Hartman, June 6, 1918, in FRUS, *1918,* 411.

43. Norman Hezekiah Davis, undersecretary of state, to Hartman, December 8, 1920, in FRUS, *1920,* 2:203.

44. Quoted in Clark, *Redemptive Work,* 194.

45. Quoted in Loewenfeld, "Guayaquil and Quito Railway," 76.

46. Loewenfeld, "Guayaquil and Quito Railway," 24.

47. Clark, *Redemptive Work,* 37.

48. Treatment of the Galápagos Islands is drawn from E. Taylor Parks and J. Fred Rippy, "The Galápagos Islands, A Neglected Phase of American Strategy Diplomacy," *Pacific Historical Review* 9 (1940): 37–45; Lauderbaugh,

"United States and Ecuador"; Walter V. Scholes and Marie V. Scholes, "The United States and Ecuador, 1909–1913," *Americas* 19, no. 3 (January 1963): 276–90; and Rosenberg, "Dollar Diplomacy."

49. Quoted in Parks and Rippy, "Galápagos Islands," 38.

50. "Message of President Leonidas Plaza G. to the National Congress of Ecuador," August 10, 1904, in FRUS, *1904*, 296.

51. Quoted in Parks and Rippy, "Galápagos Islands," 43.

52. Report from the U.S. consul in Guayaquil, January 28, 1911, in U.S. Department of State, General Records of the Department of State.

53. Sections on health conditions in Guayaquil are drawn from FRUS, *1908, 1912, 1913, 1914;* U.S. Department of State, General Records of the Department of State Relating to Political Affairs in Ecuador, 1910–29, correspondence January 9–March 22, 1912, and February 16, 1914; MRE-CR, *1901–1914;* Lauderbaugh, "United States and Ecuador"; and Pineo, *Social and Economic Reform in Ecuador.*

54. Hartman to secretary of state, February 14, 1914, in FRUS, *1914*, 269.

55. Bryan, secretary of state, to Hartman, February 16, 1914, in FRUS, *1914*, 269.

56. U.S. minister to Ecuador to secretary of state, November 7, 1913, in FRUS, *1913*, 519.

57. Instructions to Rafael H. Elizalde, legation in the United States, in Ecuador, Ministerio de Relaciónes Exteriores, *Communicaciónes dirigidas a la legación del Ecuador en Estados Unidos, 1916–1922.*

58. Data drawn from Pineo, *Social and Economic Reform in Ecuador*, 2, 133–34.

## Chapter 4

1. Economic data in this chapter are drawn from Rafael Lopez Quintero and Erika Silva Ch., *Ecuador: una nación en ciernes* (Quito: Abya-Yala, 1991), 1:373, 404, 444, 445, 471; Alberto Acosta, *Breve historia económica del Ecuador* (Quito: Corporación Editora Nacional, 1995), 73, 75; David Corkill and David Cubitt, *Ecuador: Fragile Democracy* (Nottingham, U.K.: Russell Press, 1988), 13–14; Wilson Miño Grijalva, "La economía Ecuatoriana de la gran recesión a la crisis bananera," and Fabio Villalobos, "El proceso de industrialización hasta los años cincuenta," in Enrique Ayala Mora, ed., *Nueva historia del Ecuador: época republicana IV,* (Quito: Corporación Editora Nacional, 1983), 10:53, 59; Paul W. Drake, *The Money Doctor in the Andes: The Kemmerer Missions, 1923–1933* (Durham, N.C.: Duke University Press, 1989), 12, 13,

16, 127, 168; Linda Alexander Rodríguez, *Search for Public Policy: Regional Politics and Government Finances in Ecuador, 1830–1940* (Berkeley: University of California Press, 1985), 167; Agustín Cueva, *The Process of Political Domination in Ecuador,* trans. Danielle Salti, (New Brunswick, N.J.: Transaction Books, 1982); Osvaldo Hurtado, *Political Power in Ecuador,* trans. Nick D. Mills Jr. (Boulder, Colo.: Westview, 1985), 80–81; and Carlos de la Torre, *Populist Seduction in Latin America: The Ecuadorian Experience* (Athens: Ohio University Center for International Studies, 2000), 39.

2. Data on Ecuadorian demography in this chapter are drawn from Enrique Ayala Mora, *Resumen de historia del Ecuador* (Quito: Corporación Editora Nacional, 1995), 125; Quintero and Silva, *Ecuador,* 480; Acosta, *Historia económica,* 75; and de la Torre, *Populist Seduction,* 33, 36, 41.

3. See especially the discussion in Catherine M. Conaghan and James M. Malloy, *Unsettling Statecraft: Democracy and Neoliberalism in the Central Andes* (Pittsburgh: University of Pittsburgh Press, 1994), 205.

4. Rodríguez, *Search for Public Policy,* 164.

5. Correspondence, January 13, 1930, MRE-CR, *1928–1931.*

6. For the competing interpretations see Enrique Ayala Mora, *Nueva historia del Ecuador: época republicana I,* vol. 7 (Quito: Corporación Editora Nacional, 1983); Quintero and Silva, *Ecuador;* Óscar Efrén Reyes, *Breve historia general del Ecuador,* tomos 2–3 (Quito: Imprenta del Colegio Tecnico Don Bosco, n.d.); Gabriel Cevallos García, *Historia del Ecuador: Ecuador republicano* (Cuenca: Publicaciones de Editorial "Don Bosco" del Ecuador, n.d.); Rodríguez, *Search for Public Policy;* Cueva, *Process of Political Domination;* David W. Schodt, *Ecuador: An Andean Enigma* (Boulder, Colo.: Westview, 1987); and Ronn Pineo, *Social and Economic Reform in Ecuador: Life and Work in Guayaquil, 1870–1925* (Gainesville, Fla.: University Press of Florida, 1996).

7. Drake, *Money Doctor,* 162.

8. Ibid., 250.

9. Ibid.

10. Ibid., 162.

11. Ibid., 6.

12. Data on the economic decline are drawn from Ayala, *Resumen de historia del Ecuador,* 125; Quintero and Silva, *Ecuador,* 480; Acosta, *Breve historia económica del Ecuador,* 75; and de la Torre, *Populist Seduction,* 33, 36, 41.

13. Correspondence, March 17, 1934, MRE-CR, *1934.*

14. Dick Steward, *Money, Marines and Mission: Recent U.S.–Latin American Policy* (Lanham, Md.: University Press of America, 1980), 23.

15. Bryce Wood, *The Making of the Good Neighbor Policy* (New York: Columbia University Press, 1962), 25.

16. Peter H. Smith, *Talons of the Eagle: Dynamics of U.S.–Latin American Relations* (New York: Oxford University Press, 1996), 70.

17. Drake, *Money Doctor*, 22.

18. Correspondence, February 17, 1936, MRE-CR, *1935–1936*.

19. Ibid.

20. Data regarding the war with Peru are drawn from David H. Zook Jr., *Zarumilla-Marañón: The Ecuador-Peru Dispute* (New York: Bookman, 1964), 159, 165, 177; George M. Lauderbaugh, "The United States and Ecuador: Conflict and Convergence, 1830–1946" (Ph.D. diss., University of Alabama, 1997), 237; Quintero and Silva, *Ecuador*, 472–73, 480; and Reyes, *Breve historia general del Ecuador*, 295.

21. See the excellent discussion of these matters in Lauderbaugh, "United States and Ecuador," 237.

22. Zook, *Zarumilla-Marañón*, 175.

23. Ibid., 185.

24. Memorandum by Robert M. Scotten, U.S. ambassador to Ecuador, May 1, 1944, in FRUS, *1944*, 7:1061.

25. See, for example, *La prensa* (Guayaquil), December 15, 1942.

26. Scotten to secretary of state, May 29, 30, 1944, in FRUS, *1944*, 7:1036.

27. Later, in December 1942, the United States assigned two vessels to the port of Guayaquil to train Ecuadorian naval personnel. In 1943 Washington also sent a technical director to head up Ecuador's military college.

28. After the Río Conference in January 1942 most Latin American states broke relations with the Axis. Chile and Argentina did so later, breaking relations in 1943 and 1944, respectively. Ecuador would wait until 1945 to issue a formal declaration of war against the Axis, taking this action so that it could be included at the Inter-American Conference on Problems of War and Peace in Mexico City and the United Nations Conference on International Organization, held in San Francisco.

29. Correspondence, June 13, 1940, MRE-CR, *1937–1940*.

30. John Sanbrailo, former director of USAID mission in Ecuador, personal communication, October 17, 2004. In an effort to encourage the impulse for cooperation and exchange, U.S. Vice President Henry A. Wallace followed up on Arroyo del Río's visit to the United States in 1942, traveling both to Quito and to Guayaquil in April 1943.

31. Correspondence, January 28, 1936, MRE-CR, *1935–1936*.
32. Quoted in Alfaro to Quito, October 20, 1939, MRE-CR, *1937–1940*.
33. Discussed in Wood, *Making of the Good Neighbor Policy*, 268; and in Jorge W. Villacrés Moscoso, *Historia diplomática de la república del Ecuador*, (Guayaquil: Lit. e Imprenta de la Universidad de Guayaquil, 1976), 4:266.
34. Discussed in Wood, *Making of the Good Neighbor Policy*, 272; and in Villacrés Moscoso, *Historia diplomática*, 4:267.
35. Discussed in Villacrés Moscoso, *Historia diplomática*, 5:37, 39.
36. *El globo* (Bahía de Caraquez), December 19, 1941, and April 1, 1942.
37. James F. Byrnes, secretary of state, to Scotten, August 13, 1945, in FRUS, *1945*, 9:1015.
38. Memorandum by White, ambassador to Peru, temporarily in Washington, D.C., to James Clement Dunn, assistant secretary of state, August 27, 1945, in FRUS, *1945*, 9:1017.
39. Ibid., 1018.
40. Memorandum by Henry Dearborn, State Department, January 17, 1946, in FRUS, *1946*, 11:838–39; Memorandum of conversation by Dearborn, February 11, 1946, 11:843–44.
41. Memorandum of conversation by Dearborn, February 26, 1946, in FRUS, *1946*, 11:846–47.
42. Robert P. Patterson, secretary of war, and James Forrestal, secretary of the navy, to secretary of state, March 21, 1946, in FRUS, *1946*, 11:850.
43. Scotten to secretary of state, July 3, 1946, in FRUS, *1946*, 11:855.
44. Dean Acheson, acting secretary of state, to Scotten, August 27, 1946, in FRUS, *1946*, 11:858.
45. *El mercurio* (Cuenca), November 3, 1940, 30.
46. Ibid., 5.
47. Guy Poitras, *The Ordeal of Hegemony: The United States and Latin America* (Boulder, Colo.: Westview, 1990), 2.
48. Boaz Long, U.S. minister to Ecuador, to Cordell Hull, secretary of state, February 26, 1941, in FRUS, *1941*, 7:291–92.

## Chapter 5

1. José R. Chiriboga Villagómez, Ecuadorian ambassador to the United States, to Ministry of Foreign Relations, October 31, 1957, MRE-CR, *1957;* Chiriboga

to Ministry of Foreign Relations, May 23, 1958, MRE-CR, *1958;* Chiriboga to Ministry of Foreign Relations, April 6, 1959, and September 14, 1959, MRE-CR, *1959;* and Chiriboga to Ministry of Foreign Relations, May 25, 1960, MRE-CR, *1960.*

2. Economic data presented in this chapter are drawn from Wilson Miño Grijalva, "La economía Ecuatoriana de la gran recesión a la crisis bananera," in Enrique Ayala Mora, ed., *Nueva historia del Ecuador: época republicana IV* (Quito: Corporación Editora Nacional, 1983), 10:67; David W. Schodt, *Ecuador: An Andean Enigma* (Boulder, Colo.: Westview, 1987), 57, 80, 93; Alberto Acosta, *Breve historia económica del Ecuador* (Quito: Corporación Editora Nacional, 1995), 99; Osvaldo Hurtado, *Political Power in Ecuador,* trans. Nick D. Mills Jr. (Boulder, Colo.: Westview, 1985), 288; Peter Pyne, "The Politics of Instability of Ecuador: The Overthrow of the President, 1961," *Journal of Latin American Studies* 7, no. 1 (May 1975): 120; and Robert H. Terry, "Ecuadorian Foreign Policy, 1958–1968: As Reflected in the O.A.S. and the U.N.," (Ph.D. diss., American University, 1972), 274, 318, 319.

3. *La nación* (Guayaquil), March 1954.

4. Data on banana production and export presented in this chapter are drawn from Schodt, *Ecuador: An Andean Enigma,* 56–59; Terry, "Ecuadorian Foreign Policy," 263, 274, 305, 318; Miño Grijalva, "La economía Ecuatoriana," 64–65; Linda Alexander Rodríguez, *Search for Public Policy: Regional Politics and Government Finances in Ecuador, 1830–1940* (Berkeley: University of California Press, 1985), 200; David Corkill and David Cubitt, *Ecuador: Fragile Democracy* (Nottingham, U.K.: Russell Press, 1988), 17; Acosta, *Breve historia económica del Ecuador,* 83–85; and Jon V. Kofas, "Politics of Conflict and Containment: Ecuador's Labor Movement and U.S. Foreign Policy, 1944–1963," *Journal of Third World Studies* 13, no. 2 (Fall 1996): 69.

5. Data presented in this chapter regarding Ecuadorian society, demography, and poverty are drawn from John D. Martz, *Ecuador: Conflicting Political Culture and the Quest for Progress* (Boston: Allyn and Bacon, 1972), 199; Enrique Ayala Mora, *Resumen de historia del Ecuador* (Quito: Corporación editora nacional, 1995), 126–27; Miño Grijalva, "La economía Ecuatoriana," 68; Rafael Quintero Lopez and Erika Silva Ch., *Ecuador: una nación en ciernes* (Quito: Abya-Yala, 1991), 1:480; Rodríguez, *Search for Public Policy,* 206–7; Magnus Mörner, *The Andean Past: Land, Societies, and Conflicts* (New York: Columbia University Press, 1985), 208; Hurtado, *Political Power in Ecuador,* 192–93, 333; Schodt, *Ecuador: An Andean Enigma,* 59, 76. 108; Lilo Linke,

*Ecuador: Country of Contrasts* (London: Oxford University Press, 1962), 2; Acosta, *Breve historia económica del Ecuador*, 86–87, 103; Terry, "Ecuadorian Foreign Policy," 265; John Van Dyke Saunders, *The People of Ecuador: A Demographic Analysis* (Gainesville: University of Florida Press, 1961), 41–47, 58–59; Dennis M. Hanratty, ed., *Ecuador: A Country Study* (Washington, D.C.: U.S. Government Printing Office, 1991), table 8; and Samuel L. Baily, *The United States and the Development of South America, 1945–1975* (New York: New Viewpoints, 1976), 6.

6. Information presented in this chapter on the Protestant missionaries and the indigenous people of the Amazon is drawn from Allen Gerlach, *Indians, Oil, and Politics: A Recent History of Ecuador* (Wilmington, Del.: Scholarly Resources, 2003), 11, 57, 59; and Acosta, *Breve historia económica del Ecuador*, 245.

7. Data on voting presented in this chapter are drawn from Hurtado, *Political Power in Ecuador*, 142, 230; Carlos de la Torre, *Populist Seduction in Latin America: The Ecuadorian Experience* (Athens: Ohio University Center for International Studies, 2000), 9; and Agustín Cueva, "El Ecuador de 1925 a 1960," in Ayala, *Nueva historia del Ecuador*, 10:114–15.

8. John Samuel Fitch, *The Military Coup d'Etat as a Political Process* (Baltimore: Johns Hopkins University Press, 1977), 173.

9. Schodt, *Ecuador: An Andean Enigma*, 89.

10. Information presented in this chapter regarding U.S., Ecuadorian, and Latin American relations is drawn from Peter H. Smith, *Talons of the Eagle: Dynamics of U.S.–Latin American Relations* (New York: Oxford University Press, 1996), 120, 148, 151, 152, 153; John Child, *Unequal Alliance: The Inter-American Military System, 1938–1978* (Boulder, Colo.: Westview, 1980), 126; Abraham F. Lowenthal, *Partners in Conflict: The United States and Latin America in the 1990s* (Baltimore: Johns Hopkins University Press, 1990), 28; Kenneth D. Lehman, *Bolivia and the United States: A Limited Partnership* (Athens: University of Georgia Press, 1999), 118; Stephen G. Rabe, *The Most Dangerous Area in the World: John F. Kennedy Confronts Communist Revolution in Latin America* (Chapel Hill: University of North Carolina Press, 1999), 27; Harold Molineu, *U.S. Policy toward Latin America: From Regionalism to Globalism* (Boulder, Colo.: Westview, 1990), 29–30; and *La nación* (Guayaquil), March 2, 1954, 1.

11. Ellis O. Briggs, U.S. ambassador to Brazil, to the Department of State, April 5, 1957, in FRUS, *1945–1947*, 7:981.

12. Department of State, "U.S. Policy toward Ecuador," October 2, 1950, in FRUS, *1950*, 2:862.

13. Dr. Julio Prado Vallejo, Ecuador's representative to the Inter-American Social and Economic Council, to the Ministry of Foreign Relations, September 5, 1956, MRE-CR, *1956*.

14. George Kennan, "Latin America as a Problem in United States Foreign Policy," in Michael LaRosa and Frank O. Mora, eds., *Neighborly Adversaries: Readings in U.S.–Latin American Relations* (Lanham, Md.: Rowman and Littlefield, 1999), 179, 182.

15. Gordon Connell-Smith, *The United States and Latin America* (London: Heinemann Educational Books, 1974), 218.

16. Félix Vega, Bolívar Pico, and Gabriel Núñez, Ecuadorian military attachés in Washington, D.C., to Ambassador Luis Antonio Peñaherrera, November 10, 1951, MRE-CR, *1950–1952*.

17. State Department to Chiriboga, September 27, 1954, MRE-CR, *1954*.

18. Lawrence A. Clayton, *Peru and the United States: The Condor and the Eagle* (Athens: University of Georgia Press, 1999), 179–80.

19. From the combined total of $5.095 billion in U.S. credits and grants to Latin America from 1945 to 1963, Ecuador received $116 million ($35 million in military aid), while Peru received $288 million ($84 million in military aid). See Jon V. Kofas, "The IMF, the World Bank, and U.S. Foreign Policy in Ecuador," *Latin American Perspectives* 28, no. 5 (September 2001): 52, 59; and Terry, "Ecuadorian Foreign Policy," 300.

20. Braden is quoted in a memorandum of conversation by Henry Dearborn, Division of North and West Coast Affairs, May 31, 1946, in FRUS, *1946*, 876.

21. Gutt is quoted in Ecuadorian ambassador Augusto Dillon to the Ministry of Foreign Relations, February 14, 1950, in MRE-CR, *1950–1952*.

22. Samuel C. Waugh, president, Import-Export Bank, to the Office of South American Affairs, July 30, 1957, FRUS, *1955–1957*, 7:991–92.

23. Chiriboga to Ministry of Foreign Relations, July 19, 1957, in MRE-CR, *1957*, quoting an Ex–Im Bank official.

24. Molineu, *U.S. Policy toward Latin America*, 100.

25. Memorandum of conversation, Edgar L. McGinnis Jr., Office of South American Affairs, July 6, 1953, in FRUS, *1952–1954*, 4:988, recounting Chiriboga's words.

26. Pyne, "Politics of Instability," 112.

27. *New York Times*, December 15, 1960.

28. Philip Agee, *Inside the Company: CIA Diary* (Toronto: Bantam, 1975), 165.

29. One main problem was that nearly all of President Kennedy's top advisers had no experience or training in Latin American affairs. These men, the "best and brightest," waved away all complaints about this perceived shortcoming as caviling. All that local detail was unnecessary, they reasoned. Instead "modernization theory"—a highly self-congratulatory view of U.S. history that sought to remake the world in its glorified self-image that was popular among some intellectuals in the late 1950s and the early 1960s, until it crashed hard against reality—taught them all they needed to know about Latin America, they believed. Only the theory mattered, and the particulars of each region or individual nations were without any importance.

30. Molineu, *U.S. Policy toward Latin America,* 29–30.

31. Jerome Levinson and Juan de Onis, "The Alliance That Lost Its Way: A Critical Report on the Alliance for Progress," in LaRosa and Mora, *Neighborly Adversaries,* 201.

32. Federico G. Gil, "The Kennedy-Johnson Years," in John D. Martz, ed., *United States Policy in Latin America: A Quarter Century of Crisis and Challenge, 1961–1986* (Lincoln: University of Nebraska Press, 1988), 18–19.

33. Agee, *Inside the Company,* 269.

34. Ibid., 75.

35. Ibid., 76.

36. Ibid., 75; see also Corkill and Cubitt, *Ecuador: Fragile Democracy,* xii.

37. Agee, *Inside the Company,* 209.

38. Kofas, "Politics of Conflict and Containment," 84.

39. Agee, *Inside the Company,* 180.

40. Chiriboga to Ministry of Foreign Relations, January 17, 1953, MRE-CR, *1953.*

41. "Memorandum of a Conversation," R. R. Rubottom, acting assistant secretary for Inter-American affairs, May 7, 1957, in FRUS, *1955–1957,* May 7, 1957, 7:988–91.

42. Dr. Julio Prado Vallejo, Ecuador's representative to the Inter-American Social and Economic Council, to Ministry of Foreign Relations, September 5, 1956, MRE-CR, *1956;* Chiriboga to Ministry of Foreign Relations, December 28, 1955, MRE-CR, *1955.*

43. Chiriboga to Ministry of Foreign Relations, December 10, 1953, MRE-CR, *1953.*

44. José A. Correa, Ecuadorian ambassador to the United States, to Dr. Neftalí Ponce Miranda, Ecuadorian minister of foreign relations, September 18, 1963, MRE-CR, *1961–1964.*

## Chapter 6

1. Population data in this chapter are drawn from: Alberto Acosta, *Breve historia económica del Ecuador* (Quito: Corporación Editora Nacional, 1995), 110–11, 155–56; Allen Gerlach, *Indians, Oil, and Politics: A Recent History of Ecuador* (Wilmington, Del.: Scholarly Resources, 2003), 6, 63; and Osvaldo Hurtado, *Political Power in Ecuador,* trans. Nick D. Mills Jr. (Boulder, Colo.: Westview, 1985), 192.

2. Data on social conditions presented in this chapter are drawn from David Corkill and David Cubitt, *Ecuador: Fragile Democracy* (Nottingham: Russell Press, 1988), 32, 58, 63–64; Enrique Ayala Mora, *Resumen de historia del Ecuador* (Quito: Corporación editora nacional, 1995), 126–27; Dennis M. Hanratty, ed., *Ecuador: A Country Study* (Washington, D.C.: U.S. Government Printing Office, 1991), table 8; Gerlach, *Indians, Oil, and Politics,* 45–46, 75, 78; Acosta, *Breve historia económica del Ecuador* 108; Magnus Mörner, *Andean Past: Land, Societies, and Conflicts* (New York: Columbia University Press, 1985), 245–46; Samuel L. Baily, *The United States and the Development of South America, 1945–1975* (New York: New Viewpoints, 1976), 6; Anita Isaacs, *Military Rule and Transition in Ecuador, 1972–92* (Pittsburgh: University of Pittsburgh Press, 1993), 40, 50; and Catherine M. Conaghan and James M. Malloy, *Unsettling Statecraft: Democracy and Neoliberalism in the Central Andes* (Pittsburgh: University of Pittsburgh Press, 1994), 43, 247.

3. Peter Pyne, "The Politics of Instability of Ecuador: The Overthrow of the President, 1961," *Journal of Latin American Studies* 7, no. 1 (May 1975): 110; John D. Martz, *Ecuador: Conflicting Political Culture and the Quest for Progress* (Boston: Allyn and Bacon, 1972), 24; Robert H. Terry, "Ecuadorian Foreign Policy, 1958–1968: As Reflected in the O.A.S. and the U.N.," (Ph.D. diss., American University, 1972), 338, 341; and Mörner, *Andean Past,* 230.

4. Quoted in John D. Martz, "The Fate of a Small State: Ecuador in Foreign Affairs," in Heraldo Muñoz and Joseph S. Tulchin, eds., *Latin American Nations in World Politics* (Boulder, Colo.: Westview, 1996), 134.

5. See especially Jorge Pérez Concha, *Frente externo* (Guayaquil: Litografía e Imprenta de la Universidad de Guayaquil, 1985); Terry, "Ecuadorian Foreign Policy," 359; and Mary Jeanne Reid Martz, "Ecuador," in Harold Eugene Davis and Larman C. Wilson, eds., *Latin American Foreign Policies: An Analysis* (Baltimore: Johns Hopkins University Press, 1975), 388.

6. N. Ponce Miranda, Ecuadorian ambassador, to Ministry of Foreign Relations, June 6, 1963, MRE-CR, *1961–1964.*

7. See especially Manuel de Guzmán Polanco, "Ecuador en lo internacional: un cuarto de siglo, 1945–1970," in *El Ecuador de la postguerra: estudio en homenaje a Guillermo Perez Chiribobga*, vol. 2 (Quito: Banco Central del Ecuador, 1992); and John Martz, "Fate of a Small State."

8. Today the United States and Ecuador both claim a two-hundred-mile fish management zone, although the United States does not include migratory fish in its exclusionary zone, whereas Ecuador does claim exclusive rights to harvest these fish.

9. Correspondence, December 15, 1919, MRE-CD, *1916–1922*.

10. Gerlach, *Indians, Oil, and Politics*, 33.

11. Isaacs, *Military Rule and Transition in Ecuador*, 3.

12. John Martz, "Fate of a Small State," 135.

13. Data on oil are drawn from Correspondence, January 25, 1938, MRE-CR, *1937–1940*; Mary Martz, "Ecuador," 390, 392; John D. Martz, *Politics and Petroleum in Ecuador* (New Brunswick, N.J.: Transaction Books, 1987), 131; Gerlach, *Indians, Oil, and Politics*, 35–36; David W. Schodt, *Ecuador: An Andean Enigma* (Boulder, Colo.: Westview, 1987), 93, 105, 107, 111, 149; Mörner, *Andean Past*, 231–32; Hurtado, *Political Power in Ecuador*, 288; Acosta, *Breve historia económica del Ecuador*, 110–11, 128; Isaacs, *Military Rule and Transition in Ecuador*, 43; Corkill and Cubitt, *Ecuador: Fragile Democracy*, 37; and Wendy Weiss, "Debt and Devaluation: The Burden on Ecuador's Popular Class," *Latin American Perspectives* 24, no. 4 (July 1997): 11.

General economic data presented in this chapter are drawn from Acosta, *Breve historia económica del Ecuador*, 102, 103, 138, 161; Jeanne A. K. Hey, *Theories of Dependent Foreign Policy and the Case of Ecuador in the 1980s* (Athens: Ohio University Center for International Studies, 1995), 34, 37, 90, 118; Hanratty, *Ecuador: A Country Study*, table 17; Terry, "Ecuadorian Foreign Policy," 319; Schodt, *Ecuador: An Andean Enigma*, 105, 111, 112, 138–39, 149–51; Enrique Ayala Mora, "Ecuador since 1930," in Leslie Bethell, ed., *The Cambridge History of Latin America: Latin America since 1930, Spanish South America* (Cambridge: Cambridge University Press, 1991), 8:719; Corkill and Cubitt, *Ecuador: Fragile Democracy*, 33, 34, 35, 79; Gerlach, *Indians, Oil, and Politics*, 5, 33–35, 39–40, 64, 65, 110–11, 114; Hurtado, *Political Power in Ecuador*, 289, 292; Isaacs, *Military Rule and Transition in Ecuador*, 45, 56; Jon V. Kofas, "The IMF, the World Bank, and U.S. Foreign Policy in Ecuador," *Latin American Perspectives* 28, no. 5 (September 2001): 51; and Conaghan and Malloy, *Unsettling Statecraft*, 51, 110–14.

14. Corkill and Cubitt, *Ecuador: Fragile Democracy*, 35.

15. Conaghan and Malloy, *Unsettling Statecraft*, 20.
16. Isaacs, *Military Rule and Transition in Ecuador*, 20.
17. Data on voting are drawn from Schodt, *Ecuador: An Andean Enigma*, 131, 159; Hurtado, *Political Power in Ecuador*, 230; and Gerlach, *Indians, Oil, and Politics*, 69.

## Chapter 7

1. Jeanne A. K. Hey, "Foreign Policy Options under Dependence: A Theoretical Evaluation with Evidence from Ecuador," *Journal of Latin American Studies* 25 (1993): 548.
2. Economic data presented in this chapter are drawn from: Alberto Acosta, *Breve historia económica del Ecuador* (Quito: Corporación Editora Nacional, 1995), 102, 103, 138, 161; Jeanne A. K. Hey, *Theories of Dependent Foreign Policy and the Case of Ecuador in the 1980s* (Athens: Ohio University Center for International Studies, 1995), 34, 37, 90, 118; Dennis M. Hanratty, ed., *Ecuador: A Country Study* (Washington, D.C.: U.S. Government Printing Office, 1991), table 17; Robert H. Terry, "Ecuadorian Foreign Policy, 1958–1968: As Reflected in the O.A.S. and the U.N.," (Ph.D. diss., American University, 1972), 319; David W. Schodt, *Ecuador: An Andean Enigma* (Boulder, Colo.: Westview, 1987), 105, 111, 112, 138–39, 149–51; Enrique Ayala Mora, "Ecuador since 1930," in Leslie Bethell, ed., *The Cambridge History of Latin America: Latin America since 1930, Spanish South America* (Cambridge: Cambridge University Press, 1991), 8:719; David Corkill and David Cubitt, *Ecuador: Fragile Democracy* (Nottingham: Russell Press, 1988), 33, 34, 35, 79; Allen Gerlach, *Indians, Oil, and Politics: A Recent History of Ecuador* (Wilmington, Del.: Scholarly Resources, 2003), 5, 33–35, 39–40, 64, 65, 110–11, 114; Osvaldo Hurtado, *Political Power in Ecuador*, trans. Nick D. Mills Jr. (Boulder, Colo.: Westview, 1985), 289, 292; Anita Isaacs, *Military Rule and Transition in Ecuador, 1972–92* (Pittsburgh: University of Pittsburgh Press, 1993), 45, 56; Jon V. Kofas, "The IMF, the World Bank, and U.S. Foreign Policy in Ecuador," *Latin American Perspectives* 28, no. 5 (September 2001): 51; and Catherine M. Conaghan and James M. Malloy, *Unsettling Statecraft: Democracy and Neoliberalism in the Central Andes* (Pittsburgh: University of Pittsburgh Press, 1994), 51, 110–14.
3. Population data in this chapter are drawn from Acosta, *Breve historia económica del Ecuador*, 110–11, 155–56; Gerlach, *Indians, Oil, and Politics*, 6, 63; and Hurtado, *Political Power in Ecuador*, 192.

4. Data on social conditions presented in this chapter are drawn from Corkill and Cubitt, *Ecuador: Fragile Democracy*, 32, 58, 63–64; Enrique Ayala Mora, *Resumen de historia del Ecuador* (Quito: Corporación editora nacional, 1995), 126–27; Hanratty, *Ecuador: A Country Study*, table 8; Gerlach, *Indians, Oil, and Politics*, 45–46, 75, 78; Acosta, *Breve historia económica del Ecuador*, 108; Magnus Mörner, *The Andean Past: Land, Societies, and Conflicts* (New York: Columbia University Press, 1985), 245–46; Samuel L. Baily, *The United States and the Development of South America, 1945–1975* (New York: New Viewpoints, 1976), 6; Isaacs, *Military Rule and Transition in Ecuador*, 40, 50; and Conaghan and Malloy, *Unsettling Statecraft*, 43, 247.

5. Data on economic performance and the debt during the Roldós and Hurtado years are drawn from Wendy Weiss, "Debt and Devaluation: The Burden on Ecuador's Popular Class," *Latin American Perspectives* 24, no. 4 (July 1997): 11, 13; Acosta, *Breve historia económica del Ecuador*, 104–5; Corkill and Cubitt, *Ecuador: Fragile Democracy*, 49, 50, 79–80; Hey, *Theories of Dependent Foreign Policy*, 41; Jeanne A. K. Hey and Thomas Klak, "From Protectionism to Neoliberalism: Tracing the Transition in Ecuador," 22, paper presented at the 1995 meeting of the Latin American Studies Association, Washington, D.C. 1995.; Gerlach, *Indians, Oil, and Politics*, 42; Isaacs, *Military Rule and Transition in Ecuador*, 130; Conaghan and Malloy, *Unsettling Statecraft*, 113; Schodt, *Ecuador: An Andean Enigma*, 151, 155; and Ayala, "Ecuador since 1930," 719–20.

6. Quoted in Conaghan and Malloy, *Unsettling Statecraft*, 114.

7. For data on the crisis see Peter H. Smith, *Talons of the Eagle: Dynamics of U.S.–Latin American Relations* (New York: Oxford University Press, 1996), 236–37, 240.

8. Conaghan and Malloy, *Unsettling Statecraft*, 5.

9. Hey and Klak, "From Protectionism to Neoliberalism," 2.

10. Hey, *Theories of Dependent Foreign Policy*, 139.

11. Ibid., 65.

12. Ibid.

13. Data on the economy during the Febres Cordero administration are drawn from Acosta, *Breve historia económica del Ecuador*, 138, 155; Ayala, "Ecuador since 1930," 725; Schodt, *Ecuador: An Andean Enigma*, 110–11, 163, 165; Corkill and Cubitt, *Ecuador: Fragile Democracy*, 79–80, 95; Weiss, "Debt and Devaluation," 11, 13; Hey, *Theories of Dependent Foreign Policy*, 36–37, 41; Hey, "Foreign Policy Options under Dependence," 553–54; Hanratty, *Ecuador: A Country Study*, table 15; Hey and Klak, "From Protectionism to

Neoliberalism," 22; Hurtado, *Political Power in Ecuador,* 289; Conaghan and Malloy, *Unsettling Statecraft,* 166; and Gerlach, *Indians, Oil, and Politics,* 42.

14. Data on U.S.-Ecuadorian trade and aid are drawn from: Hey, "Foreign Policy Options under Dependence," 553; and Hey, *Theories of Dependent Foreign Policy,* 37.

15. See especially Hey, *Theories of Dependent Foreign Policy,* chap. 6, 153–76.

16. Data on the economy under Borja and Durán Ballen are drawn from Weiss, "Debt and Devaluation," 11, 13; Gerlach, *Indians, Oil, and Politics,* 42, 84–85; Ayala, "Ecuador since 1930," 725; Isaacs, *Military Rule and Transition in Ecuador,* 130; Hey, *Theories of Dependent Foreign Policy,* 41; and Hey and Klak, "From Protectionism to Neoliberalism," 9, 22.

17. Data on the social implications of neoliberalism under Borja and Durán Ballen are drawn from Gerlach, *Indians, Oil, and Politics,* 37; Nader Nazmi, "Failed Reforms and Economic Collapse in Ecuador," *Quarterly Review of Economics and Finance* 41 (2001): 728, 730; Carlos de la Torre, *Populist Seduction in Latin America: The Ecuadorian Experience* (Athens: Ohio University Center for International Studies, 2000), 85; and Anita Isaacs, "Ecuador: Democracy Standing the Test of Time?" in Jorge I. Domínguez and Abraham F. Lowenthal, eds., *Constructing Democratic Governance: Latin America and the Caribbean in the 1990s* (Baltimore: Johns Hopkins University Press, 1996), 49.

18. Bucaram, the son of Lebanese immigrants, was one of several Middle Eastern–Ecuadorians who found success in Ecuadorian national politics in these years. Middle Eastern–Ecuadorians were generally labeled *turcos* (people from Turkey), although their forebears actually came from locations across the Levant. Mainly middle-class merchants of the Christian faith, they had left in the late nineteenth and early twentieth centuries in search of entrepreneurial opportunities, and some had found them in Ecuador. Now their offspring were using their families' earlier economic success as a springboard into national politics.

19. This section on Bucaram is drawn especially from de la Torre, *Populist Seduction in Latin America,* 93, 98–99; and Gerlach, *Indians, Oil, and Politics,* 86.

20. Quoted in Gerlach, *Indians, Oil, and Politics,* 90.

21. Ibid., 107.

22. Gerlach, *Indians, Oil, and Politics,* 107, reports Arteaga's recollection of Alexander's reaction from a telephone conversation she had with the ambassador.

23. Data on Ecuador's indigenous people are drawn from Gerlach, *Indians, Oil, and Politics*, 11, 57, 59; and Acosta, *Breve historia económica del Ecuador*, 245.
24. Quoted in Gerlach, *Indians, Oil, and Politics*, xvii.
25. Isaacs, *Military Rule and Transition in Ecuador*, 5, 6.

## Epilogue

1. Jeanne A. K. Hey, *Theories of Dependent Foreign Policy and the Case of Ecuador in the 1980s* (Athens: Ohio University Center for International Studies, 1995), 44–45.

# Bibliographical Essay

This essay offers recommendations for further readings on the history of Ecuador and on Ecuadorian and Latin America relations with the United States. For an unabridged bibliography on Ecuador, consult Michael T. Hamerly, "Bibliografía historica del Ecuador," Latin American Studies Section on Ecuador, 2000, http://yachana.org/ecuatorianistas/bibliographies/hamerly/.

## Guides, Sources, and Source Collections

There are several good guides to the literature on U.S./Latin America relations, including Richard Dean Burns, ed., *Guide to American Foreign Relations Since 1700* (Santa Barbara, Calif.: ABC-CLIO, 1983); Robert L. Beisner, ed., *American Foreign Relations since 1600: A Guide to the Literature*, 2 vols. (Santa Barbara, Calif.: ABC-CLIO, 2003); David F. Trask, Michael C. Meyer, and Roger R. Trask, eds., *A Bibliography of United States–Latin American Relations since 1810* (Lincoln: University of Nebraska Press, 1968); and Michael C. Meyer, ed., *Supplement to a Bibliography of United States–Latin American Relations since 1810* (Lincoln: University of Nebraska Press, 1979).

As of this writing, nearly all Ecuadorian foreign relations documents are unpublished. Original source documents on Ecuador's foreign relations—Ecuador, Ministerio de Relaciónes Exteriores, *Communicaciónes recibidas de la legación del Ecuador en Estados Unidos;* and Ecuador, Ministerio de Relaciónes Exteriores, *Communicaciónes dirigidas a la legación del Ecuador en Estados Unidos*—are available only at the Ministry of Foreign Relations archive in Quito.

Many U.S. source documents on U.S.-Ecuadorian relations are, however, now available on microfilm and may be obtained via interlibrary loan: U.S. Department of State, Despatches [*sic*] from U.S. Consuls in Guayaquil, 1826–1906; Despatches [*sic*] from U.S. Ministers to Ecuador, 1848–1906; and General Records of the Department of State Relating to Political Affairs in Ecuador, 1910–29.

There are several annotated and edited collections of U.S. documents on U.S.-Ecuadorian relations available in print: William Ray Manning, ed., *Diplomatic Correspondence of the United States concerning the Independence of the Latin-American*

*Nations*, vol. 1 (New York: Oxford University Press, 1925); Manning, *Diplomatic Correspondence of the United States*, vol. 2, parts 3–4 (New York: Oxford University Press, 1925); Manning, *Diplomatic Correspondence of the United States: Inter-American Affairs, 1831–1860*, vols. 6 and 10 (Washington, D.C.: Carnegie Endowment for International Peace, 1935); and U.S. Department of State, *Foreign Relations of the United States*. On the inter-American conferences see James Brown Scott, ed., *The International Conferences of the American States, 1889–1928: A Collection of the Convention, Recommendations, Resolutions, Reports, and Motions Adopted by the First Six International Conferences of the American States, and Documents Relating to the Organization of the Conferences* (New York: Oxford University Press, 1931); Carnegie Endowment for International Peace, *The International Conferences of American States: First Supplement, 1933–1940* (Washington, D.C.: Carnegie Endowment for International Peace, 1940); and Pan American Union, *The International Conferences of American States: Second Supplement, 1942–1954* (Washington, D.C.: Organization of American States, 1958).

## Overviews

There are numerous historical overviews of U.S.–Latin American relations, including the flagship book for this series, Lester D. Langley, *America and the Americas: The United States in the Western Hemisphere* (Athens: University of Georgia Press, 1989). Peter H. Smith's *Talons of the Eagle: Dynamics of U.S.–Latin American Relations* (New York: Oxford University Press, 1996) provides a worthy introduction for the general reader. Harold Molineu, *U.S. Policy toward Latin America: From Regionalism to Globalism* (Boulder, Colo.: Westview, 1990), takes a thematic approach, with a focus on events of the 1980s. Dick Steward, *Money, Marines and Mission: Recent U.S.–Latin American Policy* (Lanham, Md.: University Press of America, 1980), offers a readable and highly critical account of U.S. foreign policy, looking especially at developments in Central America. Gordon Connell-Smith's *The United States and Latin America* (London: Heinemann Educational Books, 1974) is a valuable work from the "realist" perspective, a school of thought that sought to correct earlier scholarship, which had tended to offer an uncritical account of U.S. actions. J. Lloyd Mecham, *A Survey of United States–Latin American Relations* (Boston: Houghton Mifflin, 1965), is a classic work, especially strong in coverage of the inter-American conferences.

There are several overviews of Ecuador's history. The leading works in English include David W. Schodt, *Ecuador: An Andean Enigma* (Boulder, Colo.:

Westview, 1987). Schodt's is the best single volume treatment of Ecuadorian history, even if he focuses most of his attention on events of the late twentieth century. David Corkill and David Cubitt, *Ecuador: Fragile Democracy* (Nottingham, U.K.: Russell Press, 1988), provides many keen cultural insights. Osvaldo Hurtado, *Political Power in Ecuador*, trans. Nick D. Mills Jr. (Boulder, Colo.: Westview, 1985), offers a left-wing analysis of leading developments in Ecuadorian history by the former president, who since has become a born-again neoliberal. Dennis M. Hanratty, ed., *Ecuador: A Country Study* (Washington, D.C.: U.S. Government Printing Office, 1991), is a brief but steady mainstream summary. Agustín Cueva, *The Process of Political Domination in Ecuador*, trans. Danielle Salti, (New Brunswick, N.J.: Transaction Books, 1982), offers not so much a comprehensive history of Ecuador as a series of loosely connected if highly provocative essays. Magnus Mörner, *The Andean Past: Land, Societies, and Conflicts* (New York: Columbia University Press, 1985), contains some useful information. Mörner focuses especially on socioeconomic history, attempting to cover the full sweep of Peruvian, Bolivian, and Ecuadorian history. The classic study of the region, Frederick B. Pike, *The United States and the Andean Republics: Peru, Bolivia, and Ecuador* (Cambridge, Mass.: Harvard University Press, 1977), is still valuable. Several earlier historical overviews of Ecuador are now largely outdated: John D. Martz, *Ecuador: Conflicting Political Culture and the Quest for Progress* (Boston: Allyn and Bacon, 1972); George I. Blanksten, *Ecuador: Constitutions and Caudillos* (New York: Russell and Russell, 1964); and Lilo Linke, *Ecuador: Country of Contrasts* (London: Oxford University Press, 1962).

Overviews of Ecuadorian history in Spanish include Rafael Quintero Lopez and Erika Silva Ch., *Ecuador: una nación en ciernes*, tomo 1 (Quito: Abya-Yala, 1991), which offers a marvelously detailed and closely argued treatment of Ecuador's history. This book is required reading for all serious students of Ecuadorian history. The second and third volumes continue the authors' analysis with essays focusing more on the present. Enrique Ayala Mora, *Resumen de historia del Ecuador* (Quito: Corporación editora nacional, 1995), offers a quick and reliable summary. Other efforts in Spanish include Gabriel Cevallos García, *Historia del Ecuador: Ecuador republicano* (Cuenca: Publicaciones de Editorial "Don Bosco" del Ecuador, n.d.); and Óscar Efrén Reyes, *Breve historia general del Ecuador*, tomos 2–3 (Quito: Imprenta del Colegio Tecnico Don Bosco, n.d.). Humberto Oña Villarreal's encyclopedic *Presidentes del Ecuador* (Quito: n.p., 1987), is a handy reference.

On Ecuador's economic history see Alberto Acosta, *Breve historia económica del Ecuador* (Quito: Corporación Editora Nacional, 1995), which supplies much of the data. Acosta's effort now supersedes Luis Alberto Carbo, *Historia montetaria y cambiaria del Ecuador* (Quito: Imprenta del Banco Central del Ecuador, 1978).

Luis Robalino Dávila, *Orígenes del Ecuador de hoy* (Puebla: Editorial José M. Cajica Jr., 1967–1970), is a classic seven-volume history of Ecuador by a former diplomatic representative of the nation and includes particularly worthwhile detailed interpretative accounts of key developments in Ecuador's diplomatic history. Jorge W. Villacrés Moscoso, the founding father of Ecuadorian diplomatic history, has many works to his name: *La política económica internacional de los estados hispanoamericanos (iniciativas y contribución del Ecuador)* (Guayaquil: Imprenta de la Universidad, 1955); the multivolume *Historia diplomática de la república del Ecuador* (Guayaquil: Lit. e Imprenta de la Universidad de Guayaquil, 1967, 1976, 1978, 1982); and *Historia de las relaciones culturales de la república del Ecuador* (Guayaquil: Universidad de Guayaquil, 1991), which together provide a wealth of details and opinions on nearly every episode in Ecuador's foreign policy.

## The Nineteenth Century

On Ecuadorian independence Roger Paul Davis's "Ecuador under Gran Colombia, 1820–1830: Regionalism, Localism, and Legitimacy in the Emergence of an Andean Republic" (Ph.D. diss., University of Arizona, 1983); and "The Local Dynamics of National Dissent," *Historian* 55, no. 2 (Winter 1993): 289–302, offer carefully researched and convincingly argued analytical treatment of the coming of Ecuador's independence. The dissertation is now slated for publication in Spanish in Ecuador. On the United States and the process of Latin American independence, Arthur P. Whitaker, *The United States and the Independence of Latin America, 1800–1830* (New York: W. W. Norton, 1964), continues to deserve its reputation as a sturdy classic, especially valuable for its detailed treatment of the Monroe Doctrine.

On Ecuador's relations with the United States, George M. Lauderbaugh's excellent "The United States and Ecuador: Conflict and Convergence, 1830–1946" (Ph.D. diss., University of Alabama, 1997), is an enormously valuable treatment of the leading U.S.-Ecuadorian foreign policy exchanges. Joedd Price, "Ecuadorean Opinion of the United States in the Nineteenth Century: An Attitudinal Study" (Ph.D. diss., University of North Carolina, 1968), is a good study of outlooks and a solid overview of leading events. Two highly readable travel accounts, William Eleroy Curtis, *The Capitals of Spanish America* (New York: Praeger, 1969), originally published in 1886; and Friedrich Hassaurek, *Four Years among Spanish Americans* (New York: Hurd and Houghton, 1967), written by the U.S. ambassador to Ecuador, reveal at least as much about American attitudes as they do about Ecuadorian realities.

On Ecuador's nineteenth century political history see Frank MacDonald Spindler's descriptive narrative, *Nineteenth-Century Ecuador: An Historical Introduction* (Fairfax, Va.: George Mason University Press, 1987). Mark J. Van Aken's *King of the Night: Juan José Flores and Ecuador, 1824–1864* (Berkeley: University of California Press, 1989) is a superb biography of Ecuador's first president. Peter H. Smith, "The Image of a Dictator: Gabriel García Moreno," *Hispanic American Historical Review* 45, no. 1 (February 1965): 1–24, provides a brief, sound assessment of this leading Ecuadorian political figure. Linda Alexander Rodríguez's prize-winning *The Search for Public Policy: Regional Politics and Government Finances in Ecuador, 1830–1940* (Berkeley: University of California Press, 1985), is an excellent assessment of Ecuadorian fiscal history, with many insights into the play of regionalism in Ecuadorian politics. Ronn Pineo, *Social and Economic Reform in Ecuador: Life and Work in Guayaquil, 1870–1925* (Gainesville: University Press of Florida, 1996), contains information on turn-of-the-century Guayaquil. A strong overview of the cacao age is provided by Lois Weinman's "Ecuador and Cacao: Domestic Responses to the Boom-Collapse Monoexport Cycle" (Ph. D. diss., University of California, Los Angeles, 1970).

There are several fine books in Spanish on nineteenth-century Ecuador. Enrique Ayala Mora, ed., *Nueva historia del Ecuador: época republicana I*, vol. 7 (Quito: Corporación Editora Nacional, 1983), includes several very good essays, among them, Ayala Mora, "La fundación de la república: panorama histórico 1830–1859"; Ayala Mora and Rafael Cordero Aguilar, "El período Garciano: panorama histórico 1860–1875"; and Gonzalo Ortiz Crespo, "Panorama histórico del período 1875–1895." Jorge Pérez Concha, *Frente externo* (Guayaquil: Litografía e Imprenta de la Universidad de Guayaquil, 1985), seeks to cover a wide-ranging mix of topics, offering especially worthwhile treatment of Ecuador and the nineteenth-century wars among the Pacific states of South America.

## 1900 to Mid-Twentieth Century

A. Kim Clark, *The Redemptive Work: Railway and Nation in Ecuador, 1895–1930* (Wilmington, Del.: Scholarly Resources, 1998), offers much detail on the railway. Clark's work, however, does not supersede Eva Maria Loewenfeld's splendid

"The Guayaquil and Quito Railway," (M.A. thesis, University of Chicago, 1944), which provides an incisive summary of this critical issue in U.S.-Ecuadorian affairs. Loewenfeld's essay is available only through interlibrary loan from the University of Chicago. Also worth consulting are Walter V. Scholes and Marie V. Scholes, "The United States and Ecuador, 1909–1913," *Americas* 19, no. 3 (January 1963): 276–90; and Emily S. Rosenburg, "Dollar Diplomacy under Wilson: An Ecuadorean Case," *Inter-American Economic Affairs* 25, no. 2 (Autumn 1971): 47–54.

Paul W. Drake, *The Money Doctor in the Andes: The Kemmerer Missions, 1923–1933* (Durham, N.C.: Duke University Press, 1989), is a clearly written and analytically powerful contribution. John Child, *Unequal Alliance: The Inter-American Military System, 1938–1978* (Boulder, Colo.: Westview, 1980), provides an invaluable study of U.S.–Latin America military relations. On the U.S. bases in Salinas and the Galápagos see E. Taylor Parks and J. Fred Rippy, "The Galápagos Islands, a Neglected Phase of American Strategy Diplomacy," *Pacific Historical Review* 9 (1940): 37–45.

David H. Zook Jr., *Zarumilla-Marañón: The Ecuador-Peru Dispute* (New York: Bookman, 1964), is an evenhanded look at the long-running border dispute, with detailed treatment of the 1941 war. Bryce Wood, *The United States and Latin American Wars, 1932–1942* (New York: Columbia University Press, 1966), is the best brief treatment of the Peru-Ecuador boundary dispute and the war of 1941. For coverage of the continuing disputes after the war, see David Scott Palmer, "Peru-Ecuador Border Conflict: Missed Opportunities, Misplaced Nationalism, and Multilateral Peacekeeping," *Journal of Inter-American Studies and World Affairs* 39, no. 3 (Fall 1997): 109–48.

Alvin M. Goffin, *The Rise of Protestant Evangelism in Ecuador, 1895–1990* (Gainesville: University Press of Florida, 1994), offers a passionate account of indigenous peoples' struggles to defend their native ways. The essays by Jon V. Kofas, "Politics of Conflict and Containment: Ecuador's Labor Movement and U.S. Foreign Policy, 1944–1963," *Journal of Third World Studies* 13, no. 2 (Fall 1996): 61–188; and "The IMF, the World Bank, and U.S. Foreign Policy in Ecuador," *Latin American Perspectives* 28, no. 5 (September 2001): 50–83, are very well-argued and valuable works that fill large gaps in the historiography. Worth consulting is John Van Dyke Saunders, *The People of Ecuador: A Demographic Analysis* (Gainesville: University of Florida Press, 1961), which sums up the numbers from the nation's first census.

Enrique Ayala Mora, "Ecuador since 1930," in Leslie Bethell, ed., *The Cambridge History of Latin America: Latin America since 1930, Spanish South America,* vol. 8 (Cambridge: Cambridge University Press, 1991), is a quick summary of some events of the twentieth century in Ecuador. Better is Enrique Ayala Mora, ed., *Nueva historia del Ecuador: época republicana IV*, vol. 10 (Quito: Corporación Editora Nacional, 1983), especially Agustín Cueva, "El Ecuador de 1925 a 1960."

## The 1960s to the Present

On the U.S. and Ecuador, Mary Jeanne Reid Martz, "Ecuador and the Eleventh Inter-American Conference," *Journal of Inter-American Studies* 10, no. 2 (April 1968): 306–27, offers a unique look at this failed conference. John D. Martz, "The Fate of a Small State: Ecuador in Foreign Affairs," in Heraldo Muñoz and Joseph S. Tulchin, eds., *Latin American Nations in World Politics* (Boulder, Colo.: Westview, 1996), focuses especially on the period from the 1960s and to the early 1990s. Robert H. Terry, "Ecuadorian Foreign Policy, 1958–1968: As Reflected in the O.A.S. and the U.N.," (Ph.D. diss., American University, 1972), offers a wonderful overview of Ecuadorian foreign policy and is particularly strong in explaining how Ecuadorian views of Peru did much to give shape to Ecuador's foreign policy. For a quick overview see Mary Jeanne Reid Martz, "Ecuador," in Harold Eugene Davis and Larman C. Wilson, eds., *Latin American Foreign Policies: An Analysis* (Baltimore: Johns Hopkins University Press, 1975). Philip Agee, *Inside the Company: CIA Diary* (Toronto: Bantam, 1975), provides a chilling look behind the scenes of clandestine CIA operations. Stephen G. Rabe, *The Most Dangerous Area in the World: John F. Kennedy Confronts Communist Revolution in Latin America* (Chapel Hill: University of North Carolina Press, 1999), is a powerful and convincing reinterpretation of the reasons for the failure of the Alliance for Progress. Jeanne A. K. Hey, the best scholar of recent U.S.-Ecuadorian relations, offers, in *Theories of Dependent Foreign Policy and the Case of Ecuador in the 1980s* (Athens: Ohio University Center for International Studies, 1995), a detailed and closely reasoned analysis of contemporary developments. Also by Hey are "Foreign Policy Options under Dependence: A Theoretical Evaluation with Evidence from Ecuador," *Journal of Latin American Studies* 25 (1993): 543–74; and, with Thomas Klak, "From Protectionism to Neoliberalism: Tracing the Transition in Ecuador," paper presented at the 1995 meeting of the Latin American Studies Association, Washington, D.C., 1995.

On Ecuador's recent history see Steve Striffler, *In the Shadows of State and Capital: The United Fruit Company, Popular Struggle, and Agrarian Restructuring in Ecuador, 1900–1995* (Durham, N.C.: Duke University Press, 2002), which is now the new standard on Ecuador's banana boom. John Samuel Fitch's *The Military Coup d'Etat as a Political Process* (Baltimore: Johns Hopkins University Press, 1977) is still a worthy contribution to understanding Ecuadorian political history. Anita Isaacs, *Military Rule and Transition in Ecuador, 1972–92* (Pittsburgh: University of Pittsburgh Press, 1993), is packed with information and offers highly perceptive comparative analyses. This is easily the best book on Ecuador's military government in either English or Spanish. Also see Isaacs's "Ecuador: Democracy Standing the Test of Time?" in Jorge I. Domínguez and Abraham F. Lowenthal, eds., *Constructing Democratic Governance: Latin America and the Caribbean in the 1990s* (Baltimore: Johns Hopkins University Press, 1996). John D. Martz, *Politics and Petroleum in Ecuador* (New Brunswick, N.J.: Transaction Books, 1987), offers ample detail on the Ecuadorian oil industry. Catherine M. Conaghan, *Restructuring Domination: Industrialists and the State in Ecuador* (Pittsburgh: University of Pittsburgh Press, 1988), is one of the most sophisticated studies of Ecuadorian politics. This book is essential reading for the serious student of Ecuadorian history. Equally valuable is Conaghan and James M. Malloy, *Unsettling Statecraft: Democracy and Neoliberalism in the Central Andes* (Pittsburgh: University of Pittsburgh Press, 1994), a wise and highly perceptive comparative analysis of the links between neoliberalism and democratization in the three Andean republics. Also see Conaghan's "Party Politics and Democratization in Ecuador" in James M. Malloy and Mitchell A. Seligson, eds., *Authoritarians and Democrats: Regime Transition in Latin America* (Pittsburgh: University of Pittsburgh Press, 1987). Also see Wendy Weiss, "Debt and Devaluation: The Burden on Ecuador's Popular Class," *Latin American Perspectives* 24, no. 4 (July 1997): 9–33. Carlos de la Torre, *Populist Seduction in Latin America: The Ecuadorian Experience* (Athens: Ohio University Center for International Studies, 2000), provides insightful treatment of José María Velasco Ibarra and Abdalá Bucaram. Allen Gerlach, *Indians, Oil, and Politics: A Recent History of Ecuador* (Wilmington, Del.: Scholarly Resources, 2003), gives good coverage on the collapse of the Bucaram and Mahuad presidencies. Paul Beckerman and Andrés Solimano, eds., *Crisis and Dollarization in Ecuador: Stability, Growth, and Social Equity* (Washington, D.C.: World Bank, 2002), is a workmanlike presentation of the World Bank's views. Similar is Vicente Fretes-Cibils, Marcelo M. Giugale, and José Roberto López-Cálix, eds., *Ecuador: An Economic and Social Agenda in the New Millennium* (Washington, D.C.: World Bank, 2003). Andrés Mejía Acosta et al., "Political Institutions, Policy Making Processes, and Policy Outcomes in

Ecuador," Inter-American Development Bank, 2004, finds much of the fault for Ecuador's continuing economic problems in the nation's dysfunctional political system. Michael Shifter, "Breakdown in the Andes," *Foreign Affairs* 83, no. 5 (September–October 2004): 126–38, examines recent problems in the process of democratization in Bolivia, Peru, and Ecuador, finding many parallels in their historical experiences.

In Spanish, Ayala Mora, *Nueva historia del Ecuador,* vol. 10, provides some very worthwhile essays, including Alexei Páez Cordero, "El movimiento obrero Ecuatoriano en el periodo (1925–1960)"; Wilson Miño Grijalva, "La economía Ecuatoriana de la gran recesión a la crisis bananera"; and Fabio Villalobos, "El proceso de industrialización hasta los años cincuenta." Manuel de Guzmán Polanco, "Ecuador en lo internacional: un cuarto de siglo, 1945–1970," in *El Ecuador de la postguerra: estudio en homenaje a Guillermo Perez Chiribobga,* vol. 2 (Quito: Banco Central del Ecuador, 1992), is chiefly an anti-Peru polemic by a former diplomat.

# Index

255